G000090936

Beyond the Green Door
Six Years inside the FAI

Beyond the Green Door

Six Years inside the FAI

Brendan Menton

BLACKWATER PRESS

Editor
Ciara McNee

Design & Layout
Paula Byrne

Cover Design
Melanie Gradtke

ISBN
1 84131 636 9

© 2003 Brendan Menton

Produced in Ireland by
Blackwater Press
c/o Folens Publishers
Hibernian Industrial Estate
Greenhills Road
Tallaght
Dublin 24

All rights reserved. No part of this publication may be reproduced or transmitted in any form or by any means, electronic, mechanical, photocopying, recording, or otherwise without prior written permission from the Publisher.

The book is sold subject to the conditions that it shall not, by way of trade or otherwise, be lent, re-sold, hired out or otherwise circulated without the Publishers' prior consent in any form or cover other than that in which it is published and without similar conditions including this condition being imposed on the subsequent purchaser.

Brendan Menton was born in September 1951 and grew up in Clontarf on the north side of Dublin. Brendan was educated at St Paul's College Raheny, a rugby school, but football always took priority. He played his first competitive match for Home Farm FC in 1961, the club his father cofounded in 1928. A mediocre football career, reaching the heights of the AUL premier division, was cut short by a broken ankle in 1973.

Brendan studied economics in UCD, receiving first-class honours degrees both as a Bachelor of Arts and Master of Arts. In the early 1990s, he received a first-class honours Master of Science degree in Investment and Treasury. He subsequently lectured in DCU on a part-time basis.

Brendan worked as an economist for the Economic and Social Research Institute, the Confederation of Irish Industry and Allied Irish Bank. He left AIB in 1995, to establish a financial training company, but soon afterwards was enticed into the FAI at the time of Merriongate. He served as Acting General Secretary in 1996 for six months, Honorary Treasurer for four and a half years (1996–2001) and General Secretary for eighteen months (2001–2002). He is now Director of National Associations and Clubs for the Asian Football Confederation, based in Kuala Lumpur.

Brendan has been married to Linda since 1975 and they have four children, Ronan, Aisling, Ailbhe and Niamh.

Dedication

To Linda
my centre half

To Ronan, Aisling, Ailbhe and Niamh
my midfield and strikers

To my father, Doc Menton, who gave me my love for football

All the worlds a stage,
All the men and women merely players;
They have their exits and their entrances;
And one man in his time plays many parts.

Shakespeare's *As You Like It*

Acknowledgements

I would like to thank the following: my great friend Declan Mullen, who brought Blackwater Press and me together; Ger Kenneally, who read the initial pages during our pilgrimage to Seville for the UEFA Cup Final and encouraged me to go for it and expunge my hurts; Lucy and John Keaveney, who 'celebrated' their twenty-fifth wedding anniversary reading the manuscript and encouraged me to continue; my son, Ronan, who set up the e-mail system which ensured privacy and capacity for large volumes of text across 8,000 miles – from Kuala Lumpur to Tallaght to Meath; my daughters Aisling, Ailbhe and Niamh, who interrupted study time to spend hours in libraries and on the web establishing facts and locating references; my sister Mary and brothers Kevin, Colm and Malachy, who bore with fortitude my six years beyond the green door; Pearce Mehigan for his steadfast advice; my friends in Home Farm, on whose support I could always depend. The club will always remain my base in football; my many football friends who cannot be named; publisher John O'Connor; editor Ciara McNee, who managed the process brilliantly for me across a distance of 8,000 miles; Paula Byrne and all in Blackwater Press.

In memory of my dad, who had every newspaper cutting on the FAI and Irish football since 1996.

The author would like to thank Mick McCarthy for permission to quote from his *World Cup Diary 2002*, TownHouse/Pocket Books, 2002.

Contents

Introduction

The year 1996 was to be a year of celebration for the FAI. The organisation was seventy-five years old, having split away from the Irish Football Association in 1921. Most football associations would have a year of events to mark the occasion, including international matches against major opposition and celebratory dinners. It should be a time for good public relations and promotion of the game, a time of looking forward and making plans for future development. None of this happened in the FAI. The anniversary was officially marked by the publication of the seventy-five-year history of the Association, *The Football Association of Ireland 75 Years,* written by Peter Byrne, then soccer correspondent of *The Irish Times.* No other event was organised. There was nothing much to celebrate.

The manuscript had to be finished by mid-March in order to get it to the printers on time. However, I got a brief mention on page 208, the third-last page:

> *Within a week... Brendan Menton, a member of the Home Farm club, was nominated Acting General Secretary.*

Merriongate exploded at the end of February 1996, even though the ticket scandal it related to occurred during the World Cup in the US, nearly two years previously. The scandal brought me into the top echelons of the FAI, as I was invited to take over as General Secretary[1] in order to sort out this and other messes.

---

1. The FAI has a dual structure: the professional staff of Merrion Square and the voluntary officials who serve on committees and become the directors and officers of the Association. The General Secretary is the bridge between the two, leading the professional staff, attending the committee meetings and liaising with the officers.

I believe I did this very satisfactorily. At the end of my six-month tenure as Acting General Secretary (31 August 1996), the Association was back on an even keel.

I was disappointed not to be offered a contract to remain as General Secretary. This I suppose was my first lesson in the politics of the FAI. I was perceived as being from the wrong side of the football tracks: League of Ireland rather than junior football. Even the long association of my club, Home Farm, with schoolboy football counted for nought. Power and control would be seized where politics permitted.

I was urged to stay involved in the FAI by standing for the vacant position of Honorary Treasurer[2]. After a few weeks reflection, I decided to do so and was nominated for the vacant position by Dr Tony O'Neill of UCD. I quickly learned my second lesson in football politics: those who had urged me to stay involved in the FAI had nominated a rival candidate for the position. I won the contest because I managed to get my politics right: nearly all the league clubs supported me.

My tenure as Honorary Treasurer, November 1996 to May 2001, was my best time in the Association, although the last two years were marred by the bitter and divisive rows over Eircom Park. The officers of the Association used to be treated with respect. The role of Honorary Treasurer had a particular aura, as the person who held the position controlled the purse strings of the Association and, hence, was perceived as being influential in giving out grants. It is a powerful position and this power can be used to achieve positive developments or political advantage. For two years, there was some money for development grants. However, the black hole of Eircom Park put an end to that.

In May 2001, when a second chance arose to become General Secretary, I took it. I went for the job on a political basis and won the support of the majority, but by no means all, of the Board members.

---

2. Bernard O'Byrne's selection as General Secretary caused this vacancy.

Becoming General Secretary was something I wanted to do, so I went for it. I knew that I was moving from having a respected political position to becoming a general dogsbody. Every Board member believes that they own the General Secretary and that he should do what they want as a matter of course. Some Board members carry this to a ridiculous extreme.

I have no regrets about my involvement in the FAI. I love football and wanted to do my best for it. Let other people judge my contribution, but please not the media, some of whom I have come to distrust, particularly those who seldom bother to get their facts totally right. The story is often more important than the truth.

There are many journalists that I do respect. These are the foot soldiers for Irish football. You are more likely to meet them at league grounds on a Friday night than in a five-star hotel on away international trips or in an English Premiership stadium. They understand the importance of the domestic game and support it as best they can, blemishes and all. It is one of the ironies that the FAI is often portrayed as a blazer brigade, only interested in the free trips. There are a lot more journalists on the Irish team plane than FAI officials.

If I had stayed as Honorary Treasurer, rather than becoming General Secretary in May 2001, I believe that I could still be involved in the FAI. I am glad that I am not. I would have been burnt out by this stage. I have come to understand, belatedly perhaps, that the flaws within the structure and culture of the FAI run deep. I was portrayed as a thwarted reformer. I did not have the ability and strength to change the organisation. Does anyone? Those who look to the Genesis Report for a solution will be disappointed; it is a political cop-out. Genesis addresses none of the fundamental issues. Widespread political reform is needed, together with the increased administration resources proposed. Political reform is only marginally on the Genesis agenda, which is why the FAI have seemingly embraced it with enthusiasm.

If I had remained as Honorary Treasurer, I would have missed the opportunity to work for the Asian Football Confederation[3]. I have got the better part of the bargain. Life is full of cause and effect. I am glad that this opportunity presented itself to me. I can again enjoy being involved with the game I love. If I had to suffer the trauma of eighteen months as General Secretary of the FAI to arrive where I am today, then so be it.

This book does not purport to be a history, unofficial or otherwise, of the Football Association of Ireland. It does take up the story where Peter Byrne's book left off, however. Plenty has been written about the events I describe by outside observers, by players, managers, and the media. Giving the inside story from beyond the green door provides a new perspective. This book is my account of the major events that happened during my six years of involvement with the Association. It is a very different story about very familiar events; it is my story.

I had a very eventful six years in the FAI. It started with Merriongate and progressed to Eircom Park. The whole World Cup 2002 campaign was fantastic from the kick-off against the Netherlands to the final penalty by Mendieta in Suwon. I was there; no one can deny me my great memories.

For those who want to judge the Saipan controversy, please study the Genesis Report in detail. The arrangements for the World Cup in Japan and Korea were excellent. Saipan had its good points in terms of preparation, but also its drawbacks. The FAI did not get everything right, but we had made very substantial progress since USA '94 and Italia '90. Tony Cascarino recently referred to the 'smelly hotel' era of his playing days. I think someone should tell Tony that those days were long over before he retired. Why this kind of diatribe is still

---

3.   I am currently employed as Director of National Associations and Clubs with the Asian Football Confederation. My role is to assist the development of football in Asia in the Vision Asia project. My position is funded by UEFA, the governing body for football in Europe.

being published, when it is nearly ten years out of date, I do not understand. The players who took part in the 2002 World Cup were impressed by the arrangements – just read their comments in Genesis. Would one of them mind telling Cas?

I am still proud of the Sky TV deal. It was the right one for Irish football. Most people involved in football understood it and accepted it. The armchair fans were the ones upset and they won out in the end, aided in no small part by the vested interests of RTÉ. Perhaps the way the FAI announced the deal could have been improved, but if any inkling of the deal had leaked, powerful forces would have tried to undermine it. The money from Sky was needed to sustain and develop the game at all levels. The government will not replace this money. Our young players are the losers. Let me state my basic belief: it is more important to have a young person play a game than watch one on television.

Irish football thrives despite the FAI. I speak from experience. The FAI seldom discusses important football issues. Its meetings are dominated by petty politics. The rows are more important than the issues. Dealing with matters arising from the previous meeting's minutes can take hours, as people try to score points off each other. The Association's committees simply do not function and achieve nothing positive for the game. The President's job is as impossible as the General Secretary's. Neither can give constructive leadership, because as soon as they come up with a good proposal, it is knocked. The FAI as an organisation knows what is wrong with any proposal, but can never bring itself to focus on the positive.

I came to hate the organisation and its poisonous atmosphere. However, I love Irish football. I had to give it a go. It took me six years to realise that if you want to achieve something for Irish football, you have to stay away from the FAI.

I wish I had been able to give a full account of all the significant issues that I was involved in.

I ran out of both time and space and, hence, stories like the 'Paul Marney'[4] affair, and the Euro 2008 bid remain untold. I am particularly sorry not to describe the Marney affair in detail, for two reasons: The first is that it demonstrated everything that is wrong with League of Ireland football and its clubs. The second is that one of the main characters involved rang my publisher and tried to persuade him to omit the story and demanded an assurance that his name would not be mentioned in the book. The publisher did not tell him that the Marney story would not feature. At this stage, he was encouraging me to include it. He had a good laugh after the telephone call. It convinced him that what I have written about the behaviour of FAI people is true.

I had another chapter planned, entitled 'Angels on a Pin Head'. This was going to deal with some of the never-ending petty rows within the FAI that probably still continue. It would have included the attempt by the Schoolboys Football Association to undermine Brian Kerr as manager of Ireland's underage international teams. One league club also wanted Brian out because he had once managed St Pats. At Board meetings, the current Honorary Treasurer also launched several attacks on Brian during his tenure as technical director of the Association. Success does not bring you support in the FAI; it makes you a target.

One of the key things I achieved during my time in the FAI was the production and publication of the first strategic plan for the

---

4. The 'Paul Marney' affair was the dispute between Shelbourne and St Patrick's Athletic over an error in registering Paul Marney to play for St Pats. St Pats were deducted fifteen points after a bitter dispute, when it emerged that a second player, Charles Mbabazi Livingston, was also not registered by St Pats for five games. The row involved league committees, appeal hearings, arbitration and a court case. The court case upheld the FAI arbitration, procedures and findings. The row also involved interminable meetings and telephone calls between the principals involved, going around in never-ending circles. The two dominant individuals in the two clubs had a poor relationship. In the end, Shelbourne were the official winners of the league, despite St Pats winning more points on the pitch. Shelbourne got the prize money, entry into the Champions League and the very large cheque that goes with that. (Shelbourne lost to a team from Malta.)

development of football in Ireland. Surely, here was a project that everyone would support. Wrong! We involved the Honorary Secretary of the Schoolboys Football Association of Ireland in the development of the strategic plan; he was on all the committees and chaired some of the workshops. When the plan was published, the Schoolboys Football Association of Ireland, led by this individual, rejected it on the basis of lack of consultation. I think what had happened was that the Honorary Secretary of the Schoolboys Football Association had not consulted with his own members. The proposals were hugely beneficial for the schoolboy game. I doubt that many of the officials of schoolboy football read the plan, because if they had they should have endorsed it loudly. It was again about petty politics, rather than the real issue of developing and improving the game.

There is no end to the stories of stupidity that I could relate. Maybe there should be a second volume.

The title for this book, *Beyond the Green Door*, was chosen to reflect the strange behaviour of the FAI. The title was my wife Linda's idea. The green door of the FAI is probably the best-recognised doorway in Ireland. The word 'beyond' reflects the surreal behaviour that happens when people meet in the name of the FAI. It is often beyond reason, beyond comprehension and frequently beyond football.

In this book, I have a go at many people, on a wide range of issues. This is not motivated by revenge, but by frustration. If this book is the mirror in which the FAI sees itself through the eyes of one of its own, then maybe it will help to bring about change. I won't be holding my breath. I am not bitter about what happened to me in the FAI. The decisions to get involved, to change roles and to move on were mine alone – decisions I have never regretted. I have no problem taking responsibility for my own actions.

My departure from the FAI was as scandalous as anything that happened during my six years' involvement. The manner in which the FAI dealt with my complaints over the Mick McCarthy bonus issue was a significant motive for writing and publishing this book. I needed to set the record straight. I wanted to purge my soul of the stupidity I had encountered – putting it down on paper was a good way of doing this. The book was well under way when a publisher approached me out of the blue.

Let those members of the FAI who are upset by the contents of this book examine the behaviour of the Association in the first three months of this year, when dealing with the McCarthy bonus issue. Can any one of them say that it was dealt with honourably and honestly? If so, please telephone me!

I have made many friends in football; some of them are still involved in the FAI. These friendships are important to me, and I know that they will survive this book. My friends know the truth of what happened and understand why I wrote this book. I know that I am still welcome at most football grounds in Ireland. On the flip side, there are many people whom I am happy are now firmly in my past.

I am proud of what I achieved in my eighteen months as General Secretary of the FAI, between May 2001 and November 2002. Nobody ever gets everything right, but I believe my balance sheet shows a very healthy positive balance. You won't have read much about my positive achievements in the media. I am going to indulge myself here, because as author of this book, I can do so without constraint. If you don't want to read about them, step through the looking glass and enter beyond the green door into the *outré* world of the FAI; go straight to Chapter 1.

The Association's strategic plan, *One Game One Association,* was published in November 2001. It was completely the internal work of FAI staff and committee members. It is a good document, involving the most extensive consultation process ever undertaken in the FAI. We got little thanks for this. The name seemed a good idea at the time, but now seems so far removed from reality as to border on the ridiculous. The plan is largely gathering dust; it was certainly a document that fell on stony ground. The one exception is the Technical Department who, led by Brian Kerr and Packie Bonner, have since devised their own Technical Development Plan. That, too, will be criticised!

Ten new development officers were appointed to the Technical Department in 2001. These appointments not only completed the regional structure of development officers, but also saw development officers appointed to women's football, to the schools, for referees and to the special needs groups (Football For All is the terminology now used). The first joint meeting between the four special needs groups (Special Olympics, Special Schools, Cerebral Palsy Ireland and Blind Sports), who all play football to a good standard, was held in that year. I doubt if any other sporting organisation does half as much to support these groups. A development officer was appointed to run the FAI summer soccer clinics; in two years, the number of kids attending has more than doubled to over 15,000. In my opinion, the FAI camps far surpass the rival Samba camps, in terms of the standard of coaching provided and the supervision available. A professional national children's officer was also appointed, and a development officer was given responsibility for Futsal, the official indoor version of football. Futsal is a fabulous game. At fifty-two years of age I have started playing it on the AFC pitch in Kuala Lumpur. It is great fun and good exercise. Unfortunately, few people in the FAI recognise its potential.

As Honorary Treasurer, I introduced a system of annual budgeting and quarterly management accounts. This was the first attempt to plan activity and expenditure in the FAI. It is a basic management procedure in any organisation. I hope it has continued.

During my tenure, the FAI developed excellent working relationships with the Department of Sport and the Irish Sports Council. We worked very closely with the Department of Sport on the allocation of government development grants, and, in most cases, they heeded our advice. This was a totally new development and I believe that the department recognised its merits. The appointment of the first development executive in the FAI, John Byrne, was a major contributing factor to this success. The FAI now had someone to support and assist the clubs and leagues in their development.

In late 2001, the government allocated an additional €1 million to the three main sporting bodies through the Irish Sports Council. The Sports Council accepted the expenditure plans the FAI drew up, which included money for the League of Ireland clubs to support the initiation and development of the national U21 League. In time, this league will succeed in greatly raising playing standards. It has already expanded football at this level to Kerry and Mayo. We managed to persuade the Sports Council that some of the money should go directly to the thirty-two Schoolboy Leagues around the country, not that this was appreciated. The Schoolboy Leagues complained that they should have been given more, whereas in reality, the money they received was stretching the bounds of what was permissible under the grant.

We totally revamped the FAI website in early 2002. It is now a sophisticated site and has one of the highest levels of hits of any Irish site. It even won website of the week. Visit it and you will see why.

As I was leaving the FAI, the process of upgrading the technology was well underway. In support of this, many of the basic management processes were being reviewed internally, led by Ian O'Callaghan, a consultant on assignment with the FAI. This work preceded Genesis. This revamp was allied to a new technology sponsor, HP, brought into the Association in early 2002.

The commercial sponsorship of the Association, which is a vital source of revenue, was streamlined, with three categories of sponsors pinpointed and an appropriate package of benefits identified for each category. Through renegotiation with existing sponsors and the introduction of new sponsors, the revenue to the Association was greatly increased.

Through the introduction of touchline seats, we managed to increase the capacity at Lansdowne Road for competitive matches by close to 1,500 seats. These were first used for the match against the Netherlands in September 2001. Peter Buckley of the Finance Department can be given credit for the idea.

The process for introducing the FAI club licence system[5] was firmly established. As I ended my involvement with the project in March 2003, very significant progress had been made.

---

5. The FAI club licensing is derived from the UEFA club licence. A club must meet standards in facilities, player development, finance and administration, among other areas, before receiving a licence to become eligible to play in European competitions. The FAI club licence was due to commence for season 2004, as I exited the FAI.

I created both International and Domestic Football Departments in the FAI: the latter should really be called the Competitions Department. I know of no other association that operates without specialised expertise in these areas.

I reformed the arbitration system, with the goal of reducing the number of silly disputes within the FAI that are allowed to drag on. As Honorary Treasurer of the FAI and also the League of Ireland, I played a significant role in bringing about the transition to summer soccer. I firmly believe this change will prove to be the most important reform of the professional game in Ireland.

An official doping-control system was introduced into the League of Ireland in cooperation with the Irish Sports Council. This system is operated to the highest standards. Under this system, FIFA's list of prohibited substances are banned. Players are randomly tested at a number of league matches throughout the season.

Finally, and perhaps most significantly in the light of all the criticisms about the World Cup preparations, it was reported on the FAI's website that the Association made a profit of €3.3 million from the 2002 World Cup. This compared with losses incurred in both 1990 and 1994. I let the 2002 figure speak for itself. Despite this profit, the FAI had an overall surplus of just €300,000 for the year. This reveals how precarious the Association's financial position is.

I list these things just to show that, as Honorary Treasurer and General Secretary of the FAI, I actually did some important work and achieved a few positive things for Irish football. I do not dwell on these in the book – that is about a different set of issues. As you turn over the page to begin Chapter 1, you are entering a totally different world. As you step beyond the green door, you will not lose your sense of reason. You may well conclude that this is what happens to FAI officials who remain beyond the green door for too long... I escaped in time!

Brendan Menton
Kuala Lumpur
October 2003

1

Merriongate

Merriongate, the scandal of the FAI's handling of tickets for the 1994 World Cup in the US, was my introduction to the centre of the FAI. Whether it happened by accident or design, I still do not know. Sean Connolly had resigned as General Secretary of the Association on 16 February 1996, after five years of service. This was a bolt from the blue at the time, but soon the reasons became obvious. Sean's resignation was not at the core of the Merriongate crisis, but was the factor that brought me into the FAI as Acting General Secretary.

My appointment as Acting General Secretary came about in a strange way. I bumped into Des Casey, Honorary Secretary of the FAI, while I was in the arrivals hall of Dublin Airport on Monday evening, 19 February, awaiting the arrival of a business colleague from London. I think Des was leaving someone to catch a flight. As I had been involved in football with Home Farm Football Club for nearly twenty years and, indeed, peripherally involved in the FAI, I knew Des well. I was aware of the controversy in the FAI. Des spoke to me in a quiet corner. He asked me if I would be interested in taking over as Acting General Secretary of the FAI for an interim period. As Honorary Secretary, Des assumed the powers of the General Secretary in the latter's absence and was well within his authority in asking me this. The appointment would, of course, be subject to approval by the FAI Executive Committee[1], which was meeting on Wednesday. I do not know whether Des had intended

---

1.　Forerunner of FAI Board of Management.

asking me in any event or whether our chance meeting prompted the proposal.

I was surprised to say the least. Des wanted to know whether I could give him a response in advance of the Executive Committee meeting of the FAI on 21 February. I told him that I would think about it overnight and talk to him the following day. I had never really considered working in football on a full-time basis before this. On reflection and after discussion with Linda, the opportunity was attractive to me. The FAI was in crisis and there were many problems that needed to be sorted out. However, I was enough of an outsider that I would be seen as a new broom. The idea of working full-time in a game I loved was alluring. I rang Des the next day and told him that I was interested. He told me that he would propose it at Wednesday's Executive Committee meeting.

At that time, I was running my own financial training company. I had left AIB in late 1995, after sixteen years as chief economist and working in the dealing room, and had linked up with an established financial training company in London. The lure of working within football proved too strong. I had someone working for me part-time who could take over running the company in the interim. She agreed to do so and Dympna Gavin is still running the company, seven years on.

I decided not to tell my wider family at this stage, as I felt that they would advise against it. This was particularly true of my father, who had been President of the FAI in the early 1980s. I know that he was very relieved when his term of office was up and was more than happy to withdraw from the FAI and pursue his other interests, particularly Home Farm Football Club.

On the evening of the Executive Committee decision, I was entertaining my colleague from the UK. He had played some professional football with Crystal Palace, so had a big interest in football. At 9 o'clock, I was sitting at the bar in Larry Murphy's pub in Baggot Street when the main evening news came on. The FAI's crisis press conference on World Cup tickets figured prominently. I was mentioned as the new Acting General Secretary of the FAI. This was the way that I heard the news. My mobile phone battery had died and I have no doubt that Des Casey was fully occupied with the chaotic press conference in Merrion Square.

I was back in the realm of the contactable some time after 10 pm, when I plugged my phone into the car charger. I was able to telephone Linda and my father. He was delighted for me, if this was what I wanted to do, but warned me to be very careful. Merrion Square, in his view, was a very difficult place. My sister, Mary, was having a TV dinner, which ended up on the floor when the news was announced. The home phone did not stop ringing, but I did not arrive home until late that night.

My prior involvement in the FAI was as Home Farm's representative on the FAI National Council, supposedly the supreme policy-making body of the Association, which meets about four times a year. I was also a member of the FAI Finance Committee at the time.

From what I had heard, the Executive Committee agreed readily enough to Des' proposition and I was to become Acting General Secretary of the Football Association of Ireland, starting the following Monday, 26 February 1996. It was the beginning of six and a half years of very interesting involvement at the core of Irish football.

*****

The FAI was in crisis. It was not just Merriongate and the World Cup ticketing scandal. During the first week in my new role, the list of crisis issues that crossed my desk included:

- The previous General Secretary had voluntarily resigned from the post, yet had been paid off by the Association. The media were chasing the details of this story.
- The Association was in dispute with Sean McHale and Associates, the agency contracted to market and sell the ten-year seats at Lansdowne Road. The contract had been lost in the FAI. There was a disputed bill of IR£75,000 outstanding.

- There was a dispute with Millwall FC over the appointment of Mick McCarthy as Ireland's international manager. Millwall were demanding compensation of Stg£100,000. No one had thought to check and resolve this issue before offering Mick the position as manager.

- Maurice Setters, assistant manager to Jack Charlton, was taking legal action against the Association over his contract. Apparently, when Jack was asked to leave his position, no one from the Association thought to speak to Maurice.

- The financial accountant of the Association, Michael Morris, was leaving in disputed circumstances. The then Honorary Treasurer, Joe Delaney, said it was voluntarily. Michael Morris was obviously very unhappy with the nature and timing of his departure. This ended in legal action, with the Association conceding a substantial compensation payment.

- The ticket debtor situation was appalling, with over IR£230,000 outstanding. Michael Morris stated publicly that he had been ordered by officers to write off the ticket debts of some people, including some officers.

- The Association had refused to accede to Mick McCarthy's wishes and appoint Ian Evans as his assistant on a full-time basis.

- The 'Bring Wimbledon to Dublin' campaign was in full flow. Sam Hamman, Chairman of Wimbledon, had visited Dublin on 8 February 1996 and met with senior Association and club officials. He had visited Tolka Park.

- The technical director of the Association, Joe McGrath, also resigned and took legal action against the Association. Once again compensation was obtained from the Association.

- There was a distinct possibility that the referees could go on strike, thus forcing the cancellation of football matches. Two referees had sued the Association in the high court and won substantial damages.

- And then there was Merriongate – the ticket scandal of the 1994 World Cup in the US. The Association had denied that there was any shortfall in ticket receipts from the 1994 World Cup, but this was far from the complete truth. The media, led by Veronica Guerin who broke the story, were investigating hard.

Welcome to the FAI, Brendan!

I will look at these issues, before dealing in full with the Merriongate scandal. Sean Connolly's resignation on Friday, 16 February, had taken everyone in football by surprise. Sean had been a football outsider when selected to succeed Tony O'Neill, who resigned not long after the 1990 World Cup. Sean had a football background as a player but had not been previously involved in football administration. I believe that Bernard O'Byrne, who figures largely in the history of the FAI during the six years under scrutiny, was a serious contender for the position of General Secretary at the time of Sean's appointment.

Let me start by quoting the public statement put out by the FAI on the Friday evening of Sean's departure:

> At a meeting this evening, the Executive Committee of the Football Association of Ireland accepted the voluntary resignation of its General Secretary/Chief Executive, Sean Connolly.

Sean issued his own statement later that evening, saying:

> I have spent the last ten years in the public eye – five years with the IRTC [Independent Radio and Television Commission] and five with the FAI. I feel that the time is now right to move on to pastures new, at the same time as the FAI have changed their international manager.

Two very brief and uninformative statements after five years at the top! Surely if the parting had been amicable, there would have been at least some sign of regret and some recognition of Sean's contribution to the Association.

The media were suspicious, partly because of the terse statements and partly because they had received no inkling of this development. The FAI was leaking like a sieve at this time, with different stories, often contradictory, coming from the General Secretary and the officers. The media were also aware that some officers had tried to oust Sean on a number of occasions. They wanted to know more. It emerged at the FAI Executive Committee meeting on the following Wednesday that Sean had received a settlement from the Association as part of the termination agreement. Why was this payment made if Sean was resigning voluntarily? The media's antennae were now fully extended.

The story is a complex one and the full truth has probably not emerged. I am relying here on Sean's own statements on the issue to an RTÉ *Prime Time* programme on the FAI in February 2003:

Narrator: *In February 1996, Sean Connolly resigned under pressure, the final issue revolving around FAI money he had used for personal purposes.*

Interviewer: *But there was the question of some money that was said you used for personal purposes in your house rather than for the FAI.*

Sean Connolly: *Yes.*

I: *And was that true?*

SC: *That was absolutely true. I had got a loan. I forget exactly how much at this stage, about £5,000.*

I: *Six.*

SC: *£6,000, which was subsequently repaid to the organisation long before I left. That was not an issue at all.*

I: *But it did contribute to your going.*

SC: *To some extent it did, yes. I have no doubt at all about that, but I think the point I was making, that even before that became an issue, I think that they were – how shall I put this? When you are anxious to get someone to move on, it is very easy to find little chinks which you can hammer people with and off they go.*

I: *So you think…*

SC: *I have no doubt that it became the final stick to beat somebody with, the sort to see him off the premises.*

I believe that Sean's departure was a combination of the loan issue and the desire of some of the officers to oust him. There was media speculation that these officers wanted to run the Association on a day-to-day basis.

The issue about the missing contract with Sean McHale and Associates, who were contracted to sell ten-year tickets for internationals at Lansdowne Road, was very strange. The ten-year ticket scheme was designed to create a fund, the interest on which would be used to provide development grants to football clubs and leagues. About 1,400 tickets were sold, creating a fund of less than IR£3 million. When interest rates were high, this fund provided some revenue for development grants; when interest rates fell, the contribution of the fund was small. In any event, the remainder of the fund disappeared into the black financial hole of Eircom Park. In my judgement, a return of just 1,400 ten-year seat sales was a very poor outcome, given the success of the international team at the time.

The scheme was running out of steam in early 1996 and was costing more than it was bringing in. Let me quote Brian Carey's summary of it in the *Sunday Business Post* of 3 March 1996:

> The 10-year scheme was a flop, selling a mere 1,300 [sic] tickets, but McHale earned £350,000 commission on the scheme.

The decision was taken to end it and make do with the fund as it had accumulated at that time. Thus, the need to reach a final settlement with Sean McHale and Associates arose. This is where the problem erupted. How much money was owed? McHale claimed one figure; the FAI disputed it. However, the FAI could not find its copy of the contract and so was stymied. I believe that Sean Connolly took the blame for this in the FAI, but let me quote Sean on the subject from the *Evening Herald* of 28 February 1996, the day after the story broke in the same paper:

> The physical copy of the contract went missing, which was most odd.

I inherited Sean's office and found the system of filing and the storing of important documents to be well managed. In the end, the FAI had no choice but to pay the money McHale had claimed.

The Association was also in dispute with Millwall FC and this time the amount in question was Stg£100,000. Millwall claimed that they were owed compensation for the loss of Mick McCarthy as their manager. Mick stated that he had a 'get out' clause in his contract, if he was offered the position as Irish manager. The problem for the FAI was that they did not know the truth of the situation. They had not explored this prior to offering Mick the manager's job and were now caught. If Millwall were owed compensation, the FAI would have to pay it.

President Louis Kilcoyne and Honorary Treasurer Joe Delaney travelled to London to meet with the directors of Millwall FC on 19 February 1996. The impasse remained. Millwall claimed that they were owed the money. The FAI denied this, but, as they were operating without full knowledge, their hands were tied. Millwall were threatening legal action. Mick stood on the sidelines, happy to be the Republic of Ireland's new manager. Though judging by his public utterances at the time, he was appalled by what was happening within the FAI.

In late March, I visited Millwall FC in the company of Donie Butler, then the Association's commercial manager. We got no further than Kilcoyne and Delaney. Without the knowledge of what actually was in Mick's contract with Millwall over a release clause, we could only bluster. Then we got lucky. In April, Millwall FC went into financial administration, bringing about a change of management and the departure of the directors. We heard nothing more. The Association got away with this one through Millwall's misfortune.

Maurice Setters, who was Jack Charlton's assistant manager during his ten-year reign, was the forgotten man. When Jack was asked to leave as Irish manager, at a meeting in the AUL Complex in Clonshaugh in December 1995, no one in the FAI thought to speak to Maurice Setters. Maurice had a contract with the FAI as assistant manager. A letter was received from Maurice's solicitor and this resulted in the Association having to make another financial settlement.

As I was taking up the position of Acting General Secretary, Honorary Treasurer Joe Delaney was having discussions with the FAI's financial accountant, Michael Morris, about Michael's imminent departure. Michael had a serious issue with the timing of the departure, as it followed closely after Sean Connolly's resignation and coincided with the eruption of Merriongate. Michael's departure had nothing to do with either of these issues. Joe Delaney had brought Peter Buckley in to work in the Finance Department of the Association shortly before this.

This whole episode is a clear illustration of what was fundamentally wrong with the Association at the time and continues to hamper its efficient operation. The officers of the Association, under their own rules, do not have an executive role in administrating the Association. The rules of the Association give decision-making powers to the Executive Committee (Board of Management). The professional staff is there to implement the decisions and to manage the day-to-day affairs of the Association. This is a model for Associations that works well all over the world.

However, at the time, the FAI officers were meeting regularly, at least weekly, as an Officer Board. They were usurping the authority of their own Executive Committee and also interfering in the administration of the Association. They were acting as executive directors, but did not have the authority to do so. This is how the mess came about. On rereading some of the media coverage at the time, one of the major criticisms was the excessive amount of time some of the officers spent in Merrion Square.

In a public statement issued on 1 March, announcing that he was going to take legal action for constructive dismissal against the Association, Michael Morris denied reports that he was not pressurised into resigning and that he had another job to go to:

Above all I object to the timing of my resignation, a date fixed by Joe Delaney, and the circumstances with which it coincided. I asked Joe Delaney on a number of occasions on Thursday 15 (February) and Friday 16 to change the date but he would not do so.

The Association made an out-of-court settlement on this issue with Michael Morris, paying him a substantial sum of money.

One of the effects of Michael's departure was that the person who had worked in the Finance Department of the Association during the critical period of the 1994 World Cup and who had handled the financial side of ticket sales, was removed from his position. This area was about to come under intense scrutiny and investigation. Michael, from outside the Association, cooperated fully with the subsequent investigation.

The second part of Michael Morris' statement was more damning and was more directly related to the Merriongate ticket scandal, which had broken in the media on Sunday, 18 February. Michael stated that he had queried the World Cup ticket situation in November 1994 and had been assured by Joe Delaney that there was no reason to be concerned. Michael Morris's statement then raised a further issue:

During my term of office, I was also periodically instructed by officers to edit the lists of ticket debtors, prior to advising the finance committee/senior council and this editing would have included officers' names. I was never happy about this.

The FAI ticket system was a mess. At this time, the debtors amounted to about IR£230,000, much of it relating to the play-off against the Netherlands in Anfield in November 1995. A significant amount also related to earlier matches. More than three months after the Netherlands match, a very significant proportion of the money had not been collected. The FAI ticket system was the responsibility of the FAI Finance Department and the General Secretary but the Honorary Treasurer had assumed a hands-on role.

Let me relate a personal incident of FAI ticketing procedures. During the 1994 World Cup, I visited the team hotel in Orlando to purchase tickets for the round-of-sixteen match against the Netherlands. I was not on the FAI Council at the time and was there as a fan, at my own expense. I visited the famous ticket room. Tickets were strewn in bundles all over the floor. Recording was done manually. I offered to assist in acquiring a credit card system to make payment more efficient. I was politely told that it was cash only. It is my information that the hotel safe was raided during Ireland's stay in Orlando, though I do not know whether any FAI ticket money was taken.

The ticketing systems were antiquated and the controls were non-existent. In his *Prime Time* interview, Sean Connolly intimated that he was prevented from introducing a new ticketing system. After taking over as Acting General Secretary, I put pressure on the ticket debtors to pay up. Unsurprisingly, it was not too difficult a job, given the media attention. No one wanted to be named and shamed. I recall that, in the end, some IR£20,000 was written off.

What made the matter worse was that very sophisticated computer-based ticket-recording systems were readily available and were not expensive. All English Premiership clubs had them. In the summer of 1996, as Acting General Secretary, I had one installed in the FAI. It worked a treat. With this new system, 99.5 per cent of all ticket income from any game was quickly collected. The remainder probably related to lost tickets and the non-return of unsold tickets.

The statement by Michael Morris that he had been instructed to edit the ticket debtors list was never fully investigated. It got lost in the wider issues of Merriongate.

Mick McCarthy was offered the job as Irish international team manager on Wednesday, 7 February 1996, and accepted it the following day. He was introduced to the media as Ireland's new manager at a press conference in Lansdowne Road on the Friday. There was a bad start to his relationship with his new employers. FAI President, Louis Kilcoyne, admitted in a radio interview that Kenny

Dalglish and not Mick had been his first choice. Mick's selection had been on a three-to-two vote. I believe that it was Kevin Moran who was the loser in the vote, as Dalglish had earlier withdrawn his application. Louis' gaffe annoyed some of his colleagues on the selection panel and there were demands for a statement of full support for Mick. Now in fairness to Louis, he was just being honest, but it would have been better left unsaid. I have no doubt that if Merriongate had turned out differently, and Louis had stayed on as President of the FAI, he would have been very supportive of Mick. Once a decision is made, everyone needs to get behind the new man.

As is always the case in football, a manager selects and brings his own team of technical staff. His assistant manager is the most important of these. Mick wanted to bring in Ian Evans as his number two. Ian had played with Mick at Barnsley and had been his assistant at Millwall. The FAI had no problem with the selection of Ian, but initially refused to make the position a full-time one. In addition, the FAI did not want the assistant manager running the U21 team, a system that had been disastrous under Maurice Setters in the Jack Charlton era.

In the end, there was a classic FAI fudge, as *The Star* reported on Monday, 19 February:

> 'The Assistant Manager will be brought in on a part-time basis,
> but his job will be almost full-time,' said one senior FAI source
> last night.

I have no idea what this meant; one possible interpretation is that the FAI wanted Ian to work full-time, but only to pay him a part-time salary. In effect, Ian worked full-time for the Association. The FAI also later reversed its decision on the U21 position and Ian managed the U21 team for four years, until Don Givens took over in February 2000. All this was not a good start for the working relationship between the FAI and Ireland's new manager.

At this time, the 'Bring Wimbledon to Dublin' campaign was back in the news. I was, and still am, totally opposed to the imposition of an outside club onto Irish football. This is a solution that suits the 'armchair' fans, but would damage the structure of football. The League of Ireland may not be great, but it is improving, as evidenced by its slow progress up the UEFA ranking list. If there were a major professional club based in Dublin and playing in the English Premiership, then the very existence of the League of Ireland would be in danger. The major club would attract virtually all the commercial sponsorship and merchandising support. This would impact not only on football clubs but on other sports as well. The fans would have little money left after paying perhaps IR£50 for a ticket and IR£60 for a replica shirt that costs less than IR£10 to make. Bringing Wimbledon to Dublin was about money, not football.

Sam Hamman had visited Dublin on 8 February 1996, met with officials of Shelbourne FC and had been shown around Tolka Park. He had also met with officials of the FAI, some of whom supported the Wimbledon move to Dublin. This was a hugely controversial issue within football and its resurrection at this point in time only served to further inflame divisions within the game. Luckily, it has died as an issue. Wimbledon's relegation from the Premiership, allied to Sam Hamman's takeover at Cardiff, has probably buried it – deeply, I hope.

Joe McGrath had been the technical director of the Association for a number of years and had done a reasonable job with limited resources. Joe McGrath and Maurice Price, an FAI coach, had managed the underage international teams, eliciting credible performances, but not qualification for European underage championships. At that time, the FAI Technical Department consisted of three coaches, with one person providing secretarial support. Now there are at least twenty-five people in the department, with expenditure on coaching and the underage international match programme probably close to €3 million per annum.

Joe McGrath was interviewed in *The Star* on Monday, 19 February 1996, threatening to resign if he did not get the required support from the Association to enable him to develop football in Ireland. Joe and I get on well, but I believe his timing was atrocious. It may have been determined by the fact that Joe had been offered the position as technical director of the New Zealand Football Association. The development of football is a vital issue, but this was not the time to raise it, immediately following the shock resignation of the General Secretary of the Association. Joe was in England with the U16 team on the Monday, but carried through with his decision to resign when he returned to Dublin on the Tuesday. The FAI were now also without a technical director, a position that took nearly eighteen months to fill, when Brian Kerr was appointed in 1997.

Joe McGrath immediately took up the three-year position as technical director of the New Zealand FA. Before his departure from the FAI, he issued proceedings against the FAI for constructive dismissal. This again was settled out of court, requiring another substantial pay out by the Association.

At the time, the FAI had a serious problem with their referees, who were threatening to strike, starting 1 March 1996. Without referees, there would be no football. The basis of the dispute was the attempt by the FAI to introduce seminars for referees. The seminars were in fact tests of the physical fitness of referees and their knowledge of the laws of the game. Based on the results of these seminars and on their experience, referees would be graded and hence allocated to different leagues and different levels of football. Football referees get paid at all levels. It varies from perhaps €10 for a seven-a-side game at U8 level to in excess of €100 plus expenses for a League of Ireland game. Hence a referee's grade was directly related to his earning potential from football.

Two League of Ireland referees, Mick Tomney and Tommy Traynor, had refused to attend their seminar and had been subsequently downgraded by the Association. It was reported in the media that one of them had ended up refereeing an U12 match. Both referees had operated at the highest level for a good number of years and had obtained their UEFA badges, which meant that they were eligible for selection to referee competitive European and international matches.

The problem was the way the FAI reacted to Tomney and Traynor's refusal to attend the seminar. It was a new system and a good system, but it needed to be introduced by agreement. The unilateral demotion of the referees by the FAI led to the referees taking legal action against the Association. In a court ruling on 12 February 1996, Judge Cyril Kelly said that the FAI's decision to demote or re-grade the referees was outside the rules of the Association and was invalid. Judge Kelly awarded damages totalling IR£40,000. When costs for both sides were taken into consideration, the total bill for the FAI must have been close to double that amount.

What was worse for the Association was that shortly prior to the court hearing, an out-of-court settlement had been reached. This tentative settlement agreed an all-in figure of damages and costs of just IR£3,500. It was the FAI who decided to fight the case, much to its cost. Worse was to follow: The FAI misinterpreted the judge's ruling. On Wednesday, 14 February, the FAI sent letters, signed off by Sean Connolly, to 142 referees around the country, informing them that because of their failure to complete a seminar they were now deemed ineligible to referee. This letter directly contradicted the court ruling; each of these 142 referees was now entitled to sue the Association. Luckily, the letters were withdrawn and serious behind-the-scenes negotiations took place. Peace was restored, the strike was called off and the seminar system was successfully introduced, without further cost to the Association.

Let me summarise the FAI's crises at the time of my appointment as Acting General Secretary:

- Sean Connolly 'voluntarily' resigned as General Secretary, yet was paid a substantial termination payment.
- Sean McHale and Associates were paid IR£75,000 more than the FAI thought it owed them.
- The Association was lucky in escaping a compensation payment to Millwall FC of Stg£100,000.

- Maurice Setters, assistant manager under Jack Charlton, was paid a substantial termination payment.

- Michael Morris, the FAI's financial accountant, was paid a substantial termination payment in an out-of-court settlement.

- The Association did manage to recoup some IR£100,000 from its ticket debtors.

- The former FAI technical director, Joe McGrath, was paid a substantial termination payment in an out-of-court settlement.

- Two referees had been awarded a combined IR£40,000 in damages. Legal costs would have doubled the Association's bill.

And people wondered where the FAI's money had gone.

*****

And then there was Merriongate[2] – the scandal of the World Cup 1994 tickets. The late Veronica Guerin broke the Merriongate story in the *Sunday Independent* on 18 February 1996, just two days after the shock resignation of Sean Connolly. Let me be clear, the two events were unrelated.

In an exclusive by Veronica, entitled 'FAI in Crisis after Referees' Court Ruling', Veronica dealt with the referees dispute. However, in the second half of the article, she broke the story on the ticket losses of the 1994 World Cup. It is worth quoting in full:

> *In an unrelated matter, senior FAI personnel have confirmed that a London-based ticket agent absconded with Stg£200,000, which was revenue from tickets relating to the 1994 World Cup. The ticket agent told this newspaper that he had secured tickets for Irish games from the FAI but was not due to pay for them until after the World Cup. However,*

---

2. Three different currencies are used in this chapter, Irish pounds, sterling and dollars. The World Cup tickets were priced in dollars, whereas the money paid to the FAI by Joe Delaney was in sterling. I have converted the ticket values from dollars to Irish pounds at the exchange rate of IR£1 = $1.60.

unfortunately for the FAI the agent, Tio Marcos, absconded with the funds.

A senior FAI official has denied that the tickets given to Mr Marcos were for any of the Irish matches. He said that the FAI had traded quarter-final, semifinal and final tickets with Mr Marcos for Irish tickets. He said that the Stg£200,000 owed by Mr Marcos was in fact 'paid by someone else' in November 1994. As a result, he added, 'we are not unduly concerned about them'.

The FAI said that they were dealing with Mr Marcos in his capacity as a 'ticket agent'. They understood that Mr Marcos was selling tickets at face value to corporate enterprises.

The FAI told this newspaper that they are now satisfied Mr Marcos was not a recognised ticket agent[3] and they were naive to deal with him.

We understand that the FAI is also to conduct an investigation into how Mr Marcos secured Stg£200,000 worth of tickets without paying for them.

The FAI is not prepared to reveal who paid the shortfall of Stg£200,000 left by the agent or how this money was paid. It is our information that two cheques, one for Stg£130,000 and another for Stg£70,000, were paid to the Association in the name of a senior FAI official.

The issue of match tickets is a source of concern to the Association. Insiders in the FAI say that there has never been a balance between the revenue gained and the ticket sales.

A senior FAI official, who did not wish to be named, confirmed yesterday that this was the case. However, he added, 'It's not of such massive proportions that it causes concern'.

The representatives of the League of Ireland, Amateur League and Schoolboy Leagues do not agree with the views of

---

3.   The wording here has been slightly altered from the original for legal reasons.

this official. The matter is to be raised at the next meeting of the Association.

Readers may be surprised that it was Veronica Guerin, crime correspondent of the *Sunday Independent,* who broke this story. Veronica was an ardent football fan. Where she picked up the trail of the ticket story, I have no idea. But once she was on a story, there was no letting go. I was the recipient of a number of middle-of-the-night phone calls from Veronica, as she continued to chase the story. It did not end with the departure of Louis Kilcoyne and Joe Delaney from the Association. She was getting deeper and deeper into the story and had identified new twists. Unfortunately, her murder on 26 June 1996, ended the media investigation into the 1994 ticket scandal. I suspect that there were many additional explosive facts that never surfaced. I was in Glasgow on FAI business when I heard that Veronica had been ruthlessly murdered. I was absolutely shocked and deeply saddened by this news. During the Merriongate crisis, she had been very supportive of me. She showed her great passion for the game, through her determination to get to the bottom of the story surrounding the Merriongate scandal.

Veronica had continued to telephone me at intervals during the preceeding months. She had an arrangement to meet me to ask me about additional information she had come across. However, the meeting was scheduled for the day Garda Gerry McCabe was killed; she phoned me to cancel, as she had to go to Limerick. Veronica told me she had uncovered more interesting information. Alas, I never got to meet her to find out what she had discovered.

Reading the *Sunday Independent* report suggests to me that Veronica had excellent sources. Nearly all her information was subsequently proven to be correct, with the exception that it was non-Irish match tickets that were the subject of the scam. Even her payment amounts were virtually spot-on. The two payments had been Stg£140,000 and Stg£70,000, totalling Stg£210,000. The unnamed FAI spokesman quoted was obviously well briefed on the issue; at that time many of the FAI officers were unaware of the situation in the detail provided.

However, some of the details must have come from other sources, both inside and outside the FAI.

One of the funny things about the FAI quotes is the claim that Mr Marcos, a ticket agent, was selling tickets at face value to corporate enterprises. Come off it! No agent transacts business without collecting a fat fee. Veronica's story states that a senior FAI official made good the Stg£200,000 shortfall. This was crucial in what followed. It was officially denied by the FAI, but shortly afterwards the FAI Honorary Treasurer, Joe Delaney, admitted that it was true and that he had paid Stg£110,000 to the Association.

Let me put the situation into perspective. The FAI had purchased nearly IR£300,000 (over 3,000 in number) worth of non-Ireland match tickets, including semifinal (1,200) and final (500) tickets. These were expensive tickets. The average price of a World Cup final ticket was over IR£200.

What was the FAI at? It seems that the strategy was to purchase tickets for non-Irish matches and trade these with other Associations for tickets for the Irish games. There was a major problem with this strategy. Most other Associations do not get involved with such activities and, hence, the number of tickets other Associations would have for Irish matches and, thereby, available for swapping would be small. After the Associations, the next recourse for tickets for Irish matches was ticket agents, and here the FAI was out of its depth.

Let me describe the FIFA ticket strategy for a World Cup. It did not change much between the US in 1994 and Korea/Japan in 2002. Each Association is entitled to buy 8 per cent of the ground capacity for the matches in which it participates. It can also buy a limited number of tickets for other matches, including quarter-finals, semifinals and the final. A good number of tickets go to sponsors, commercial partners and the travel trade. The rest of the tickets are put on general sale to the public in the host country or via the Internet. A key difference is that all tickets bought from FIFA for 2002 had to be paid for in advance, whereas in 1994, the payment date was November, four months after the World Cup.

For USA '94, the FAI took up their full allocation of tickets for Ireland's matches and for selected quarter-finals, the semifinals and the final. They also bought tickets for selected first and second-phase matches, for which they thought that there might be a demand. They did this in order to have tickets with which to barter for Irish games. As an example, they purchased 200 tickets for the Germany v. Spain game in Chicago. Why did they do this? The FAI saw themselves as having a responsibility to provide a ticket for every Irish fan that wanted to attend the Irish games. To my knowledge, no other Association does this. They simply buy and sell on to their supporters the tickets to which they are entitled and let the rest fend for themselves. I don't know what it is about the psyche of the FAI, but they bring trouble on themselves by getting involved in areas that other Associations avoid. I thought that the notion of the FAI being a ticketing agent for the Irish fans would have died after Merriongate, but it came back in a limited way for the round-of-sixteen match against Spain in Korea in 2002.

The FAI's ticketing strategy in 1994 had little or no effect. Let me use the match against Italy in the Giants Stadium as the initial example. This was the only game for which the FAI obtained additional tickets. The FAI had received 4,082 tickets directly from FIFA. Through their acquisition policy, the FAI managed to source just a further 314 tickets, bringing the total provided by the FAI for that game to 4,396. I was one of those lucky enough to be among the 70,000 attending that game, having bought and paid for my ticket directly from the FAI. I estimate that there were about 45,000 Irish supporters at the game. Where did the other 41,000 Irish fans get their tickets, as it certainly wasn't from the FAI?

Irish fans are well able to look after themselves when it comes to tickets. World Cup 2002 again proved this. The FAI were entitled initially to 3,800 tickets for the match in Ibaraki against Germany. When Germany did not take up their full allocation, we got perhaps 1,500 more. The Association and, indeed, FIFA were paid in advance for these tickets. Perhaps 12,000 Irish fans attended that game. Many fans had to, and succeeded in, sourcing their tickets from outside the FAI. There were no complaints.

My third example brings us back to USA '94, this time to the round-of-sixteen match against the Netherlands in Orlando. The FAI bought their full allocation of 3,394 tickets from FIFA. They sourced no additional tickets. Many fewer Irish fans than expected turned up, as some of those supporting the team in the first phase had gone home. Tickets could not be given away before the game – I know, as I had five too many. Luckily, one of the people who had asked me to acquire tickets organised a whip-round to reduce my loss. The FAI were left with 385 unsold tickets to the value of IR£20,000 for this game.

That was 1994. The FAI had similar problems with ticketing in 1990 and incurred a loss of IR£154,000 on ticketing, made up of IR£80,000 on unsold tickets and IR£74,000 on ticket trading. Complimentary tickets were a further cost to the Association of IR£101,000. Tickets for the round-of-sixteen game against Romania in Genoa could not be given away. Yet again, I know because I was there, this time with one surplus ticket. The mistake was repeated for the quarter-final in Rome. Let me quote Dr Tony O'Neill, who was FAI General Secretary during Italia '90, from the *Irish Independent* of 27 February 1996:

> The audited accounts for 1990 made reference to a ticket discrepancy and this would explain at least some of the alleged shortfall. We had found ourselves with extra tickets for the Brazil v. Argentina last 16 game in Turin. We applied for them because there was a chance that we could have played there. Louis Kilcoyne went to Turin to try and offload the tickets. He was detained by the authorities outside the ground and an amount of money and tickets were confiscated.
>
> For the quarter-final in Rome we bought more tickets than we could sell. We squeezed as many tickets as we could out of FIFA but the expected numbers didn't come over for the game, so

we lost money there. I am not sure what the final figure was, but it was certainly noted in the accounts for 1990.

Given the 1990 experience, which was Ireland's first World Cup, one would have expected the FAI to pursue a different strategy for the next major championship. The maxim, 'once bitten, twice shy' did not seem apply to the FAI.

Neither did the maxim, 'when you are in a hole, stop digging'. In the week after Veronica's exposé, FAI Treasurer Joe Delaney managed to make a large excavation into which he, his fellow officers and the whole FAI were in danger of disappearing. There was little media reaction to Veronica Guerin's exclusive in the days that followed. The missing ticket money got one or two mentions in passing, but the hacks didn't have the information or, indeed, didn't know where to get it. However, the crisis meeting of the FAI Executive Committee on Wednesday, 21 February, provided them with a focus. The main topics were the replacement of the Chief Executive, the compensation row with Millwall and the threatened referees' strike.

The FAI turmoil was attracting a wider media interest. News editors and investigative news reporters were becoming involved. The press conference after the Executive Committee meeting on Wednesday, 21 February, was to be the catalyst for trouble. The FAI did not usually hold a press conference after the Executive Committee met, but the pressure of the resignation of Sean Connolly and revelations by Veronica Guerin the previous Sunday forced them to do so.

The press conference was a disaster. Most of the officers were not aware of the whole truth and thus ended up defending the indefensible and misleading the media. The headlines in Thursday's *Irish Independent* were 'Irish Soccer Smokescreen' and 'Denials and Silence the Order of the Night'. The report stated that the three-hour Executive Committee meeting had been studded with discord. One member was reported to have stormed out. Des Casey led the press conference in his role as Acting General Secretary. I believe that at this stage the full truth of the ticket issue was known only by

Joe Delaney. I believe that both Des Casey and Louis Kilcoyne gave answers at the press conference that they believed to be true, based on the information available to them at the time. As Eamon Dunphy reported in the *Sunday Independent* of 25 February:

> *Joe Delaney sat quietly beside his colleagues as, knowingly or not, he misled his colleagues.*

As reported in the *Irish Independent* the following morning, five key questions raised by the media each got a blunt 'no' for an answer.

- Had the executive any knowledge of a IR£200,000 shortfall for World Cup tickets? – No!
- Would there be an internal investigation into this matter? – No!
- Had any member of the Officer Board considered resigning his post? – No!
- Had the Officer Board anything to add in relation to Sean Connolly's resignation? – No!
- Were the officers concerned that three of their four full-time officials (staff members) had resigned in the space of five days? – No!

What was said was what caused the problem. You can only stonewall the press to a limited extent. Particularly in a group situation, someone is likely to say the wrong thing or say more than was intended. It was the comments at this press conference that turned Merriongate into an unstoppable force.

Louis Kilcoyne accepted that officers had dealt with a known ticket dealer – Tio Marcos, aka Theo Saveriades, aka George the Greek – though they (the officers) claimed 'naivety':

> *We dealt in good faith as best we know. We were not aware that the man named in a newspaper article was a tout. I don't know how many tickets were involved. This was one of many transactions we would have done but we know that we got paid every penny.*

Louis Kilcoyne believed this to be true when he said it. It was what he had been told by Joe Delaney. Indeed, it had been reported to the

Finance and Executive Committees of the FAI in November 1994 that no money was outstanding from World Cup tickets.

Des Casey prefaced Louis' remarks by reading from minutes of this 1994 Executive Committee meeting, which revealed that the officers had been told that there was no evidence to suggest a shortfall. I refer the reader to the portion of the statement issued on Michael Morris' behalf by his solicitor on 1 March that deals with this issue.

> *Also an incomplete account was given at the FAI press conference on Wednesday 21 February, regarding the alleged shortfall of Stg£200,000 in money accrued from the FAI's allocation of 1994 World Cup tickets. All statements quoted in respect of monies owing were attributed to me, but prior to the November 1994 (Finance and Board) meetings I had queried Joe Delaney, who was not only the Treasurer, but also the person who handled all of the World Cup ticket trading, and he had assured me that there was no reason to be concerned.*

Not only had the FAI Executive Committee been misled, but now the media had also been given incorrect answers, albeit unwittingly by the people who spoke. Joe Delaney had remained largely silent. The chase was now on. The media had smelt blood, and there would be no stopping the hounds until that blood had been spilled.

*****

I had been appointed as Acting General Secretary at this Executive Committee meeting. It hardly merited a mention in the papers the following morning.

The pressure was also mounting within the FAI. Finbarr Flood of Shelbourne resigned from the Executive Committee. The threat of a vote of no confidence in the officers, singularly and collectively, quickly raised its head. The League of Ireland delegates led it, but comments in the media suggested that there was widespread dissatisfaction. This threat split the apparent unity in the Officer Board. It was now every man for himself.

On Friday, 23 February, the crisis deepened. Treasurer Joe Delaney issued a statement in which he admitted that he personally covered a Stg£110,000 shortfall from ticket losses. What had happened between the Wednesday and the Friday to bring about this disclosure? Delaney's statement read as follows:

> *I wish to clarify my role in the acquisition and management of match tickets for the World Cup in America in 1994. In spring '94, the FAI ordered tickets for matches in other groups. These tickets were used to barter for extra tickets for the FAI and, in turn, for Irish fans.*
>
> *This was not the easiest of tasks but the object was to get as many extra tickets as possible for Irish fans. The exchange and purchase of tickets between national associations and, indeed, with agents is common practice at major championships. In 1994, one of these agents, with whom I had dealt on behalf of the FAI, proved less than trustworthy. The FAI was facing a shortfall of Stg£110,000.*
>
> *As the error of judgement in dealing with this agent had been mine, I felt honour-bound to personally meet this shortfall to ensure that the FAI was not at a loss. I now realise that I should have informed the FAI Senior Council of the facts in November 1994.*

The FAI had sourced just 314 additional tickets for one game!!

The truth had been withheld from the Finance and Executive Committees of the FAI. Some FAI officers had unwittingly given wrong information to the media. As Vincent Hogan described it in Saturday's *Independent* (24 February):

> *With each hour the diagnosis seems to worsen. In its blackest week, the Football Association of Ireland looked inwards and found only an open sewer. The wash of recriminations forced open cliques, dismantled time-worn friendships.*

The latter was true. Two members of the Officer Board, long-time friends, have not spoken to each other since. Writing of the press conference, Hogan continued:

*The press conference that followed amounted to a pathetic nadir
on the slide towards self parody.*

The media coverage was intense in the days that followed, reaching a crescendo at the weekend. Many an editorial was written on the need for the FAI to clean up its act. The Wednesday press conference had made matters worse. Rather than resolving anything, Joe Delaney's statement on the Friday created more problems. The questions remained unanswered.

Veronica Guerin added fuel to this fire in the *Sunday Independent* of 25 February with another exclusive, headlined: 'FAI Treasurer Paid Out Further £100,000'[4]. This was in direct contradiction to Joe Delaney's statement that he had personally met a shortfall of IR£110,000. Within two days, the 'clear the air' statement by Delaney had come under scrutiny. Veronica also raised the loss on the Italia '90 tickets, bringing the total loss to the FAI to well over IR£300,000.

Veronica obviously had very good sources within the FAI. Some of her information was surprisingly accurate and was shown to be so in the subsequent inquiry. Let me quote some of the key sentences in her article:

> The shortfall in ticket sales in the 1994 World Cup – met by treasurer of the FAI, Joe Delaney, was Stg£210,000, not the Stg£110,000 Mr Delaney admitted on Friday night. The Association also lost a further IR£130,000 during Italia '90.
>
> The 1994 World Cup shortfall came about because of a ticket sting by two international ticket touts, who claimed that they had been left with unpaid bills by the FAI from a previous ticket transaction.
>
> Documents within the FAI show that there were two payments made to the Association by Mr Delaney – one for

---

4. Veronica Guerin's first article found a shortfall of Stg£200,000. By the second article one week later, she had the accurate figure of Stg£210,000. The Stg£100,000 referred to in the headline was the additional amount to the Stg£110,000 admitted to by Delaney.

Stg£140,000 and one for Stg£70,000. On Friday, Mr Delaney confirmed that he had made up a shortfall of only Stg£110,000 from his personal funds.

The Sunday Independent *has learned that the money was paid by electronic funds transfer from an English bank to the sterling account of the FAI at the Bank of Ireland, Baggot Street, Dublin, in late November and early December 1994. The EFTs were made payable to the FAI and show the source of the funds as Joe Delaney.*

Last week's Sunday Independent *report that the 1994 shortfall had been met by an officer of the Association was denied by the President Louis Kilcoyne and by Mr Delaney, before the Treasurer made his statement on Friday night.*

Our information, which has been confirmed on two separate occasions by four senior FAI officials, is that two separate sums totalling Stg£210,000 were paid by Mr Delaney to the Football Association in November and December 1994. Mr Delaney refused to answer any questions.

The second paragraph claims that the sting was organised by two international ticket dealers, who believed that they were owed money by the FAI. This is supported by a finding by Bastow Charlton that there was no evidence in the FAI of an acknowledgement from a London ticket agent of a cash payment of IR£43,000, a matter which was the subject of a claim against the FAI.

Let me state clearly that I believe Louis Kilcoyne's statement at the Wednesday press conference reflected the facts as he believed them to be.

The timing of the payments in late 1994 was significant. This was when a report was made to the Finance and Executive Committees that there was no shortfall. It was when Michael Morris was querying the situation within the FAI and was told that there was nothing to worry about. It is also my information that the President of the Association, Louis Kilcoyne, wanted to bring in the Association's auditors at that time but was prevented from doing so.

That was not the full story, but it was all that got into the media. A further IR£18,500 was received subsequently and a deficit of IR£6,700 still remained.

Joe Delaney restated his position in an interview with Paul Lennon in *The Star* on Monday, 26 February, providing his response to the fresh allegations by Veronica Guerin. He denied repaying Stg£210,000 to the FAI for World Cup tickets and said he had no intention of quitting:

> I made my statement on Friday and I am standing over it now. I will give a full account of actions to the FAI Council meeting on 8 March. I'll stand over that and either stand or fall by my case.

When asked if he had made any additional payment relating to the 1994 World Cup final, he stated: 'No'.

Another aspect of the story was becoming a little clearer. It was emerging that the FAI had dealt with a well-known ticket dealer during Italia '90. In his article, Paul Lennon wrote that: David Ginger Browne had dealt with the FAI before and during the World Cup in Italy. The FAI dealings with Browne in Italy are believed to be the root cause of the supposed Stg£210,000 shortfall carried out by another dealer, Tio Marcos, also known by the second names of Mavros and Saveriades and 'George the Greek'. Browne, who was based in New York, was a familiar figure during the World Cup finals in the US. Lennon wrote that Browne supplied tickets for matches right up the World Cup final itself.

The suggestion appears to be that the FAI had short-changed Browne during Italia '90 and he had got his revenge with interest during USA '94. The other question was where he had sourced the tickets for the World Cup final. The answer is obvious.

*****

The day following Veronica Guerin's second revelation, Monday, 26 February 1996, was my first day in Merrion Square as Acting General Secretary. For me, everything had happened within seven days. Within the FAI, the mess had got worse. I remember Linda driving me into Merrion Square, as my car was going for a service; I arrived about 9 am. I rang the front doorbell, but got no response. The FAI did not officially start business until 9.30 am. I did not know this, nor did I know that there was a back entrance, off Fitzwilliam Lane. I stood ringing the doorbell for about ten minutes. Not an auspicious start.

When I finally gained entry and got through the reception area, the first person I met was none other than Joe Delaney. He wanted to speak to me. We went up to the General Secretary's office to have the discussion. Joe told me that the report in the *Sunday Independent* was accurate in the sense that he had paid Stg£210,000 from his bank account. However, he said some Stg£100,000 of this had been given to him for tickets he had sold, so Veronica's exclusive was not wholly accurate. We were getting into semantics. Joe had paid Stg£210,000, but only Stg£110,000 of this was his own money. The other Stg£100,000 was money he had received as payment for tickets.

Was Joe Delaney telling me that the money from the FAI's World Cup tickets went through a personal account rather than the FAI's account? He seemed to be. This was getting more bizarre. What a start!

The situation was getting rapidly out of control. I had spoken about an internal enquiry to establish the full facts. I quickly realised that this would not be sufficient. There was no one within the Association with the independence and expertise to carry out such an investigation. Political wrangling and manipulation would easily undermine an internal investigation. No, what was needed was a thorough and independent external investigation. Thus, my first decision as Acting General Secretary of the FAI was to request an accountancy firm, Bastow Charlton, to undertake an investigation into the US and Italian World Cup tickets and to have an interim report available in time for the National Council meeting set for Friday, 8 March. This was less than two weeks hence. It was a tall order. However, as there were likely to be motions of no confidence in the officers at this meeting, it was vital to get as much factual information as possible for the Council members. FAI politics would not be delayed for the full truth to be established.

I telephoned each of the officers to inform them of what I was doing. None of them had any objection. None of them could!

Bastow Charlton started work immediately and had a comprehensive interim report available for the Council meeting. The report established a lot of facts. It also identified areas where it was going to be impossible to get at the full truth. The report was available for the Council members.

By early March, the major revelations on Merriongate had been well aired in the media. Little new occurred for the next week. However, there was daily comment and analysis. The FAI troops were getting restless and were conveying their feelings through the media.

The next instalment of the great FAI soap opera occurred at a meeting between the officers and the league clubs on Monday, 4 March. The meeting had been demanded by the clubs in an attempt to get answers. By this stage, motions of no confidence in the officers had been tabled by Bohemians FC and also by the Schoolboys FAI. The politics of survival were underway.

There was only one item for discussion on the agenda of that meeting, but even that was pre-empted. Just as the meeting was about to start, Honorary Secretary Des Casey and Vice President Pat Quigley entered the room and asked to address the meeting. They disclaimed all knowledge of the payments by Joe Delaney and announced that they were resigning as officers of the Association. If the FAI Council wanted to reinstate them at Friday's meeting, then that was its prerogative. They issued statements, which converged on several key points. They stated that they had asked both Louis Kilcoyne and Joe Delaney to resign and when they declined, Des and Pat decided to resign.

In his statement, Des Casey stated:

> *At no time had I ever had hand, act or part in any irregularities, either directly or indirectly, nor as a non-executive director of the FAI had I ever knowingly contributed to the mismanagement of*

the Association's affairs. I believe that my honesty and integrity will stand up to any scrutiny and am confident that I will be exonerated by the ultimate findings of the investigation.

I telephoned Louis Kilcoyne and Joe Delaney and suggested that their positions were untenable and that they should resign. Having received no positive response, I have no option but to tender my own resignation as Honorary Secretary.

Pat Quigley said that:

The external enquiry, which I have always welcomed, is a positive move. It has and will continue to have my fullest cooperation. I look forward to the enquiry fully and completely exonerating my good name. In the interests of soccer in Ireland, I have over the past forty-eight hours requested Mr Louis Kilcoyne and Mr Joe Delaney to tender their resignations. Neither has taken this course of action to date. I now consider my position to be untenable and resign forthwith.

Des and Pat were clearly acting in concert. The Officer Board was now openly split. Des and Pat had distanced themselves from the other officers and would stand or fall in front of Council together. Des and Pat left the meeting before it had formally started. They had taken everyone by surprise, including their fellow officers.

The meeting continued for about three hours, ending at about 10 pm. Little was achieved and there was no indication of any movement by any of the remaining officers. No additional information was forthcoming. Positions seemed to be entrenched.

I was in my office upstairs immediately after the meeting, when Michael Hyland entered and tendered his resignation as an officer. He had his resignation already written out. Why he chose to do it in this fashion rather than announce it at the meeting, I can only guess. Michael was always his own man and would sink or swim on his own. I have no doubt that he was confident of getting enough votes to be reappointed. As Chairman of the League of Ireland and with a strong background in junior football, he was unlikely to lose out.

Michael had hardly left my office when Joe Delaney entered and told me he also was resigning. This was a surprise, as just two hours earlier a statement had been issued on his behalf saying that he 'would announce his decision at the Council meeting on Friday'. He gave the reason for his change of mind as:

> I have said all along that I wanted the opportunity to tell my side of the story to Council. When I heard that Des Casey and Pat Quigley were being afforded that facility on Friday, I made my decision to resign on the basis that I would be given the same courtesy.

Four down and one to go: Louis Kilcoyne was now the most isolated officer.

Why did the officers resign? I believe that Des, Pat and Michael wanted to distance themselves from Louis Kilcoyne and Joe Delaney. These three officers had been involved in the FAI for something like a combined seventy-five years. Their involvement in football had lasted even longer. It cannot have been an easy decision for them to resign. This was particularly true for Des Casey, who was a member of the UEFA Executive Committee, a position that was also on the line. These officers probably believed that they had increased their chances of surviving a confidence vote. I have less understanding of Joe Delaney's reasons. He might have wanted to isolate Louis or may have felt that resignation was a signal that he accepted that things had gone somewhat awry. He certainly fought hard to win the vote of confidence. Resignation was not a signal that he was bowing out of football.

*****

There was one funny incident that night. The media were camped on the doorstep of Merrion Square, looking to get a photograph or a quote from the league delegates as they left. Nothing of much significance was disclosed at the doorstep. This would happen later by mobile phone. One of the FAI staff members from the press office was leaving late that night. As she exited the front door, there was one lone photographer left. She told him that everyone had gone.

I had stopped briefly in Home Farm Football Club on my way home, when I received a phone call from Linda telling me that a local radio station was announcing on its news bulletin that all five officers had resigned. This puzzled me, as we had informed the media that four officers had resigned. I eventually found out the source of the information. I quickly realised what had happened. The FAI staff member had said that all the officers had gone – out the back gate – and there was no one left to be photographed. The photographer interpreted this as everyone had resigned.

This anecdote is a good illustration of how the media treat the FAI. The following day, the *Irish Independent* claimed that the incorrect news that Louis Kilcoyne had resigned was due to an erroneous report from Merrion Square. This was not true. The incorrect report emanated from one of their own, a photographer, who totally misinterpreted the situation, thought he had a scoop and tried to make a name for himself. The report had been picked up and broadcast on national and local radio and one newspaper ran with the story in its early edition. I had to try to correct the situation at midnight.

*****

Louis Kilcoyne was the only one still in office. I spoke to Louis on a number of occasions during the following days. I believed that he had a better chance of surviving if he held his hands up, admitted that these things had happened under his stewardship and resigned. I know he had outside advisers who were telling him differently: their advice was to stand his ground and fight. If Louis had bowed out, along with Des Casey, Pat Quigley and Michael Hyland, it might have left Joe Delaney solely in the firing line. However, Delaney resigned first and it was Louis who was left isolated. This was how he wanted it, but I am not sure that it was the right decision for him.

The scene was now set for the Council meeting on Friday, 8 March. In football, this meeting is known as the night of the long knives, courtesy of a headline in the *Evening Herald*. The meeting was scheduled to take place in the Westbury Hotel, starting at 5 pm. What the hotel had done to deserve the circus that was performed there that night, I do not know. What the hotel guests, who had paid a hefty rate for quietness, luxury and comfort, made of it is equally a mystery. There were hundreds of media personnel present from every sector of the industry. If memory serves me well, RTÉ interrupted its scheduled broadcasts until close down to bring the latest news to the nation. There was hourly coverage on radio news up until 3 am.

The meeting lasted for nearly ten hours. After a certain point, it was decided to fully resolve the matter in one session, regardless of how long it took.

The meeting took place in a suite of rooms (the Kildare Suite) to the left of the lobby. The journalists were camped in the bar and in the lobby, which are normally host to afternoon tea to the strains of a piano. The main problem with this arrangement from an FAI perspective was that the toilets were on the far side of the lobby and the meeting lasted until 3 am the following morning. Going to the loo was a daunting task, as the media were more interested in asking questions than in the comfort of one's bladder. The media were well supplied with leaks!

Before the formal start of the meeting, the Council members received and studied the interim report on the ticket investigation from Bastow Charlton. The firm effectively had eight days to work on it. They produced a thirty-two-page document with an additional fourteen pages of appendices. The report laid out most of the facts and clarified many matters, although it could not be conclusive on all areas. Two partners from Bastow Charlton presented the report to the Council in the Kildare Suite prior to the meeting. The presentation was followed by a question-and-answer session to clarify issues. Then, the Council members were given time to study the report in detail. It is likely that most of this time was taken up by caucus meetings rather than perusing the report.

The Bastow Charlton report was a damning indictment of the way the FAI managed its ticketing operation. Its findings fell into two categories: those specific to the Merriongate saga and those of a more general nature dealing with financial procedures and controls. The report was leaked to the *Evening Herald* and the details published on Friday, 15 March 1996. How it took so long to get into the media amazed me. The findings and recommendations were also published as the last two pages of Peter Byrne's official history of that FAI – a fitting tribute to its first seventy-five years! I have used the figures in the Irish pound values, as that was the currency at the time. The tickets were valued in dollars in the report. The findings of the report as published in the *Evening Herald* were as follows:

- The FAI purchased IR£296,000 ($474,000 for some 3,120 tickets) of 'other match' tickets (tickets for games in which Ireland was not involved) for USA '94.

- The five officers entrusted this amount of readily marketable tickets to one person, Mr Joe Delaney.

- Normal supervisory responsibility regarding these tickets was withdrawn from Chief Executive, Mr Sean Connolly, and the accountant, Mr Michael Morris.

- It appears likely that Italian, Brazilian and other fans paid over 'face value' for the FAI's final and semifinal tickets (1,700 tickets).

- Mr Delaney advised Bastow Charlton that he handed over IR£296,000 worth of World Cup tickets to an unfamiliar agent, without checking his creditability/reliability and without security, other than a $30,000 third-party cheque drawn in favour of another unknown third party.

- The custody, exchange and/or sale of these tickets were entirely uncontrolled and remained undocumented.

- The 'other match' tickets (and/or the corresponding cash) were outside the control of the FAI (and put in the sole custody of Mr Delaney) from May 1994 through November 1994, when most of the face value of these tickets was paid to the FAI. In November 1994, an amount of Stg£210,000 was paid to the FAI (in two separate bank transfers of Stg£140,000 on 2 November 1994 and Stg£70,000 on 9 November 1994). These monies were paid in by Mr Delaney, apparently to clear the balances on his account for the 'other match' tickets. However, it now appears that this payment still left a balance unpaid of IR£25,200. The records show that IR£18,500 was paid subsequently, leaving a deficit of IR£6,700.

- There were inordinate delays in the receipt and lodgement of USA '94 ticket sales. At 1 November 1994, over IR£334,000 remained to be collected and lodged.

- FAI records indicate balances of IR£39,000 still outstanding for USA '94 tickets (nearly two years later).

- There have been considerable delays between the receipt of cash/cheques and subsequent lodgements. On occasions, large amounts of both Irish and foreign currency were held in the FAI safe for prolonged periods without obvious explanation.

- Unsold tickets (still in Merrion Square and including tickets for the Italy game) totalled IR£37,000.

- Ticket allocation for the Italy, Mexico and Norway games were recorded in May 1994 and are adequately documented, although there were weaknesses in accounting control and debt collection.

- Ticket allocation for the Holland match was poorly controlled and documented. Details of sales and receipts were not recorded until April 1995 (nine months after the match).

- There is no written evidence that any of the IR£296,000 of 'other match' tickets were ever exchanged for Irish match tickets, other than IR£9,000 of Irish match tickets (314) distributed for the Italy game.

- Ticket losses in the US were IR£109,000 (over and above the scam).

- There is evidence that the executive functions of senior staff were restricted and their role in controlling FAI finances were inhibited by the involvement of certain officers in the day-to-day management of the FAI.

- There is evidence that expenditures were authorised and payments were made without the proper authorisation of two cheque signatories. In particular, certain authorised cheque signatories pre-signed blank cheques.

- There is some written evidence that cash (as opposed to tickets) of IR£86,000 was received by the Honorary Treasurer for 'other match' tickets before the World Cup (but not accounted for in the FAI's records until late July and November 1994).

- There is evidence that the FAI officials dealt with ticket dealers in the past and that FIFA expressed concern about this prior to the World Cup.

There are a number of observations that can be made on the report's findings:

- The FAI gambled nearly IR£300,000 on buying over 3,000 match tickets for non-Irish matches. Yet, they managed to obtain just 314 additional tickets for the Ireland v. Italy game.

- Joe Delaney paid Stg£210,000 to the FAI, as claimed by Veronica Guerin, but some of this money was FAI money that had been sitting in a personal bank account for up to six months. This was part payment by the ticket dealer. In addition, there appears to have been a third payment received of IR£18,500, but even this still left a balance owing of over IR£6,700.

- Brazilian and Italian fans, among others, were ripped off, in having to pay exorbitant prices for semifinal and final tickets originally bought by the FAI, but passed to a dealer by Joe Delaney. George the Greek not only scammed at least Stg£110,000 of the FAI's money, but also made another small fortune by ripping off Brazilian and Italian fans.

The second-last point in the Bastow Charleton conclusions is very strange indeed. Some of the 'other match' tickets were sold for cash prior to the World Cup. I would love to know why. I thought the whole idea was to barter these tickets for additional Irish tickets.

One new item in the *Evening Herald* article of 15 March was a table showing the allocation of tickets for the Ireland v. Italy game. The FAI had published its intended allocation of the original 3,325 tickets from FIFA. However, an additional 942 had been received from FIFA, and, of these, 754 had been allocated to the officers and the General Secretary's office.

*****

With the presentation made and all the questions asked, the meeting was again adjourned to allow for final discussions. The caucuses again met and reaffirmed their voting intentions on the reappointment of officers. This was important. In the FAI, it is by no means a secret ballot with one man, one vote. A number of affiliates to the FAI vote in blocks. It is one man, one vote within these affiliates, but when a majority of the delegates from that affiliate are in favour of one decision, then all the votes go in that direction as a block vote.

Let me illustrate this, using the Leinster Football Association (LFA) as an example. With nine votes, the LFA was the largest such affiliate. The twenty-two league clubs at Council all voted individually. Bernard O'Byrne was President of the LFA at that time. The LFA votes were crucial, as nine votes swinging one way or another was very significant in deciding which of the officers would survive. In the end, the votes of the LFA were vital on all motions. Although they were far from unanimous amongst themselves, the LFA voted nine votes to zero in favour of some officers and nine votes to zero against others. The LFA sit as a group at meetings and show each other their votes to ensure their system is adhered to. The Munster Football Association (five votes) and the Junior Council (two votes) vote in a similar manner.

There were forty-seven votes in the room. The Council numbered fifty-two at the time, but four of the five officers had resigned and the President, Louis Kilcoyne, as Chairman of the meeting, only had a casting vote in the event of a tie. Twenty-four votes were needed to survive.

The real business of the meeting started just after 8 pm, three hours after the Council members convened. The four officers who had resigned were excluded from the meeting until this point. They had been given a copy of the report as soon as it was available. They had sat in a private room, just off the Kildare Suite, since arriving at the hotel. I would have loved to have overheard their conversations.

Shortly after these resigned officers entered the Council meeting at 8 pm, a statement was issued to the press on Joe Delaney's behalf, giving a detailed account of his version of events. It is reproduced as Appendix A to this chapter. The timing of this was unfortunate, as Delaney did not get to address the Council until some hours later. As a result, the media had access to his statement long before the Council. This was not well received by Council members, who heard of it during breaks from the meeting.

With all the resigned officers present, there was more discussion on the Bastow Charlton Report, and this time the officers had the opportunity to question the authors of the report. This continued until about 9.30 pm, when the motions of no confidence in the officers began to be heard. The procedure was that each officer in turn was allowed to address the Council and answer questions put by Council members; then the motion of no confidence was put formally to the floor.

I cannot remember the precise order in which the motions were put, but my best recollection is that Pat Quigley was first, followed by Michael Hyland, Joe Delaney, Des Casey and, finally, Louis Kilcoyne.

Pat Quigley stated that he had asked Louis Kilcoyne and Joe Delaney to resign and this was still his position. Pat performed brilliantly on the night, and this, coupled with his resignation on the previous Monday, left him in a strong position. He succeeded in winning the vote of confidence, by a good margin. This must have been good news for Des Casey, although he would have to wait another few hours before having his fate finally determined. It was 10.30 pm when Pat Quigley was reinstalled to Council and as Vice President of the FAI. Pat Quigley then issued a statement to the press.

Next up was Michael Hyland. Michael had done his political work behind the scenes and was never really in danger. His presentation on the night was less strong than Pat Quigley's, and he was less critical of some of his fellow officers. Nonetheless, Michael also won his confidence vote easily. Two votes concluded and still there had been no sacrificial lamb.

The officer at the centre of the mess, Joe Delaney, was up next. This was the crucial vote. If Delaney survived, then there was unlikely to be any casualties. Delaney read his pre-released press statement to Council. In Delaney's version of events, it had all been done to provide tickets for the Irish fans (all 314 of them). Ireland's defeat to Holland had left the Association with many unusable tickets. The gamble that Ireland would at least qualify for the quarter-final had failed. The tickets were worthless if brought back to Ireland. He took a calculated risk, one he now bitterly regrets, and gave the tickets to 'George the Greek' and received assurances that all monies would be paid before November. He apologised for allowing his fellow officers to mislead the public and the media.

In his statement, Delaney also raised unrelated issues, such as a perceived attempt to link him to misappropriation of Manchester United tickets to the amount of 200 per game and said that the suggestion he had anything to do with the touting of these tickets was disgraceful. He refuted that he had a personal allocation of 2,000 tickets for Irish home matches. He denied that he had sold tickets for the same section of the stadium to both Irish and English fans for the match in Lansdowne Road in February 1995.

Delaney had some support at Council, but in the end he was badly beaten in the vote of confidence. His margin of defeat was in double figures. The LFA had voted nine to nil against Delaney. With a reversal of the LFA vote, he might just have survived. It was just after midnight when Delaney left the Council meeting. He would only answer questions from the media based on his statement. Nothing was clarified.

Des Casey was up next. Like Pat Quigley and Michael Hyland, he was never in serious danger. His long service to the game, his position in UEFA and the fact that he had decided to resign were all very much in his favour. He won easily, by the biggest margin of the night. Only the Council die-hards wanted a complete clear-out of the officers.

It was 1 am when Louis Kilcoyne began his address to the Council. Louis had vacated the chair and I, as General Secretary, chaired the rest of the meeting. This was somewhat unusual, but as the Chairperson did not have a vote, no one with a vote wanted to be Chairperson. The re-elected officers, to the best of my recollection, took no part in the meeting or the voting.

The question was whether the dismissal of one officer was sufficient to satisfy Council. There was no doubt that Joe Delaney was the prime culprit for Merriongate, but would he also drag down Louis Kilcoyne? Louis started from a disadvantage. Many of the league clubs, his political base, would vote against him, due to his perceived involvement with the loss of Milltown to football.[5] Could he overcome this?

Louis put on a spirited performance. He was the wrong man in the wrong place when the wheels came off. He had tried to get an investigation the previous November but had been thwarted. Louis had many supporters on the Council, including some league clubs, but many of the big players from junior football were opposed to him continuing as President. The vote was taken at around 2.30 am and the result was announced just before 3 am. Louis had been defeated. No official result was announced, but I know that the margin was just three votes (twenty-five to twenty-two). It had been very close. The nine LFA votes, led by Bernard O'Byrne, had gone against him.

Louis accepted his fate with dignity. He had his friend, Eamon Dunphy, as his media adviser on the night. He emerged into the media scrum and spoke of his disappointment. Louis showed no bitterness and announced that he would not appeal the decision of Council. One of my clearest memories of that night was an embrace between Louis and myself, even though I had presided over his

---

5. Glenmalure Park in Milltown, the home of Shamrock Rovers, was sold for housing development in 1987. At the time, the Kilcoyne family controlled Shamrock Rovers and Louis Kilcoyne was general manager of the club.

departure from football. Louis is a gentleman and, whether or not I agree with him over football matters, I count him as a friend.

Thus ended the FAI's night of the long knives. As Vice President, Pat Quigley took over as acting President until he was confirmed in that position at the AGM in June. The FAI also needed a new Honorary Treasurer; Bernard O'Byrne was duly elected to this position at the following Council meeting in April.

At the Association's AGM in July 2002, Joe Delaney was made an honorary life member of the FAI.

*****

Bastow Charlton completed their work and produced a full report. It made many recommendations. Those dealing with ticketing and financial control were implemented; those dealing with other structural and political reforms were largely ignored. Instead, a further report was commissioned from consultant Ray Cass. This report was the most far-reaching and radical ever produced for the FAI. The scope of its proposed reforms went far beyond the Genesis Report. It dealt not only with the administrative structures and staffing of Merrion Square, but also looked at reform of the political structures, something Genesis ignored. It advocated a ten- to twelve-man Board, but the FAI decided on a twenty-two-man board. The Ray Cass Report recommended that members, clubs and players should have a larger say. The FAI cherry-picked the recommendations they implemented. We got new committees and formally became a Board rather than an Executive Committee. This was window dressing. The real meat of the proposals was rejected. Let me admit that, at the time, I supported the partial implementation of the Cass Report, something with hindsight I would change.

*****

As a postscript to Merriongate, some weeks later I received a phone call from Joe Delaney, asking whether I could meet with him, as there were some matters he would like to discuss with me. The meeting would have to take place outside of Merrion Square. We met in the

Conrad Hotel for coffee. Joe Delaney asked me for his Stg£110,000 back! I was shocked. I said 'No'; the meeting ended. I never raised this request with other people in the FAI. In the context of what had happened, it was preposterous. I never heard about it again. I often wonder if some future events were in any way related to this refusal by me.

There was one other infamous incident that summer. In May, it was brought to my attention that FA Cup final tickets supplied to the FAI had been sold to one of our major sponsors through a ticket agency. What was worse, this sponsor had requested tickets from the FAI and had been told that there were none available. Imagine his surprise when he got two tickets from alternative sources, stamped with the FAI's name. He brought the matter to my attention.

The two tickets in question had been allocated to the FAI commercial manager, Donie Butler. It was Donie's responsibility to look after the Association's sponsors. Tickets allocated to Donie Butler should only have been used for sponsors. Getting to the truth of the matter was difficult, as the people involved did not want to point the finger. However, in the end it was confirmed that Donie Butler was the source of the tickets and their convoluted path through the ticket agency to the sponsor was clarified.

As this matter was coming to a head, I was about to depart to France on holiday. I called into Merrion Square on my way to Rosslare and spoke to Donie Butler. He had no intention of resigning from his position and was still protesting his innocence. I left for a two-week break, believing that the matter could be dealt with on my return. Forty-eight hours later, as I opened the door to my accommodation in south-west France, the phone rang. It was Des Casey telling me that Donie Butler was resigning. Des asked whether I could come back. The next day, I drove to Nantes and got a flight to Dublin via Gatwick. When I landed, I took a taxi to the Berkeley Court Hotel, where an emergency Executive Committee meeting was about to start. What I was unaware of was that during my travelling time, the officers of the Association had negotiated with Donie Butler and had come to a termination agreement with him, involving a very substantial payment. Donie had instigated this process. He obviously thought that he could get a better deal in my absence, as I was the one person in possession of the full facts. The meeting of the Executive Committee was a rubber-stamping exercise. My journey back had been wasted.

*****

The FAI needed to appoint a permanent Chief Executive/General Secretary at the end of my six-month tenure (31 August 1996). They decided to advertise this position, which I suppose was fair enough, though I was a bit disappointed. I thought that I had been doing a good job. I had extracted the Association from the Merriongate mess and had stabilised its operations. I felt that they might offer me an extended contracted. It was not to be. On one occasion, Bernard O'Byrne asked me if I was going for the position and, when I replied 'yes', he said that he would not oppose me. This was not to be either; Bernard applied for the position.

Interviews were held during August; an aptitude assessment was carried out as well. What I did not realise at the time was that Bernard was interviewed some weeks in advance of the other candidates, as he was going to the US with the Athletic Union League. There was a five-person selection panel, made up of President Pat Quigley; Charlie Cahill of the Leinster Football Association; Bill Attley, the chief referees inspector; Niamh O'Donoghue of the Ladies Football Association; and Michael Cody of Cobh Ramblers. I knew that I would not receive the support of the first two – they were from junior football, as was Bernard. Nonetheless, I thought that I still had a chance. Bill Attley and Niamh O'Donoghue were two professionals with a lot of experience in personnel recruitment. Michael Cody was from a league club, my football base.

I heard that it was a tight decision, with the assessment scheme used unable to split Bernard and me. In the end, it came down to a vote and I lost out by three votes to two, with, I believe, Michael

Cody of the league joining the two people from junior football in voting in favour of Bernard. I was hugely disappointed when I was informed in advance of the September Council meeting. I know that many Council delegates were shocked that my name was not put forward, but such is the FAI.

After the meeting, I was encouraged by everyone to remain in football and the FAI. Some consolation! They told me the position of Honorary Treasurer was again vacant and, given my financial background, I had the experience and expertise to do the job. I said I would give it consideration. When I decided that I would seek election as Honorary Treasurer, I found that a candidate, supported by people who had originally asked me to stand, was opposing me. Fergus McArdle from Dundalk is an accountant and a successful businessman. He had previously been involved with Dundalk FC. Fergus travels to all the Irish games and we get on well. In the end, I won by a two-to-one margin from the fifty-plus votes cast. The league clubs backed me solidly and this was enough to win the day.

Thus, on 25 November 1996, I became the Honorary Treasurer of the Football Association of Ireland.

*****

Appendix A

Statement by Joe Delaney, March 8 1996

When I asked for the opportunity to address you this evening, it was for a very fundamental reason: to set the record straight about my role as Treasurer of the FAI, specifically in relation to the purchase and allocation of tickets. I also wish to expose as untrue the shameful allegations made that I somehow acted improperly and abused my position in the Association in order to benefit myself.

It is because, first and foremost, I am answerable to you (the FAI Council) that I have refused to publicly comment on recent press allegations. But for quite some time now, I have been subjected to the most appalling smear campaign of innuendo, half truths and whisperings, which has at its root the belief that, as the person in charge with the responsibility of satisfying the huge ticket demands of Irish fans, I enriched myself in the process. That is an appalling calumny and a denial of the value of twenty years of work that I have done willingly, voluntarily and without charge to the FAI, because of my love of the game and my delight at being part of a wonderful era in Irish football. Indeed, the success that Ireland achieved in the Charlton era, which generated an unprecedented support for the national team over eight years, is at the heart of the problems now laid at my door.

The initiatives that I took on behalf of Irish fans over these years are now being misrepresented by many people who were at the time delighted and grateful that the results of my actions meant that they and their friends could attend and support the Irish team in person in stadia throughout the world. It is easy to be wise after the event, but I want to go back to 1990 and the chaos we experienced in relation to tickets during Italia '90.

It was at Italia '90 that the practice of trading tickets originated. My most vivid memory of ticket chaos was prior to our game in Genoa. Indeed, the euphoria of our subsequent win over Romania was lost on me due to sheer fatigue of the bartering process I became engaged in.

The days leading up to the game were manic, trying to barter and secure tickets [for fans] outside stadia, who had queued for hours and even days in extreme heat. Tony O'Neill, then General Secretary, and I spent many hours trying to negotiate tickets for the fans. In the end, we secured 3,000 tickets through a Novant (Italia '90) Tour ticket agent. At the time, nobody was concerned as to the source of the tickets, nor did the Association conceal that we dealt with a ticket agent.

As you are aware, we defeated Romania and were on our way to Rome. However, what was forgotten was that the Association suffered a loss, as the fans refused to pay face value of £80 a ticket, the only ones we had left, and we had to sell them for only £40.

Our next match was in Rome. We had reached the quarter-finals of the World Cup. As you can imagine, the pressure was enormous to acquire tickets and the government of the day even sent the Minister for Sport, Mr Frank Fahy, TD, to help us with our long and tedious negotiations.

We bartered whatever semifinal and final tickets we had left, for tickets for the Italian game. And, in fact, by miscalculating our requirements we were left with surplus tickets, showing a loss to the Association in all ticket transactions for Italia '90. I have often reflected on the fact that if we had beaten the Italians, we had nothing left to barter with and God only knows what we would have done.

The whole episode left me mentally and physically drained and I resolved that the Association should never be exposed to such a situation again.

When we qualified for USA '94, in consultation with my fellow officers, I was delegated to take charge of the conversion of tickets we acquired for non-Irish games into Republic of Ireland tickets. I was determined that the follies and losses of Italia '90 would not be repeated, and I decided to take full control of all transactions. I was approached by a ticket agent named Theo Saveriades, who gave assurances that he was in a position to acquire tickets for all Irish games through other Associations. The objective of trading was to secure as many tickets for Irish matches as possible. All transactions were conducted at face value on all tickets on a barter system.

All dealings were reasonably controlled at the point of departure of the Republic of Ireland team from the World Cup. Because of the Irish team's exit from the World Cup and the anticipated reduction in demand for tickets for the Holland game, I now found myself in a situation where we were returning home and I had surplus tickets. Had we qualified for the next round in Dallas, these tickets would have been used but now they were non-returnable to FIFA and worthless if brought home. I then took what I considered at the time to be a calculated risk, but one which I now bitterly regret: I gave the tickets to Theo Saveriades. I received assurances from him that all monies due to the FAI would be paid on or before the FIFA settlement date in November of 1994. In all, I received £100,000 in the form of tickets, drafts and cash – some before we left Ireland and more while still in America. But on several occasions I went to London to try and secure the remaining funds without success. Despite many deadlines and further assurances no monies were forthcoming.

It was at this stage that I considered myself responsible for the debacle I now find myself in and decided to bridge the outstanding monies to the Association. I did so in two credit transfers of £140,000 and £70,000, respectively. As I retrieved some £100,000 back from Theo Saveriades as already stated, the shortfall I personally met was £110,000, as I declared in my statement of 23 February.

Before I embarked on this course of action, I now fully realise that I should have consulted my fellow officers for guidance. I truly regret not doing so.

I should state at this stage that I fully expected to retrieve all monies owing, but in the early months of 1995 it became clear that Theo Saveriades had vanished and, with him, his debts. At this point in time, the Association had suffered no financial loss and stubbornly I decided to try and let the matter rest. For me to have allowed my fellow officers to mislead the public and the media by my silence was unforgivable and has cost me, and is costing me, a lot of pain. I wish to apologise now to the officers and to the Council for my silence. As to the misadventure with the tickets, I have paid the ultimate price for a foolish decision made for the best of reasons in the euphoria of the World Cup.

I now want to return to recent allegations in the media. These allegations have caused me much personal pain and have also, of course, injured my family, friends and colleagues. Let me unequivocally state that I regard these accusations as malicious, without foundation and wholly hurtful to my reputation.

An attempt has been made to link me to the misappropriation of Manchester United tickets to the amount of approximately 200 per game. The suggestion that I or the FAI had anything to do with the touting of these tickets is disgraceful. I have been attending games at Old Trafford for the past twenty-five years and have built up a relationship with Manchester United officials of trust and integrity.

I have received a small number of tickets for matches from time to time, and have credit card statements and faxes to attest that these were allocated to Council members and not sold to touts.

Since the alleged misappropriation, I have attended Old Trafford on numerous occasions. My honesty has never been called into question there. I have never abused the tickets they have provided me with and I deeply resent the suggestion that I might have.

The suggestion that I personally had a ticket allocation for home [Ireland] matches of 2,000 tickets is ludicrous in the extreme. FAI records over the last two years show my personal average ticket allocation at around 250 tickets per home match. To inflate that figure by 800 per cent is unfounded and malicious.

Recent reports that I owe a substantial amount to the FAI for tickets are also fictitious. Nothing could be further from the truth, and I hold a letter from the FAI in support of this.

I want to take this opportunity also to deal with a possible misinterpretation by some people regarding ticket prices for the 1994 World Cup. The FAI prudently added a small premium to the ticket prices as a hedge against currency. This premium resulted in a surplus to the FAI of $49,000.

Finally, it deeply saddens me that it has been suggested that I or any member of the FAI was somehow responsible for the tragic scenes in Lansdowne Road last year during the Republic of Ireland v. England match. This I regard as perhaps one of the most callous allegations made. Having acted as security chief of the FAI for ten years, nobody would be more conscious than I of the inherent danger of mixing tickets and fans in such an emotionally charged atmosphere. I have documented seating arrangements for all tickets I issued and I am distraught, as is my family, that anyone should think I had any involvement in the barbaric scenes which we all so sadly witnessed.

I want to thank you for listening to me and for your support over the years. I want to thank my wife, Joan, and my family and colleagues for their strength and encouragement of the past month. It has been very tough on us all. I have given twenty-five years of my life to the game of soccer and I have lived for every moment – the bad times as well as the good. During those years, on every occasion that I acted for the FAI, I always did so in good faith, with the needs of the fans my top priority. My only regret is that I am now forced to retire from an Association, which has become a huge part of my life. I wish Mick McCarthy and the Irish soccer team the very best of luck in the future and promise all my support wherever I can give it.

2

Eircom Park and the National Stadium

Eircom Park started out in a blaze of enthusiasm. Everyone in football wanted a stadium. The concept was good. A multi-functional 45,000 capacity stadium, costing just IR£65 million, would meet the needs of Irish football. The cost was 'cast in stone'. The project would be self-financing. It would generate huge profits for the Association, money that would be used to develop the game at all levels. It was everyone's dream come true at the wave of a magic wand. Unfortunately, it was too good to be true.

At the outset, I was a strong supporter of Eircom Park. However, after some time, I began to question the financial assumptions on which the project was based. It took me some months to realise that they were totally unrealistic and could bankrupt the Association. The main reason for this delay was the difficulty in getting access to information and getting answers to the questions I asked. This was despite the fact that I was Honorary Treasurer of the Association and a director of the stadium development company.

I strongly support the concept of a national stadium and sports campus at Abbotstown. This is not due to politics; it is based on the needs of all sports in this country. It should be built regardless of the state of the public finances and the political wrangling of the government parties. Travelling with the Irish team, I have seen superb sporting facilities in numerous countries, many of them, such as Iran and Macedonia, with a fraction of Ireland's wealth per capita. The facilities in Malaysia are superb. In every case, the state has built or largely financed them. Provision of a national stadium is seen as the responsibility of the state. These facilities are beneficial to the people of these countries. They take pride in them.

The Lansdowne Road site is too small for a 65,000-capacity stadium. I was very surprised that the May 2003 joint FAI/IRFU study came up with Lansdowne Road as a practical solution to the stadium problem. It is my belief that previous studies had come up with the opposite conclusion. A city centre stadium may be optimal if the site is large enough, but that is not the case at Lansdowne Road or, indeed, at any other city site that has been suggested.

I believe that the government has an obligation to provide adequate sporting facilities as part of its social responsibilities, not only for the major sports, but for all sports, as is the plan for Abbotstown. If the government set aside just €50 million a year for the next ten years, Abbotstown in all its glory would quickly become a reality. This is just 0.01 per cent of the government's annual expenditure – a drop in the ocean in overall financial terms. After it became obvious to me that Eircom Park was not viable, it was my view that the government's National Stadium was, and still is, the only option. A joint FAI/IRFU stadium will run into the same problems as Eircom Park, unless it gets significant state financial support. To me, the National Stadium should not be the subject of any debate. Just build it!

I am very disappointed that the Abbotstown project was shelved because of petty political wrangling. From talking to them, all the main political parties, with the exception of the PDs, support the National Stadium. The infrastructure cost argument is also fallacious. The west and north-west of Dublin are the most rapidly developing areas of the city. I know, because I lived in east Meath and commuted to Dublin for twenty years. I have seen rapid change over the last five years. Whether Abbotstown gets built or not, new roads and rail systems are needed. The M50 is currently unusable at certain times of the day.

The Aquatic Centre at Abbotstown is a fabulous facility and something for us to be proud of. It would be a great pity if it became an isolated development.

The current situation with regard to a stadium for international matches is unsustainable. Lansdowne Road is an antiquated stadium and is unsuitable in very many respects for international events, both rugby and football. The FAI have been using Lansdowne Road as its international venue since 1981. My late father, also Brendan Menton, was President of the FAI at the time and was instrumental in obtaining the agreement with the IRFU over the use of Lansdowne Road.

While the IRFU have been very supportive of the FAI in providing Lansdowne Road, the agreement is restrictive in many ways. The IRFU are the landlords and the FAI are very much the tenants. The IRFU get a commission on every penny the FAI generate at football internationals in Lansdowne Road. In addition, the FAI have to meet all the expenses of managing the stadium on match days; these are considerable, particularly when the temporary seats have to be installed on the terraces for competitive games. The IRFU built and own the stadium and are entitled to their income. However, in its present condition, Lansdowne Road's days as an international venue are numbered.

The main problem with Lansdowne Road is its limited capacity and facilities. It is very old and, with the exception of the new East Stand, it has not been renovated. From a rugby perspective, it is very far behind the new stadia at Twickenham, Murrayfield, Cardiff and Stade de France. It has just 23,000 seats in the two stands, although some 1,500 touchline seats augment this. Its total capacity is 49,000 for rugby internationals, and either 35,000 (all-seated) for competitive football internationals or 45,000 when the terraces are used at friendly matches. The FAI imposed their own capacity of 45,000 – put it this way, I would not like to be on the terraces when there are 49,000 people in the ground.

Let me relate one of my first experiences when I was Acting General Secretary of the Association in 1996 and, as such, event controller for football matches at Lansdowne Road: Ireland were playing Celtic in a testimonial for Mick McCarthy. There were in excess of 40,000 people in the ground, on a sunny Saturday afternoon. Many of them had been in the local pubs before the game, and, as is usual with Irish sports fans, were leaving it late to get into the ground. I was walking around the ground, getting a general feel for what happens on these occasions. I was behind the South Terrace and could see crushes of people trying to make their way onto the terrace through the access passageways, which are called vomitaries! I suppose the name derives from people being pushed in at one end and spat out at the other. However, on this occasion, the terrace was full and the exits onto the terraces were blocked. It was a very dangerous situation and the stewards were under pressure. The pushing and shoving was intense. Many people were trapped in the crush and couldn't go either backwards or forwards. Luckily, no one was injured. It was a very early lesson for me in crowd safety at Lansdowne Road.

On the same occasion, I received a complaint from a fan who was trying to get onto the terrace with his two-year-old daughter in his arms. He had obviously been given the responsibility of minding the child for the afternoon, but he wasn't going to miss the match, nor, indeed, had he missed his pints in the pub beforehand. He was the worse for wear. We accommodated him and his daughter in stand seats. I would hate to think of what might have happened had he actually succeeded in getting onto the terrace.

Let me assure supporters that the FAI run an excellent safety operation in Lansdowne Road, under the control of FAI safety officer, Declan McClusky, and FAI chief security officer, Joe McGlue. The procedures have been hugely improved since 1996, and the safety of spectators is paramount at football internationals. Under the FAI, Lansdowne Road operates to the highest international standards on match days, despite its limitations as an old stadium. We have international observers sent by FIFA and UEFA at competitive games, and they never find anything wrong with the management of the events.

For competitive international matches, the FAI have to convert the stadium to an all-seating format. This is an expensive and costly operation. FIFA have dictated that competitive matches must take place in an all-seated stadium. I have no doubt that in many countries, this rule is not strictly observed. There is good reason for the all-seated edict. There have been numerous instances of death and injury due to overcrowded stadia and, indeed, due to the collapse of temporarily installed seating. The incident at a French Cup semifinal at the Furiani Stadium in Bastia on 5 May 1992 is probably the most telling example. Seating on a scaffolding frame collapsed. Sixteen people were killed and some 600 were injured.

Temporary seating is used at major sporting events all over the world, largely without incident. Major golf events are probably the best example. I have no doubt that the construction and safety of such stands have improved greatly in recent years and, like the temporary stands at Lansdowne Road, they are subject to many safety checks and certification. With one minor exception, the temporary seating at Lansdowne Road for football internationals has been incident free.

It costs the FAI in excess of Stg£100,000 per match to install the approximately 12,000 temporary seats, which are brought in from the UK. Depending on the exchange rate between sterling and the euro, this is equivalent to between €140,000 and €160,000. The FAI's gross income from these 12,000 seats, at an average of €25 per seat, is €300,000. Giving 15 per cent commission to the IRFU costs €45,000. Paying for the manpower to manage the seats on match days takes another sizeable chunk of the revenue. There is not much profit left for the FAI out of these 12,000 seats.

The other problem with Lansdowne Road is the lack of off-the-field facilities. Compared to any other stadium that the Irish team has played in recently, Lansdowne Road's facilities are pre-historic; I include countries such as Estonia and Cyprus in this comparison.

There are two nice dressing-rooms and a referee's room. There is one other room that is part of the players' facilities, which is used as a medical room or doping-control room as required. There is also a large function room, which can accommodate perhaps 200 VIPs. I have been in it, when in excess of 300 people have crammed into it after an international match.

There are no administration rooms or meeting rooms, and there are no proper media facilities. The press room behind the press area of the Upper West Stand is small and cramped and cannot cater for the number of media people, in terms of space or telecommunication facilities. The Lansdowne Pavilion to the left of the West Stand is used for post-match press conferences. It is old and shabby. The managers and players must walk along the pitch to get to it. There is no secure mixed zone, where journalists can meet the players for a few minutes to get their reactions to the game. We sometimes use a corridor near the dressing-room, but if there is FIFA doping control at the match, then this is off limits.

Television interviews after the match take place in the hallway. This has to be cordoned off to prevent people on their way to the after-match function crowding through and upsetting the interviews. Despite the best efforts, it is mayhem, with the interviews taking place in a noisy environment. People often stop to listen to the interviews, and security staff have to move them along. When there are two TV stations and two camera crews using different interview points, the situation becomes ridiculous. Lansdowne Road was a great stadium and has a tremendous sporting history. Now it is an embarrassment. I say this as someone from football, a sport that has never owned its own stadium in Ireland.

*****

When Bernard O'Byrne became General Secretary/Chief Executive of the Association in September 1996, he quickly set it as a personal objective to construct a stadium for football. This had been a dream for most people involved in the game, and Bernard wanted to turn it into a reality. Everyone would support him in this. The time was ripe for the FAI to consider building their own stadium. Bernard's plans fell onto very receptive ears.

The FAI established a Stadium Committee in 1998. The committee consisted of the usual (football) political representation of all such FAI committees. Relevant expertise had nothing to do with it. It met on a number of occasions to hear reports from Bernard, but it achieved nothing. The real work was being done outside the committee and was being kept within a very close circle. Even as Honorary Treasurer, I was excluded from developments. I would be told when the time was right and Bernard would decide when.

I do not know for sure, but I assume that Bernard kept FAI President Pat Quigley informed. Pat was Bernard's staunchest ally in the rows that followed over Eircom Park. Pat really believed in the project and wanted Irish football to have its own stadium. He accepted the professional advice the Association was receiving on the technical and financial viability of the project. Pat and I had many a blazing row over Eircom Park. However, at the end of it, we have remained on good personal terms. Pat always had the good grace to leave our rows in the board room. In fact, after such rows we would often sit down together to dinner at a football function and enjoy each other's company.

Bernard's decision to keep his plans within a narrow circle is typical of the FAI. On a small number of occasions, I made the decision not to divulge sensitive information, even to officers, until I thought that the time was right. This is a matter of trust; I had learned to distrust certain officers and the use they made of privileged information, especially in disclosing it prematurely to the media. I think Bernard did not trust me nor, indeed, some of the other officers, and so excluded us from his inner circle. This lack of trust is part of the culture of the FAI and is a key reason why so many rows occur. I had been Bernard's main rival for the position of General Secretary in 1996.

The lack of inclusion of the officers and directors of the Association was pivotal in the split over Eircom Park, and led to the project's ultimate demise. As the rows intensified, it became harder and harder to get accurate information, and thus the distance widened and the distrust increased between the protagonists.

I often wonder what might have happened if Bernard had widened his circle of confidants and brought more people along with him. In my opinion, his approach generated opposition. If he had listened more to internal FAI people and less to his external advisers, nearly all of whom were benefiting financially from the project, it might have gone further. It could have been adapted to what was viable and may even have been built. In reality, trust broke down very quickly and the project became surrounded with controversy and was, thereby, doomed.

*****

The real start of Eircom Park occurred in September 1998, when Bernard called a meeting of the FAI Stadium Committee, the first for a number of months. He had quietly been making progress. Few details were provided at this meeting, but the concept of a self-financing project was put forward. A traditional stadium would lose money, but a multi-functional project would be self-financing. Financial projections based on a cost of IR£65 million were discussed. This looked reasonable at the time, as new stadia such as the Riverside in Middlesbrough and the Stadium of Light in Sunderland had been constructed for less.

More details were provided at officers' meetings that took place on 18 and 26 September 1998. A number of sites were mentioned, including Ballymun, Baldoyle, Quarryvale and Ashbourne. Surprisingly, neither City West nor Clonburris, the two eventual contenders for the location of Eircom Park, were mentioned. Of course, the project was not known as Eircom Park then. This would happen in mid-1999, when Eircom purchased the naming rights for the stadium.

The proposed financial model was that the FAI would own 67 per cent, with unspecified outside equity partners owning 33 per cent. Bernard always maintained that there was outside equity interest in the project, but when push came to shove in March

2001, there wasn't. In 2001, Davy Hickey Properties Ltd offered to put up money, as a loan not equity, secured not only on the stadium project but also on the FAI's most treasured asset – TV revenues – for the next fifty years.

At this stage, the details were hazy, but at least progress was being made. The officers were content to let Bernard get on with it. We all wanted a stadium and the news we were being given was positive.

At the next officers' meeting in early November 1998, considerable progress had been made. Within the FAI, Bernard was now working more through the officers than through the Stadium Committee; this is one of the few times that there were no leaks from the Association on an important issue. The officers at the time were Pat Quigley (President), Milo Corcoran (Vice President), Des Casey (Honorary Secretary), Michael Hyland (Chairmen of the National League) and me (Honorary Treasurer). By this stage, Bernard had brought in Laurence St John, the FAI's television consultant, as his adviser on the stadium project. This group was supposedly managing the project for the FAI, but in effect was being led by the nose as it was drip-fed positive information.

By November, a site had been identified. This was the Clonburris site in Clondalkin, which was owned by Dunloe Ewart plc. It was a large site, in excess of 200 acres. Previously, there had been a proposal to develop a national distribution centre there. Situated between the Naas Road and the Galway Road and with the main Dublin to Cork railway line passing through it, the site had many good features. Despite this, it was somewhat inaccessible and would remain so until the area was developed.

Dunloe were offering the Association 40 acres of the site, free of charge. This was incredibly good news. Suitable sites in Dublin were in short supply and land was very expensive. Getting a free site was a huge boost for the stadium and made its achievement all the more feasible. Not only would we have our stadium, but we would also have enough land to build a centre of excellence for football. Based on the free site, it was now possible that the stadium could be built without outside equity and the Association would own it outright.

Dunloe weren't providing the 40 acres because they liked football; they needed planning permission to develop the full site and believed that if a stadium was part of the overall development proposal, the planners and the politicians would look on it favourably. More development might be allowed on the remaining acres, and there might be fewer planning conditions and restrictions. There is no such thing as a free gift in business.

The details of the proposal were put before a Stadium Committee meeting on 4 December 1998. The stadium would be based on the Gelderdome, the home of Vitesse Arnhem in the Netherlands, which had a capacity of 28,000 but was very innovative, with a removable pitch and a retractable roof. The stadium could easily be converted into a large multi-functional auditorium.

The key names in the project began to appear at this stage. Ascon/Rohcan would, in conjunction with their Dutch parent company HBG, bring forward a package to finance and build the stadium. HBG had built the Gelderdome and were involved in the early stages of similar stadia in Coventry and in Gelsenkirken (for Shalke 04). RHWL from Coventry would be the architects, thereby hopefully achieving synergies between the two projects in Dublin and Coventry. IMG would be our marketing partners on the project and would have responsibility for generating revenue from sponsorship and box and seat sales. A major international financial institution, which later turned out to be Deutsche Bank's London office, would also become part of the team. Finally, the FAI auditors, Deloitte Touche, were preparing financial projections for the stadium. It was decided that the project would be publicly announced early in the New Year. Eircom Park was, in effect, being born.

One other important element was added to the project team. This was a PR company. At this stage, I was working in the PR industry, with a company called Fleishman-Hillard Saunders (FHS). The role of FAI Treasurer was an honorary one, and I had to earn a living as well.

I introduced Bernard to two people in FHS, one of whom was the company's sports promotion expert and the other, Declan Kelly, was a corporate PR person. To my surprise, Bernard decided to work with Declan Kelly.

The project was being managed through the team of expert advisers and all the key decisions were made by this project team. The officers were provided with information, when Bernard thought it appropriate. This low level of involvement for the officers was certainly one of the factors that increased my level of concern. As Honorary Treasurer of the FAI, I had responsibility for the strategic financial management of the Association. The stadium project was huge financially, in terms of costs, risk and future potential income. Yet I struggled to get the basic information.

It was at this stage that a major shift occurred in the project, which had long-term consequences for it and certainly contributed to its failure. For some reason, the FAI rejected the free Dunloe site at Clonburris. This happened very quickly. On 4 December 1998, Bernard briefed the FAI Stadium Committee on the advantages of the site. However, at a meeting on 18 December in Dunloe's offices in Fitzwilliam Square, the FAI rejected the offer. Incredibly, no one from the FAI attended this meeting. The 'FAI' were represented by Laurence St John, Bernard's project adviser, and two PR consultants, Declan Kelly and Jackie Gallagher. Bernard initially denied that nobody from the FAI had attended. However, Noel Smith, Chairman of Dunloe Ewart plc, contacted me to inform me of what had transpired and provided me with a copy of the minutes of the meeting as taken by Dunloe.

What had happened to cause people acting on behalf of the FAI to turn down a free 40-acre site, which could be valued at the time at perhaps IR£10 million? Bernard O'Byrne's explanation was that Dunloe had withdrawn the offer, and this was what he told the various FAI committees. But this does not stand up from a Dunloe Ewart viewpoint. Noel Smith had raised the issue of talking to the government and trying to marry the FAI project with the government's National Stadium project, which was then in a very embryonic stage. Bernard wanted nothing to do with the government's stadium. He was fully committed to building the FAI stadium independently of the government. I believe that Bernard used Noel Smith raising the issue of the government stadium as an excuse to refuse the free site offer. This decision was never discussed in the FAI, but was presented to us as a *fait accompli*.

The other possible factor in the decision to refuse the free Clonburris site was the emergence of a new potential site in City West. The site appeared as if by magic. On 4 January 1999, Bernard reported to the FAI officers that Noel Smith was playing politics with the site and the stadium project and that the Clonburris site was no longer available. However, Bernard was exploring the possibility of an alternative site. Four days later, this turned out to be City West.

The Association were committed to announcing the project in mid-January 1999. Very elaborate plans had been made with video pieces from FIFA President Sepp Blatter and IMG Chairman, Mark McCormack, among others. All the heavy hitters in the project team were lined up to come to Dublin, and it was an impressive line-up. The project would not lack credibility due to the companies involved. However, it would look very silly if the FAI announced they were going to build a stadium, but that they had no site. Thus, the argument was put forward that we had no option but to reach agreement on obtaining the City West site for the stadium.

I rank this as perhaps the worst decision I made in my tenure as FAI Honorary Treasurer, but at the time I was accepting the information as presented and was supportive of the project. I did not know until much later that the Clonburris site might still have been available to us, as Dunloe Ewart had not withdrawn it. I have no doubt that the cost implications of the change of site were a significant factor in the ultimate demise of Eircom Park. Not only did it greatly increase the cost (by IR£16.7 million), but it also introduced the serious planning complication of being within four kilometres of Baldonnel Aerodrome, also known as Casement

Aerodrome. There is a height restriction on all developments in that zone. It the end, it was a combination of cost increases and planning issues that killed Eircom Park.

We were faced with a stark choice. Do we announce the stadium – at that stage called the Arena – without a site or do we enter an agreement with Davy Hickey Properties, the owners of City West? The decision was to get an agreement on City West. This was a rushed decision and the agreement was signed the day before the stadium project was launched. The price was IR£270,000 per acre for a total of 50 acres, which came to IR£13.5 million. Under the agreement, we had an option to purchase the site if we gained planning permission for the stadium. It involved the payment of a deposit of 5 per cent, or IR£625,000. A further condition which came back to haunt Eircom Park was that the planning permission had to be achieved within two years, by December 2000, or else the land deal was cancelled.

Eircom Park was launched in a blaze of publicity. The media were not alerted to the press conference until the morning it happened, so there was no prior speculation. The launch was impressive and successful, even if it cost a small fortune. The key objective was to achieve credibility for the stadium and this was accomplished.

On the morning of the launch, special meetings of the FAI Board and National Council were held to approve the project before it was formally announced. This was a rubber-stamping exercise; there was never going to be a problem, as everyone in football wanted a stadium. There was universal approval. It was agreed that two new companies would be established to manage the project. Centime Ltd would be the development company and Landau Ltd would be the operational company for the stadium when built. This made sense for tax reasons as Centime would be entitled to reclaim VAT, or so we thought.

This subsequently led to a row with the Revenue Commissioners, when they claimed that Centime had not carried out any development and therefore it (in effect the FAI) was not entitled to a IR£500,000

VAT refund. This row ended up in a hearing before an Appeals Commissioner, who found in favour of the FAI. However, the Revenue Commissioners subsequently decided to appeal the decision to the High Court and the issue, to the best of my knowledge, remains unresolved, one year on. The Revenue Commissioners appealed this decision because of its importance to the interpretation of Irish tax law. Thus the FAI, which are charged with running football in Ireland, became involved in a battle at the forefront of tax law in Ireland.

The directors of both Centime Ltd and Landau Ltd were the five officers of the Association, Bernard O'Byrne, as FAI Chief Executive, and Noel Kennedy from Sligo, who was a director of the FAI and a strong supporter of Bernard's. Laurence St John attended the Board meetings as Bernard's stadium adviser. Board meetings were held once a month. However, the Board of Centime did not make the key decisions on the project; Bernard and the project management team did this behind the scenes. The information provided at Board meetings of Centime was minimal. The minutes seldom extended to a second page. As the project and the rows developed, I found myself isolated as the only director of Centime to question the basis of the project and to request to see documentation.

At an early stage, I suggested to Bernard that we bring in some external directors with the requisite knowledge and experience to assist us. Bernard initially agreed to this, and we had even got as far as agreeing on the names of a construction industry expert and a banking expert. Bernard and I knew them both. They were keen football supporters. However, Bernard had second thoughts and vetoed the appointment of these external directors at the March 1999 Board meeting of Centime. Why he did this, I can only surmise. The Board was eventually extended in late 2000, after I resigned. By this stage, the project was in serious trouble.

However, everything was not as smooth behind the scenes; the genesis of the clash between Bernard and me over the stadium was happening. On the day of the purchase of land at City West, I received several phone calls telling me that I was not needed at this meeting.

However, I saw it as my responsibility, as Treasurer of the Association, to be aware and involved in all significant transactions involving FAI money. Why Bernard O'Byrne did not want me to attend the critical meeting with Davy Hickey Properties over the purchase of the City West site, I still do not understand. This was the day before the launch.

There was also a clash between Bernard and me that evening. There was a preparatory meeting before the launch, with all the parties involved in the project. Bernard afterwards complained to the officers that I was interfering, asking too many questions and making too many comments. He called a special meeting of the officers to make this complaint. I threatened to resign. This was the last thing Bernard wanted to happen: a major controversy on the day the Arena was launched. Matters were eventually smoothed over, but this was the harbinger of things to come. Bernard actually apologised to me the following morning – a unique occurrence.

Bernard had reached operating agreements with some of the project partners, such as Deutsche Bank and IMG. He did this without internal consultation and simply informed the Association of the agreements. The contract documents were never brought to the Board, and in some cases we were unaware that formal agreements had been entered into.

In the case of IMG, Bernard reached a commercial agreement with them in January 1999, covering not only the stadium project, but also all of the FAI's commercial activities. Bernard told us that IMG were working for nothing – no foal, no fee – until the stadium was built. While this may have been somewhat accurate for the first year to 31 December 1999, when IMG were just paid any commission income they earned, the agreement committed the FAI to paying IR£60,000 a month from January 2000. This memorandum of understanding, as it was called, with IMG was never presented to the FAI Board for approval.

Deutsche Bank would receive an up-front fee of IR£80,000 to be the bankers for the project. What advice they provided for this fee, I never understood.

Deloitte Touche had presented an initial business plan, which I felt was very optimistic. However, it raised no alarm bells at this stage. We were led to believe that the cost of the stadium was fixed at IR£65 million, and even with the additional cost of the land, the total cost was just above IR£80 million. This was not a cause for concern. If IMG were able to do a half-decent job in raising revenue, then the deficit would be manageable.

As long as the debt was kept to low levels, the project appeared viable. In any event, the FAI would be reselling the boxes, seats and stadium naming rights ten years after the stadium opened and this would enable any residual debt to be repaid. The initial projections put the debt at IR£15 million.

A group of FAI officers and members of the Stadium Committee, led by Bernard O'Byrne, made the pilgrimage to Arnhem in the Netherlands to see the Gelderdome and we were very impressed.

I nearly didn't get to go on the trip. I forgot my passport and only realised this at check-in. A panic call to Linda and she was on her way to the airport. Linda made the journey from Ratoath in less than 20 minutes and pulled up at the set-down zone and tossed the passport out the window to me. I grabbed it and made my dash back to the check-in desk. Luckily, the airline was sympathetic and had kept the door open until a few minutes before departure.

It was only later that we learned that the financing of the stadium had nearly bankrupted Vitesse Arnhem and had led to the sacking of the club Chairman, who had sponsored the development of the stadium. The additional non-football events to make the stadium commercially viable were not forthcoming in sufficient number and variety to generate the required income to make ends meet at the Gelderdome. Vitesse had a football match at least three times a month during the football season. Moreover, at less than 30,000 capacity, it was just two-thirds the proposed size of Eircom Park. It had cost a fraction of Eircom Park's projected cost.

The first meeting of the Board of Centime took place on 26 February 1999. All the key players were in place, with the exception of the project manager who would coordinate all activities on behalf of the FAI. A Cork-based company, J.J. Casey & Co., was subsequently appointed to this position.

All in all, eighteen different entities were paid by the FAI for this failed project. The FAI money tap had been turned on. In fairness to Laurence St John, his remuneration was on a success basis and thus he was not paid for his work on the project. If only the other agreements had been similar.

Over the course of the project, just over two years from launch to collapse, it cost the Association over IR£5 million. The bills kept rolling in. There is no doubt in my mind that the Association, which had cash reserves of IR£3.75 million in March 1999, would have had to borrow money to pay its way in 2001. Would any bank have lent us money? I doubt it. Maybe if we had pledged our headquarters in Merrion Square, but certainly not against the security of the stadium project.

Of course, one issue discussed at this initial Centine Board meeting was the directors' remuneration. FAI directors, other than the officers, who receive modest honoraria, are not paid. They receive meeting allowances, which are based on time and distance travelled. I managed to resist the payment of directors' fees, but it was agreed that the directors would receive enhanced travel allowances. These were quite modest. At the subsequent FAI Remuneration Committee meeting, Bernard was granted a substantial bonus to be paid when the stadium was completed. He got a partial payment for work achieved to date. The size of this bonus, which was reported in the media as IR£250,000, was approved by the FAI Remuneration Committee, by a vote of three to two. It was new territory for the FAI and far removed from the business of running football.

The FAI had to fund Centime and all the stadium development costs. This was done by means of a loan from the FAI to Centime. This process was supposed to put a control on the expenditure on the stadium project. While the FAI finances had improved since 1996, the level of cash reserves remained low and any downturn in income would quickly put the Association under financial pressure. The initial loan was put at IR£1.5 million, which the FAI Finance Committee approved. We were assured by Bernard that the project costs would not exceed this until a final decision on whether to proceed with the stadium had to be made.

However, this process did not work. The costs on the project simply accelerated beyond the agreed amount. As Honorary Treasurer and a director of the stadium company, Centime Ltd, I was never consulted on the expenditures or, indeed, on the very significant overruns. This made it impossible to function effectively as Honorary Treasurer, especially as any time I complained at Board level, Bernard had the votes to prevent any action being taken. I was faced with the choice of resigning or fighting. I decided to fight. Deep within me there is a stubborn streak, which is implacable when brought to the surface. I think that Bernard O'Byrne seriously underestimated me, to his cost.

The timetable we were presented with was totally unrealistic, but none of us had the experience to recognise this. At the launch, it was declared that the stadium would open within three years. Twelve months were needed for the planning process and twenty-four months for construction. When the project was abandoned, twenty-seven months later, we were still awaiting full planning permission and were facing an appeal to An Bord Pleanála and the possibility of a court case on planning, due to aviation issues. We had top-name companies advising us on every aspect of the project. Yet many aspects of the advice we received proved to be unrealistic.

It is very easy to be wise after the event. However, I still do not understand a number of key decisions that were made. In particular, why did we try to sell corporate box and seats from day one? Surely, it would have been much more sensible to wait until there was planning permission and the construction phase had started. If the stadium was under construction, then boxes and seats would have been an easy sell. Look at what is happening at Wembley (October 2003). Construction and seat sales are both going very well in tandem. The money raised from seat sales in Eircom Park was in a trust account and, therefore, could not be used for the project. The money spent by IMG on promoting the sales of boxes and seats was, in effect, wasted in my opinion.

Even at the initial meeting on 26 February 1999, the information provided was inaccurate. We were told that IMG had received 1,000 telephone calls and had ninety-five definite enquiries for boxes, and they were confident that thirty were taken. This was just five weeks after the launch. The take up was very poor, despite IMG's claims to the contrary. It seems that IMG's figures were based on their 'confidence' of turning between 20 per cent and 30 per cent of enquiries into contracts. They described this figure as 'sales'.

However, the actual seat contracts signed were kept in the Finance Department of the FAI; when I learned of this I had access to the real figures. Thus, I had no difficulty in taking on IMG publicly on this issue. The sales of seats achieved by IMG by early 2001 (in two years) were fewer than 1,400. This was less than the sales of ten-year seats for Lansdowne Road achieved in the mid-1990s. IMG were underperforming and getting paid a fortune for doing it. In two years, fifteen contracts for corporate boxes were signed and many of these were with stadium and FAI sponsors such as Eircom.

We paid Deutsche Bank their first instalment of IR£80,000 for agreeing to try to raise money for the project at some unspecified time in the future. Again, this expenditure was unnecessary.

We were spending a lot of money on very specific and detailed areas of planning. I remember one Finance Committee meeting, in which a number of small grant applications from clubs, totalling perhaps IR£25,000, were shelved. Yet the same day, I had to sign a cheque for IR£20,000 for a UK acoustics consultant. We had our priorities all wrong. As an organisation, we were gambling everything on the financial success of the stadium project.

At the Centime Board meeting of 22 June 1999, we were told that there would be seventy-six boxes in the stadium and that 75 per cent had been reserved, with an income of IR£22 million. Of the 8,000 premium and club seats, some 2,300 had been reserved, with an income of IR£10 million. With this positive information, no one could believe but that the stadium would be built. In June, the project received another massive boost when Eircom purchased the naming rights for IR£11 million. With over IR£43 million guaranteed, out of a budget cost of just over IR£80 million, we were halfway there in just six months. Later, the money guaranteed from sponsorships, boxes and seats (3,000 sold) was raised to IR£54 million, with the possibility of obtaining the land on a tax-efficient lease system. Against 'guaranteed' construction costs of IR£65 million, we were almost there. If only these figures had been true!

The sponsorship of the stadium, at a price of IR£11 million for ten years by Eircom in July 1999, was a major boost for the project. This sponsorship, together with Eircom's sponsorship of the national team and the League of Ireland, was approved at an FAI Board of Management meeting, at which only four directors were present. This is way below the quorum required for a Board meeting to be valid. In addition, all four directors present were also directors of Centime. I was not present at this meeting. It is interesting to note that the value of the naming rights for the stadium was put at IR£1.1 million per annum by IMG, whereas the value of the national team sponsorship was just IR£500,000 per annum. This still surprises me.

Even at an early stage, serious planning issues were emerging. The City West site was within four kilometres of Casement Aerodrome (Baldonnel), the main base for the Irish Air Force and a possible site for a second civilian airport for Dublin. The regulations put a ceiling of forty-five metres on the height of buildings that could be constructed within four kilometres of the aerodrome. Eircom Park, which was initially designed and sent for planning approval at sixty-two metres, was way higher than allowed under the regulations. Even after redesign, and indeed a number of redesigns, the height ceiling was still exceeded by at least two metres. All these amendments were eating up costs. Why did we submit a design that was seventeen metres too high?

The extent of the height excess depended to some degree on whether you measured the height from ground level at Baldonnel or ground level at Eircom Park. If the base point under the regulations was Baldonnel, as the Department of Defence claimed, then the excess height of the stadium was over thirty metres. The Department of Defence objected to Eircom Park on these grounds. Bernard accused the government of political interference and of manipulating the situation to impede the development of Eircom Park and, thereby, favouring the government's own proposal for the National Stadium.

*****

Despite being involved as a director of Centime Ltd, there are key aspects of the selection of City West as the site for Eircom Park that still puzzle me greatly: Why did we move from a free site in Clonburris to an expensive site in City West? It astounds me that no one from the FAI attended the key meeting with Dunloe Ewart over Clonburris, a fact that only emerged months later.

Why move to a site with very curtailed access when transport issues would form a key element of any planning approval? The Dublin Mountains bordered City West on one side, giving no road access from that direction. The approach from the north was through Tallaght. The site was about four miles past Tallaght town centre; the last two miles were 'country roads' and would require a serious upgrade. To the south, the roads went towards Blessington and Saggart, with very low traffic capacity. Saggart would be virtually cut off on event nights. To the west, access was from the Naas Road, through, perhaps, a mile of the City West Technology Park.

This is where a lot of Machiavellian speculation arose within the FAI. If planning permission for Eircom Park had succeeded (and it did receive initial approval at local authority level – although subject to many stringent conditions) then other developments in the vicinity could also be built higher. This would greatly increase the value of the land adjacent to Eircom Park, much of which was undeveloped, but zoned as commercial. Under the aeronautical regulations, a building that was 'shadowed' by a taller building could be exempted from the height restriction requirement.

*****

During 1999, the debate in the FAI mainly centred on the development costs accruing to the FAI and on whether we should meet the government in order to compare Eircom Park with the National Stadium. The assumptions of the business plan had not yet become a topic of widespread dispute within the FAI. Most of the debate took place at the Board of Centime and sometimes the FAI Finance Committee, but seldom became a serious issue at the FAI Board. All that was to change utterly during 2000!

I was continually asking for details and copies of documents and agreements, but these were denied me, even at the Board meetings of Centime. I had little support from any other director. Very often these meetings of Centime degenerated into rows between Laurence St John and me. Bernard influenced this situation to some extent, which was probably a smart move on his part. Laurence got involved, while Bernard remained aloof. Despite our 'heavy debates', Laurence and I have remained friendly and enjoy the occasional game of golf together.

I was concerned, but still wanted the stadium to go ahead. My approach at this stage was to act within the project (the Board of Centime) but not to create a major row within the FAI. I thought that reason would win the day, but I was wrong. I was up against a stubborn view that the stadium had to be built no matter what; I was painted as playing politics within the Association. I would not be surprised if it was put abroad within football that I was rocking the boat, just because I had lost out to Bernard for the position of

General Secretary. These kinds of arguments are common within the FAI and avoid the need for in-depth analysis of a situation.

Perhaps the tenor of what was happening is best illustrated by the response to a letter I wrote to Bernard, dated 6 December 1999. Bernard had described me as the Finance Director of Centime at a FAI Board meeting. This was an attempt to rope me into the project. I considered myself to be a non-executive director of Centime; I had not been included in the negotiation of any of the contracts entered into on behalf of Centime Ltd. In the letter, I pointed out that I was not the Finance Director and had not even seen copies of most of the agreements. I requested that I be given copies of all the contracts entered into and a copy of the most up-to-date business plan – not unreasonable requests from a director of the company. I also asked Bernard to institute, within the Finance Department, a system of monitoring expenses on the project, including outstanding invoices and to bring a monthly report to the Finance Committee.

I thought that my letter was polite and professional, but Bernard complained to the officers that I was criticising him personally and undermining his integrity. I was hauled before the other officers and asked to withdraw my letter. I was very taken aback by this reaction, particularly as my letter had been addressed to and sent only to Bernard. In the end, I did agree to withdraw my letter, but only on the condition that the matters I had raised in it were discussed at a meeting of the officers and at the Board of Centime. The discussions never happened effectively, and I was, in fact, accused of being disingenuous during this discussion. In what respect, I never knew. The 'solution' was that I would discuss my concerns directly with Bernard and Laurence St John. This was what I had requested in the first place.

The response I got at the subsequent meeting with Bernard was that the business plan had been drawn up by Deloitte Touche and had been approved by Deutsche Bank and IMG; what did I know about the matter in any event? I found out later that my original written comments and criticisms of the business plan had not been passed on to Deloitte Touche and, therefore, had no impact on the subsequent revision of the plan. I was fighting a losing battle.

At the December 1999 FAI Board meeting, I achieved what I considered to be a significant victory. The Board put an expenditure limit of IR£3 million on the development cost of the project. This was double the initial projection of IR£1.5 million. Bernard believed that he could maintain expenditure below this level until full planning permission had been received. I did not think that there was a hope that this could happen, given the monthly rate of expenditure on all the consultants.

I felt that this expenditure cap would bring matters to a head in mid-2000. The FAI would be faced with the decision of spending the last of its cash reserves on the project (and possibly going into debt) or abandoning it. There should at least be a serious debate on all the issues before a final decision was made. I was wrong in my presumption; the project kept gobbling money and the IR£3 million limit was exceeded. It was impossible to keep up to date on the expenditure, as many of the invoices were late in arriving to the FAI Finance Department. The final bill when the project was abandoned in March 2001 was close to IR£4 million, and this did not include the final settlement of IR£1.5 million with IMG. It usurped virtually all of the FAI's cash reserves.

All in all, the FAI was in way over its heads and was floundering. As directors of the Association and as directors of Centime, we were not in control. The FAI was footing the total bill for all of this and the money was pouring out.

I suppose part of my problem was that the directors of Centime and, indeed, the directors of the FAI knew very little about stadium development. My attempt to bring in outside directors with the required expertise had been stymied. I certainly had no expertise in this area. I believe that I have some expertise in the financial area, having a bachelor's degree and two master's degrees in the areas of economics and finance and having worked for sixteen years with AIB as their chief economist and in their dealing room. My training had taught me to analyse problems and this is what I was trying to do.

The FAI Board was made up of twenty-two people. A small minority of directors, acting in concert, could control any issue at a meeting, especially if they were vocal. At all Board meetings and on all issues, the vast majority of directors sat on the fence and stayed quiet. Six directors speaking on an issue was about the norm. In this environment, doing nothing, postponing any action, is always the easy decision. The FAI had approved the project at the outset and persuading the directors to change their minds was like stopping a runaway train. Most of the directors did not see their role as examining in detail the merits or otherwise of the stadium project, but merely giving it broad political approval. Ray Gallagher of Sligo Rovers, John Byrne of Galway United, Joe Colwell of Shamrock Rovers and Kevin Fahy of the Schools Association were the notable exceptions to this.

*****

Christmas 1999 and the New Year of 2000 was when my opposition to Eircom Park became firm, and I moved from a situation of being concerned about the proposed development to one of outright opposition. At an FAI Board meeting prior to Christmas, I had a resolution passed that the directors of Centime would be entitled to copies of all documentation on the project. This was designed to increase the quantity and speed up the timing of the availability of information to the directors.

Possibly the critical moment in my opposition to Eircom Park occurred at Christmas 1999, some eleven months after the launch. I requested a copy of all documents and contracts on the project. Bernard sent a large package of papers to my home by special delivery, arriving on Christmas Eve. All the contracts to do with Eircom Park were neatly bound in a very large document, except, as I realised when I examined them in detail, the contract with IMG. I was to discover much later that other key pieces of information were also not included.

There is an approach in the FAI that normally works: where information starvation can't kill an issue, information overload can. I do not know whether Bernard's package was an attempt to deflect me by providing me with so much information that I would lose myself in the detail. From starvation to gluttony in one Christmas package!

However, I was used to reading and analysing technical documents, and, over the Christmas holidays, I went through all the contracts and letters of appointment. I retreated into the quietest room in the house for two days. For the first time, I was able to put down on one sheet of paper the financial commitments that had been entered into on behalf of the FAI.

The May 1999 version of the detailed business plan underpinning the Eircom Park project was included in Bernard's Christmas package. I was gobsmacked. Prior to this, I had assumed, presumably like all the FAI directors, that given the stature of the companies involved in the project, the business assumptions would be conservatively based. No so. In my opinion, the assumptions did not stand up to detailed examination.

I analysed the business plan in detail and became concerned that the financial basis of the project was founded more on optimism than realism. My overall conclusion was that Eircom Park was based on a hugely unrealistic set of business assumptions and this was eventually proved correct some eighteen months later. It was at this stage that I discovered that none of my initial comments on the first business plan of September 1998 had been taken into consideration. I later learned that they had not been conveyed to Deloitte Touche.

As I read through the documents, statements made started to come back to me and missing pieces of the jigsaw started to fit into place. This was serious stuff. Where to go with this information? If it was as bad as it appeared to me, then this was the start of the demise of the stadium project. There was no way the Association could sustain this level of unchecked expenditure; there was no way Eircom Park was the golden egg it had been portrayed as. It was a very risky project.

I needed to bring this to the attention of the Board and officers. I realised that I was now setting out on a path of treading on people's dreams. I knew I had no option but to investigate and ask more questions. Linda and I discussed the consequences for me of embarking on this road. It could lead to the end of my involvement in the FAI. Who wants to be a killjoy? But we both knew where my first responsibility lay, and that was to my duty as Treasurer. I had duty of care, a moral responsibility and a legal one.

The monthly outgoings were such that it would not be long before this figure was exceeded. By then, the project would be nowhere near gaining the planning decision from South Dublin County Council. Bernard must have known this, but obviously felt that he had sufficient support to go to the FAI Board at any time and increase the FAI's commitment.

Perhaps my greatest concern was that Bernard had entered into most of these contractual obligations for the FAI without detailed consultation with and without prior formal approval from the Board of the FAI, or indeed of Centime.

The list of contracts I received that Christmas was as follows:
- Architects – RHWL of Coventry
- Architects – Henry J Lyons of Dublin
- Engineers and surveyors – Ove Arup
- Project manager – J.J. Casey & Co.
- Builders – Ascon/Rohcan and their parent company, HBG
- Planning consultant – Fergal McCabe
- Transport consultant
- PR consultants – Gallagher and Kelly
- UK lawyers – Allen and Overy
- Irish lawyers – A & L Goodbody
- Bankers – Deutsche Bank, London

In addition, there were a number of significant once-off expenditures for other experts, including aviation consultants from Ireland and Malta; an acoustics consultant from England; landscape consultants;

fire consultants; environmental consultants; traffic consultants; and model construction (the FAI spent IR£50,000 on constructing models of the stadium).

The documents I received that Christmas cemented my opposition to Eircom Park. I no longer believed that it was viable. The FAI were a small organisation with limited financial resources. We were taking on a major project that would depend on our ability to become Dublin's major entertainment company and command the lion's share of concerts and entertainment events.

Let me divide my analysis of the project into the cost side and the revenue side: Bernard O'Byrne had assured the FAI, the directors of Centime and the Irish public that the stadium would be built for IR£65 million. This figure was 'cast in stone'. He stated that he had a letter from HBG, the parent company of Ascon/Rohcan, which had built the prototype Gelderdome in Arnhem, confirming this. This letter was dated December 1998, just before the stadium was launched. At first, I thought that the actual contract with HBG had been excluded from the package of documents. However, on later enquiry I found that the only document the FAI had from HBG regarding the construction costs was that letter. Bernard was basing his guarantee on the costs on the contents of a letter. For the first time, I had sight of this letter. The letter was meaningless in the context of putting a cost on the stadium. It was no guarantee and was clearly based on very tenuous assumptions. Rather than being 'cast in stone', as the Board of the FAI was informed, the costs estimates were a puff of smoke, which were rising as fast, if not faster, than construction inflation in Ireland. The letter specifically assumed that the project would commence construction in January 2000 and finish by December 2001, which was an impossible deadline.

What was worse, although I did not know it at the time, was that the FAI were in possession of another letter, from Ascon dated August 1999, specifically warning of cost escalation due to planning delays and the rampant inflation in construction costs in Ireland.

This letter was withheld from the Board of Centime and, indeed, the FAI. I discovered it in FAI files in June 2000.

I did my own back-of-the-envelope calculations and spoke to a few people who had knowledge of large-scale construction projects and had been involved in stadium projects previously. They agreed that the IR£65 million estimate was way too low. My guestimate of the construction cost of the stadium was above the IR£80 million mark. The cost of the land, the required infrastructure improvements and the development costs would bring the total project cost to well in excess of IR£100 million. Suddenly, the debt burden on the project appeared serious – not the IR£15 million that had been contained in the business plan, but more likely somewhere between IR£35 million and IR£40 million. If IMG did not sell all the boxes and premium seats, the debt would be greater. The prospective level of debt was staggering for an organisation such as the FAI.

The operating plan for the stadium also caused me concern. What if the revenue streams fell short of expectations? What if the significant operating profits from the venue were not realised? Given the stadium's poor location on the far side of Tallaght, and with the need to bus most of the audience to events, it was difficult to see it becoming the entertainment centre of Dublin.

The running costs seemed low and the operating revenues seemed high. This combination of assumptions in the business plan guaranteed a profit, which would allow the debt to be paid off. Everything looked too good to be true. Even the football assumptions appeared to me to be optimistic – this, at least, was an area in which the FAI should know something. There were to be nine international matches a year in the stadium, as well as the FAI Cup semifinals and finals and a major club tournament.

Nine home internationals a year are an impossibility. There are just twelve international dates in the FIFA football calendar and no country uses them all. The clubs would go mad and refuse to release the players. The international trend is to reduce the number of friendly international matches. Many star players, not just Roy Keane, were refusing to play friendly international matches. Ireland plays on average two home competitive matches per season. Thus, under this plan, we would have seven home friendly matches per year. Each of these would have a full house – thereby nearly doubling the crowd who then attended friendly matches at Lansdowne Road. Ticket prices would be increased by 30 per cent on the average achieved at Lansdowne Road. This would be great business, but was it attainable? In my view, it was nonsense.

In my analysis, many of the business plan's assumptions erred on the side of optimism. When all the potential difficulties were accumulated, Eircom Park became a very risky project. My analysis over New Year 2000 was the catalyst for my strong opposition to the project. Nothing subsequently changed this point of view and, indeed, as I gathered more information over time, my opposition hardened.

During my two-day deliberation at home, I noticed that a copy of the agreement with IMG was not included in the document package. When I demanded and was given a copy of it in the New Year, I discovered that it was dynamite. Not only had Bernard entered into an agreement with IMG over the commercial rights for Eircom Park, but he had also engaged IMG to act as a commercial adviser to the FAI on all their sponsorships. If the FAI were renewing their sponsorship with Opel or Umbro, IMG would receive 15 per cent of the value of the sponsorship for delivering our own sponsors to us – 15 per cent of the gross amount, not 15 per cent of the added value. The value of contracts would have to increase by at least 15 per cent before the FAI saw an additional euro. The agreement was to last for five years, with IMG having a first option on renewal. The FAI had become married to IMG for life without knowing it. It was incredible. There was no way that this was in the interests of the FAI.

IMG were to deliver the revenue to build the stadium. When the stadium was built, IMG would provide the non-football events that would generate the revenue to ensure profitability and thus help pay for the stadium. IMG planned to sell seventy-five corporate boxes and

8,000 premium and club seats, raising a total of IR£32 million. In addition, commercial sponsorship of the stadium – such as naming rights, beer pouring rights, soft drink rights – would raise another IR£20 million. IMG were to get at least 15 per cent of this and, above a certain threshold, their commission increased to 25 per cent.

The initial debt projection on the project, according to the business plan, was IR£15 million. Bernard had assured us that Deutsche Bank had underwritten debt in the project to the extent of IR£30 million. The project was thus 'fully funded', as was frequently announced at Lansdowne Road during international matches to get the message to the public. Spin city was in overdrive.

If only things were that simple. The letter of appointment of Deutsche Bank fell far short of underwriting and, thus, of guaranteeing loans of IR£30 million to the project. Deutsche Bank had been paid an upfront fee of IR£80,000 on being appointed as bankers for the stadium project. It must have been the easiest money that they ever earned. What Deutsche Bank had promised was that they would approach other banks and ask them to lend money to the project. They would receive more money for doing this. Deutsche Bank themselves were not committed to lending one penny to the project.

When pushed, Deutsche Bank stated that they were confident of raising the required level of debt in the London market, but no, they would not be lending the money themselves. Their loans department might or might not provide some of the money, but no decision had been made. In technical terms, Deutsche Bank would act as lead banker in raising the money for the project. The lead bank makes most of the money; it's a coveted position, better than providing the actual loans. Deutsche Bank had spoken to banks in London who had expressed interest. Could we have their names? No. I admired Deutsche Bank's optimism that London-based banks would provide financing for Eircom Park at a time when these same banks were pulling the plug on the latest plan for the redevelopment of Wembley Stadium.

I found the Deutsche Bank relationship manager very difficult to deal with. At times, I felt his attitude towards the FAI bordered on the arrogant. He really got under my skin! As I had worked in a bank for sixteen years, I understood the nature of banking on such projects. His bank earned a fat fee from this failed project.

Deutsche Bank did little or nothing to earn their fee. They endorsed a project that in my view did not make financial sense for their client organisation. In the end, they had the audacity to demand the payment of the remainder of their fee. We refused; their letter of appointment had not been approved by the Board of the FAI, as it was required to be. They had made a serious error in their paperwork. My only regret is that we did not have the stomach to seek repayment of the initial fee.

I was back to writing letters in early February, this time to FAI President, Pat Quigley. I raised three issues:

1. The development costs and their impact on the cash reserves of the Association: The FAI's cash reserves were falling rapidly due to the expenditure on Eircom Park and we were projecting an operating deficit to March 2001. Finances for football in Ireland were going to get very tight.

2. The assumptions underlying the business plan, which I believed to be overly optimistic: We were assuming full houses at a minimum of twelve football matches per year[1], with increased ticket prices. There was no way that this was a 'conservative' assumption as claimed, or, indeed, even a realistic one.

3. The fact that the Board of Centime had never approved the business plan. The business plan stated that:

    The Directors of Centime accept responsibility for the information contained in this information memorandum (the business plan). To the best of the knowledge and belief

---

1. The twelve matches were made up of nine international games, the FAI Cup Final and two club tournament games.

> *of these directors, who have taken all reasonable care to*
> *ensure that such is the case, the information contained in*
> *this information memorandum is in accordance with the*
> *facts and does not omit anything likely to affect the import of*
> *such information.*

The Board had not read the plan nor discussed it. I informed Pat that I was withdrawing my implicit support for the project.

The first major row over Eircom Park at an FAI Board meeting took place in February 2000, just one year after the launch. It was here that I voiced my concerns to the wider FAI for the first time. I made little impact. The biggest row at that meeting was over the behaviour of the PR consultants to the project, Gallagher and Kelly, who by now had left FHS and set up on their own. Bernard had them lined up to provide the positive spin on the project. Everything in the garden was rosy; all projections were being exceeded; the cost was 'cast in stone'; there was nothing to worry about. Indeed, Bernard reported to the Board that he had met HBG in Holland and was discussing reductions in the cost of construction with them.

The Board row was concerned with the fact that the opponents of Eircom Park were being vilified in the media. A behind-the-scenes campaign was attempting to cast aspersions on their motivation. *Phoenix* magazine ran a feature on me, which questioned whether there was a conflict of interest between my role as Honorary Treasurer of the Association and my employment with Fleishman Hilliard Saunders, who performed PR work for the Minister for Sport. My employment was no secret to anyone in football. I raised this issue at the Board meeting simply to put it on the record that there was no conflict. In my job at FHS, I had no dealings with the Minister or department. Both John Byrne (Galway United's delegate) and John Delaney (Waterford United) then stated that they were in a similar situation. They had also been the subject of rumours fed to the media, questioning their motivation in opposing Eircom Park. John Byrne is related by marriage to the Minister of State for Science, Technology and Trade; in the case of John Delaney, the rumours concerned the role his father, Joe, played in the Merriongate scandal four years previously.

In *The Irish Times* on 5 March 2001, Emmet Malone, reviewing the whole Eircom Park saga, wrote that the FAI's public relations firm, Gallagher and Kelly, had privately briefed journalists on opponents of Eircom Park; the motives of opponents were questioned and, in one case, wholly irrelevant details relating to a club official's past were revealed in an attempt to undermine his credibility.

The pro–Eircom Park side were fighting dirty. I believe that this was a huge strategic mistake on their part, as it polarised the two camps even further and made it a fight to the finish. If Eircom Park had gone ahead, I have no doubt that my position as Honorary Treasurer of the Association would have become untenable.

*****

The Association met the Taoiseach, Bertie Ahern, in February 2000. I managed to become a member of the delegation, despite internal opposition. Basically, the Taoiseach pointed out the attractions of the Stadium Ireland option and the possible financial and planning difficulties of Eircom Park.

The Taoiseach told us, in no uncertain terms, that he believed the cost of constructing Eircom Park would run to at least IR£100 million, leaving the FAI in enormous debt. There would be severe difficulties with the planning, given the proposed site's proximity to Baldonnel Aerodrome and the large number of training flights that operated from there. Mr Ahern stated that the FAI would have no debt if it became part of the Stadium Ireland project; the FAI could also raise development funds immediately, from the sale of boxes and seats. In addition, the IR£11 million mentioned previously by the Minister for Sport, for the development of Eircom League grounds, was put on the table. We could discuss all issues with the Taoiseach's officials if we wanted to pursue this route. The offer was a forerunner of the deal agreed twelve months later. If the FAI had come on board at that stage, it would have given a tremendous boost to the National

Stadium project. Remember, this was February 2000, when the 'Celtic Tiger' economy was still in full swing.

One of the FAI's delegates made the outlandish suggestion that the Taoiseach should abandon Stadium Ireland and row in with Eircom Park. There were four FAI delegates at the meeting, and we emerged with four different views of what had been said. The official line was that nothing had changed and Eircom Park was going to be built. The Taoiseach's offer to discuss options and terms was summarily rejected.

The National Stadium project had been formally announced in January 2000. Having access to an 80,000-capacity National Stadium would solve the FAI's problems. It would guarantee us significant additional revenue of, on my estimates, about IR£4 million per year, which was about what the FAI were spending on domestic football at the time. We would, in effect, double our annual resources for administrating and developing the game. The FAI would have no risk; as tenants in the National Stadium, we would pay a percentage of revenues. To me, this was a 'no brainer', and, even if Eircom Park had been viable, we should have compared the two proposals. However, this suggestion was always obstructed.

On numerous occasions, the Board of the FAI refused to talk to the government about what may have been available for the FAI in the National Stadium, or, indeed, to commission a report comparing the pros and cons of the two projects for the FAI. I still do not understand this mentality. Surely, the purpose of the Board of the FAI is to do what is best for Irish football. How can it carry out its duties appropriately if it refuses to inform itself of the facts?

While the FAI Board may be constituted as a Board under its Memorandum and Articles of Association and under the Companies Acts, it does not act as a Board in any real commercial sense. On one occasion in March 2000, when a serious debate took place at the Board, a proposal for an internal financial assessment of Eircom Park *vis-à-vis* the National Stadium was defeated by eleven votes to five, with two abstentions. In my view, this was an appalling decision on the part of the directors. The motion of opening negotiations with the government, as part of a twin-track approach, was again put to the Board in July 2000. A wrangle ensued as to whether this should be by a show of hands or a secret ballot. This took about an hour to resolve, and eventually a secret ballot was conceded. The vote was nine to seven against. Nothing had really been achieved, but at the time I could sense that the voting gap between the two sides was closing. In the end, I spoke to the government on my own in late January 2001, without the express permission of the FAI.

*****

Over the next six months from February 2000, the arguments within the FAI intensified, but I was no nearer to persuading the Board of the FAI to seriously re-evaluate the project. An independent reappraisal at this stage might have helped me change their minds, but this was never agreed to. A minority of the FAI Board – six people – joined me in opposition to the project. They included Ray Gallagher of Sligo Rovers, John Byrne of Galway United, Joe Colwell of Shamrock Rovers, new director John Delaney of Waterford United, Kevin Fahy of the Football Association of Irish Schools and Maurice Fleming of the Schoolboys Football Association of Ireland. I had the support of four of the six league delegates to the FAI Board. I saw Michael Cody of Cobh Ramblers as straddling the fence, and I knew that Phil Mooney of St Pats was an Eircom Park proponent.

The split was along traditional lines: League of Ireland (providing five members of the opposition group, if I am included) versus junior football. The Schoolboys Association are perceived as mavericks within the Association and usually opposed most things as a matter of course. This group of seven formed itself as the opposition to Eircom Park, and firmly believed that continuing with the project was not in the interests of the Association. The opponents began to meet prior to important meetings to coordinate strategy.

Basically, the Board of the FAI quickly became divided into three fairly equal groups: Those who favoured Eircom Park and wanted to push on with the project at any cost. I can understand the motivation of most of this group – they simply wanted a stadium for Irish football. Those who sat on the fence, without analysing the pros and cons in detail and without developing a firm view one way or the other. Some members of the middle group disappointed me greatly, as I thought they had the ability to see the wider perspective. In the environment that prevailed, the fence sitters were the most frustrating – comatosed by the row and unable to move in either direction. They were waiting to see which way the ball bounced, before committing themselves completely. They will always back the winner. In the meantime, they would support the status quo – always the safe option within FAI football politics. The last group was the seven Eircom Park opponents, which included me.

We knew that we would lose any vote on the project at the FAI Board. We believed that the Board was not fully aware of the implications of the project for the Association and, indeed, had been misled on many of the facts. As such, we felt we were right to continue our opposition. It wasn't a matter of democracy, but a matter of saving the Association from a potential disaster. We avoided votes by declaring that we were in principle in favour of a stadium for Irish football, while continuing to oppose the specific project.

*****

The FAI received outline planning permission for Eircom Park in March 2000 from South Dublin County Council. It was subject to forty conditions, some of which were standard, but many of which were onerous, both operationally and financially. Among the conditions was the need to get Dúchas' advice on the relocation of badger sets!

The aviation issue was, in effect, avoided by the Council in its grant of permission. Everyone knew it would be subject to an appeal to An Bord Pleanála by the Department of Defence. Apart from this issue, there were three main areas of difficulty:

1. Securing suitable park-and-ride sites to bus most of the spectators to the stadium.

2. Reconstructing sections of the access roads to the stadium to facilitate traffic flow.

3. Making direct financial contributions of IR£3 million to the Council for public services, traffic management, water supply and the foul sewer.

My recollection is that only 3,000 cars and 150 coaches would be allowed access to and parking at the stadium. This would transport, at most, 15,000 people. Thus some 30,000 people would have to be bussed to the stadium from park-and-ride facilities or on public transport. These facilities did not exist anywhere close to the stadium site. Under the planning conditions, the stadium would have to secure long-term usages of the parking sites. This was going to be very expensive. I believe two possible sites were identified, one in Clondalkin and one near Goffs in Kill. Late one night, when travelling home from a football function in Kildare, I decided to measure the time it took to get to the City West site from Goffs. It took twenty minutes, driving on an empty Naas Road at 55 mph. Imagine the time it would take when 45,000 people were trying to access the stadium. What chaos would have ensued!

The stadium development would have to pay the cost of upgrading two roads in the area to dual-carriageway standards and the construction of a major roundabout at the entrance of the stadium and an alternative access road through Fortunestown. I estimated that the required infrastructure improvements and direct financial contribution demanded by South Dublin County Council would cost between IR£13 million and IR£15 million. The business plan contained a provision of just IR£3 million. The direct financial contribution to South Dublin County Council under the planning permission alone was put at IR£3 million. Again this shows how unrealistic the financial estimates in the business plan were.

The planning issue was always a thorny one. At the launch of the project in January 1999, it was stated that full planning permission could be achieved within twelve months. At the collapse of the project, final planning decisions were due in May 2001, some twenty-eight months after the launch. Moreover, full planning permission, if granted, was likely to be challenged in the courts by the Department of Defence. This could have taken another year. And time was money.

Another example of the way the project was managed from an FAI perspective was a June 2000 meeting between the FAI and the Department of Defence to discuss the planning/aviation issue of the proximity of Eircom Park to Casement Aerodrome. I found out that it was happening in *The Star* newspaper on the morning of the meeting. I knew that Bernard and Pat Quigley were both away in the US with the Irish team for the Nike Cup. I rang Des Casey to protest about not being involved or, indeed, not being told about it. I was making the false assumption that he, as Honorary Secretary, would be leading the FAI delegation to the meeting. I was wrong. He knew nothing about it either.

Des made some enquiries and discovered that Bernard O'Byrne had asked Noel Kennedy, Secretary of the Connacht Football Association, to travel from Sligo to attend the meeting. Noel was Bernard's strongest political ally within football and a director of Centime. In my opinion, Bernard was trying to ensure that no one who might ask awkward questions on this difficult issue would receive a briefing from the Department of Defence. Bernard never understood that there is always a back door. Some days later, I received a detailed 'off-the-record' briefing from a senior departmental official. I was parked by the side of the road at Maam Cross, as I received the briefing on my mobile. This development simply raised my antenna further.

In June 2000, I demanded access to all the files on Eircom Park. Bernard stayed on in the US for a holiday with his family after the Nike Cup. I spent a good deal of time in Merrion Square, ploughing my way through huge volumes of files. What I discovered shocked me and intensified my opposition to the project. It was also during this period that I instituted a check on the expenditure on FAI credit cards and identified a possible problem with some expenditure on Bernard's card. This I will return to later.

I discovered a number of crucial documents that had never been disclosed to the Board of Centime, who were supposedly managing the project on behalf of the FAI. Key among them was a letter from Ascon (the Irish subsidiary of HBG), which made it absolutely clear that the stadium could not be built for the 'cast in stone' figure of IR£65 million and warning of the cost impact of construction inflation and the planning delays. It specifically warned of a serious overrun in costs. The letter stated that:

> *The drawings represent a much larger building envelope than contemplated in the outline cost budget in the HBG letter of 23 December 1998... We are raising these issues in the best interests of the client and the project. We believe that it is essential that the client is fully aware of the cost implications of the present proposal prior to planning submission.*

There was also a letter from the architects, RHWL:

> *The price can be properly fixed in October 1999... after planning is received... The prices will be only as good as the drawings and specifications.*

The Ascon letter was dated August 1999 and addressed to the project manager. However, it had been sent on to Bernard immediately and, hence, had been within the FAI for nine months. The letter preceded any controversy on the stadium. The Board of Centime were being told that the construction figure was cast in stone, but the construction company had a totally different view.

No explanation was ever given as to why the letter had not been brought to the Board. When challenged, Bernard stated that he had instructed the project team to remain within the budget of IR£65 million.

I also discovered that the original land deal had been altered. We had done a minor land swap at the boundaries of the site with the owners. There was no difficulty with this. However, in April 2000 the FAI agreed to purchase an additional eight acres of land at a price of

IR£400,000 per acre. This had never been discussed or agreed. The price of land in City West had increased from IR£270,000 an acre to IR£400,000 an acre in just fifteen months. I know that land prices were rising rapidly at the time, but an increase of nearly 50 per cent in that short a time was ridiculous. How had this come about?

I saw the details of the IMG reports and realised that the sales of boxes and seats were being overstated. This incorrect information was included in the 2000 FAI annual report. I discovered that the seat contracts were held in-house in Merrion Square, so I was able to check the real sales. There were just 1,300, not the 3,300 reported. Thus, I had confirmation of what I had feared: the cost side of the stadium was mushrooming and the income side was below what was being reported. The gap in the middle – debt – was escalating. The project was not viable for the FAI.

I came across a copy of correspondence from the Air Corps to the Department of Defence, stating that:

> The Air Corps should oppose this development in the strongest possible terms. The development is incompatible with the operation of Casement Aerodrome.

We had been told that the Air Corps had no difficulty with Eircom Park. Bernard would later claim that this letter was politically motivated to obstruct Eircom Park and, thereby, improve the situation for the National Stadium. Whatever the truth, the letter was clear evidence that we faced a major battle on planning permission, a fact that should have been disclosed.

Finally, I became aware of a letter from our accountants, dated mid-May 2000, stating that they had been informed by the Revenue Commissioners that the VAT paid on the development cost would not be rebated. The cost had suddenly risen by IR£400,000 (IR£500,000 by the end of the project). The IR£3 million development cost budget was bust, but I was not informed of this, even though, as Honorary Treasurer, I had a direct responsibility in the area.

I had six bombshells in my possession. Surely, these would move the FAI Board. No! I put my discoveries and conclusions down on paper and sent a copy to each FAI director. At this stage, I consulted a solicitor and was told that I had a duty to inform my fellow directors of the situation. A special meeting of the FAI Board was convened on 5 July to deal with my letter. I made a comprehensive presentation of the information I had discovered and my objections. I felt that the Board had been badly misled on many issues, but I could elicit very little response. The parable of the sower sowing the seed comes to mind here. Some of my ideas fell onto fertile ground, but this group was already convinced of my position. Some fell onto arid ground, where they had absolutely no impact. Some fell on stony ground, where it sprouted for about five minutes until the next item on the agenda. I don't think my presentation changed anything, but simply made the existing positions more entrenched. As an aside, the emblem of my club, Home Farm, is of the sower sowing the seed.

The project manager attended the meeting and tried to answer the questions raised. This was a typical Bernard tactic. When the going got tough, he brought in the experts and he retreated to the background. The project manager gave the line that he was operating within a project budget, which was news to everyone except, I suspect, Bernard. While nothing could be tied down, he was confident of the project. The meeting degenerated into farce. Too many people, asking too many disparate questions does not allow for a focused meeting. Once again, as Bernard took a back seat, the project manager became the focus of attack.

Prior to the FAI AGM in July 2000, a famous Eircom League meeting took place, which can best be described as the 'Battle of Chief O'Neill's'. Chief O'Neill's is a restaurant and pub in the redeveloped Smithfield area of Dublin. The annual Eircom League awards ceremony had taken place there over lunch one day. In the afternoon, representatives of the twenty-two clubs sat down to discuss Eircom Park, among other items on the agenda. I led off with my usual arguments as to why it was a wrong decision for Irish football. However, I developed my presentation into an attack on the other directors of Centime, one of whom, Michael Hyland, as Chairman of the Eircom League, was presiding over the meeting. I described myself as totally isolated on the Board of Centime and only having the support of some of the club delegates on the FAI Board of Management.

Most of the league clubs supported my position. They were concerned that a financially weakened FAI could jeopardise their own development. Eircom League clubs, by and large, operate within very straightened financial circumstances, and on occasion the FAI has bailed some of them out. I was speaking on home ground and the clubs almost unanimously supported me. This time, it was Michael Hyland who was isolated.

The key decision from this meeting was that, at the forthcoming FAI AGM, the clubs would formally request Bernard O'Byrne to provide detailed answers to three issues on Eircom Park. I hoped that Bernard's written replies to these concerns would clarify many issues and possibly lead to a proper debate and decision on the project. How wrong I was. The issues were as follows:

1. A revised construction cost must be calculated by HGB, the builders.
2. IMG must provide accurate sales figures for boxes and seats and give a commitment to achieve 100 per cent of their target revenue.
3. A method of funding the debt gap must be established.

The debate at Chief O'Neill's and the decision of the league clubs to challenge the official FAI stance on Eircom Park put Michael Hyland in a very awkward position. The majority of his clubs were directly opposed to the project, and, accordingly, Michael felt he had to tender his resignation as Chairman of the league. At the end of the meeting, this issue was left unresolved and deferred to the league's AGM, which was taking place in the Iveagh Grounds in Crumlin the following week.

At this meeting, the view was expressed that Michael need not resign as long as he supported the league's position on receiving accurate information on the queries it had raised. Michael stated that he would remain on as Chairman of the league, if it were the unanimous wish of the clubs. Michael milked the situation for all it was worth. After being assured individually by the delegates from all the clubs that they wanted him to remain as Chairman, Michael then stated that he would withdraw from the room for a few minutes to decide whether he wished to remain. Whether Michael phoned his wife or went for a pint, I do not know. Eventually, he returned and stated that he would remain as Chairman. The whole episode had no impact on Michael or his position on Eircom Park, which remained one of silent approval for the project. In fairness to him, he did pursue the league's questions at meetings.

The next element of the Eircom Park circus occurred at the FAI AGM in the City West Hotel on Saturday, 8 July 2000. This provided a platform for Bernard to appeal to a wider football audience of about 150 administrators. A lot of closed conversations took place on the Friday evening, as the delegates gathered, and again on the Saturday morning. All the local politicians were lined up, including local TD and Tánaiste, Mary Harney, who was in favour of the project for her constituency. Unfortunately, she was not going to promise the state financial support that would have made it viable. It is easy to be in favour of something in principle, if you are not going to support it financially.

Bernard had put a lot of work into his AGM presentation, and his PR advisors, Gallagher and Kelly, had obviously worked hard on the speech (and, indeed, earned a fat fee). It was based purely on emotion – we needed a stadium for Irish football. The impact the controversy was having on his family got a significant mention. As he finished, about half the delegates stood up and applauded; the rest remained seated and silent. Joe Colwell of Shamrock Rovers was the first to speak. One of my staunchest allies, Joe was totally opposed to the stadium project. He described Bernard's performance as a great 'Saatchi and Saatchi speech' (Saatchi and Saatchi were Margaret Thatcher's PR company). There were large ripples of laughter. One derogatory remark and a speech that was certainly the most expensive ever delivered by an FAI person was instantly undermined.

I asked to be allowed to reply, as many of Bernard's comments had been aimed directly and indirectly at me. I had nothing prepared. However, as I had been living the Eircom Park controversy for nine months, this was not a problem. I had my difficulties with the project at the front of my mind. I made one Freudian slip in my presentation. Discussing the financial burden of Eircom Park on the FAI, I referred to its impact on the balance 'shite' of the FAI rather than balance sheet. I realised instantly what I had said and for a moment thought that I had got away with it. However, the laughter started at the back of the room and the place was quickly in uproar. I am not sure that Bernard saw the funny side of my mistake!

The stadium opponents applauded my efforts. Overall in terms of impact, the respective speeches changed nobody's minds, but I felt that more people were realising that there were genuine questions to be answered. In the *Sunday Independent*, Philip Quinn described the AGM in boxing parlance as 'Big Ben versus Little Bren' and scored the fight a draw. A draw was a good result for the stadium opponents. The AGM could have been very dangerous ground for us, if the vast majority of delegates strongly supported the project.

I felt that opposition to the stadium was slowly gaining ground. Most people in football still wanted a stadium, but the financial risks involved were now being questioned. Nonetheless, we still did not have enough support within the FAI to have the project terminated. Many of the football journalists had also begun to seriously question the viability of the project and much of the media coverage was critical of it. Some news journalists were also beginning to take an interest in the story.

Bernard O'Byrne produced a document, which purported to answer the three issues I had raised through the league, but also included answers to another seven questions of his own. This document muddied the issues further, rather than clarify anything, and I suspect that it was prepared with PR input. Bernard tried to turn the threat of my questions into an opportunity. He provided information on different points he wanted to push and also distributed the document to a wider audience within football.

His conclusions were that Eircom Park remained a highly viable project and that there were no problems. He said that the letter from HBG stated that the budget costs were fixed, up to 31 December 2001. He forgot to add that this was based on the assumption that the construction would be completed by then. Given the problems with planning permission, we would be lucky to be on site by that time. Apparently, a mystery UK firm wanted to take over the project for the same cost if HBG bowed out. IMG were a roaring success and the misinformation they were providing was repeated. Deutsche Bank was confident that the project could sustain at least IR£30 million of debt. A tax-based land lease deal, which would avoid having to buy the land up front and, thereby, reduce the debt, had been discussed in detail. This was news to me.

Furthermore, the FAI would be receiving millions of pounds in profits annually, with the prospect of IR£100 million from renewal of boxes and seats in ten years' time. All the debt would be repaid out of the stadium revenues with no recourse to the FAI. There were no problems. Eircom Park would transform Irish football. I agreed with that, but my vision of its impact was very different to Bernard's. It would impoverish us and divert resources to the stadium and away from the development of the game. That was the stark choice facing us.

I had been asking for details of the box and seat sales concluded by IMG for some months. At the July Centime Board meeting, the manager for IMG in Ireland stated that I should not be provided with this information, as I could not be trusted not to leak it to the press. Talk about double standards. The very fact that IMG took this stance proved that there was something wrong with the figures. They had been issuing press releases, stating how well they had been doing and providing supposedly accurate figures. If they had been giving out the correct information, then there should be no problem if I 'leaked' precisely the same information. If the press could have the figures, why not the Honorary Treasurer of the FAI?

Yes, I was talking to the press, but when I did, I was usually on the record. Yes, I used the press to get the debate to a wider audience. If I had not followed this strategy, I would not have achieved anything. This was a course of action I was very slow to embark on, but in the end I had no option. Some of my colleagues found my reticence in this area frustrating at times. I found their brashness in this area equally frustrating. At times, I cringed at what I read. Remember that the Eircom Park proponents were using professional PR people to spin the story in their favour. In the end, I believed that I had a right to respond and, especially, to correct a lot of misinformation.

*****

The next battleground was at a meeting of the Board of Centime in early August 2000. When I attended at the appointed time, I found that I was meeting not only with the other directors, but Bernard's experts from the project team, whom he had flown in to challenge me. I was one against, perhaps, ten. Needless to say the meeting achieved nothing, and I heard nothing to alter my views. Bernard was able to show the other directors of Centime and tell the Board of the FAI that his experts still stood behind the project. IMG were confident that they would raise the money. Six months later, these self-same experts' positions were shown to be untenable.

The builders/financiers were confident that the costs would not be exorbitant and they believed, but would not guarantee, that they could build 'a' stadium for close to IR£65 million. No longer were the project team going to build the original Eircom Park for IR£65 million, they were going to design a stadium that could be built for close to IR£65 million – a very subtle, but very significant difference. I saw it as grasping at straws. As the potential costs accelerated, Bernard was trying to move the goalposts. Who had made this decision? Certainly not the directors of Centime! Even this tactic could not rescue the project. As an expert estimate showed in February 2001, more than IR£100 million would be needed to build a bog-standard stadium.

Construction inflation was running at an extremely high level in Ireland during this period, and even with stripping the stadium down to its bear essentials, the financial gap between cost and income was widening. Stadium costs can vary greatly. A five-star, all-concrete job is very expensive; a basic steel-constructed stadium is a lot cheaper. Behind the scenes, Eircom Park was continuously being redesigned and downgraded to try (unsuccessfully) to control the costs.

At the end of the meeting, following acrimonious debates, I stated that I was considering my position as a director of Centime. I could not remain associated with a project in which I had no confidence and which I thought could bankrupt the Association. It was a spur of the moment decision on my part, prompted by the need to do something dramatic to bring home to the other directors the strength of my opposition. Having made the threat, I had no real option but to carry it through.

My brain was frying at this stage. These were the experts in their chosen fields. They were telling me it could be done, that a stadium could be built for IR£65 million, albeit a hugely downgraded one. I met with Linda and we sat in my car outside Merrion Square to discuss what action I should take. When I told Linda that they still claimed they could build a stadium for the IR£65 million, her immediate quip was: 'What, build a Tolka Park! Is that what they are talking about? They are making a fool of you.'

I felt I needed time, a half-hour perhaps. She responded that I did not need any time – I needed to get out of the mess! I sat in the car, still parked directly outside Merrion Square, and typed my letter of resignation from the Board of Centime on my laptop. I knew that my resignation from Centime could put my position as Honorary Treasurer of the Association under threat. This I had to live with. There was no going back.

When I spoke to some of my anti–Eircom Park colleagues, they urged me to resign immediately. This was certainly my intention, but I was not going to be rushed. I wanted to control the situation, if possible. However, as usual, one of my colleagues jumped the gun and told some of the media that I was threatening to resign from Centime. I was now committed, but I held off issuing any formal letter until later that night.

I had a commitment to meet with the Schoolboys Football Association that evening. I went to the meeting in the Aisling Hotel, which took me out of contact until nearly 10 pm. By that stage, the decision to resign as a director of Centime had solidified in my mind. I knew that it was the correct move, but the manner of doing it had to be carefully thought out. My primary role was as Honorary Treasurer of the Association, and it was important that the FAI directors and Council members received a direct communication from me, rather then learning about my action through the media.

I decided that I needed to send my resignation letter, addressed to Pat Quigley, to all the FAI Council members. Linda went home and printed out the letter. My supporters kept phoning the house. John Delaney was trying to hurry things up by urging Linda to issue the letter on the grounds that 'the boys [the media] have the story already'. Linda has been too long around football and certain personalities to give in to such pressure. She held off until I got home and had a chance to vet the letter before it went out.

When I got home, it was all systems go at our house. Linda and the children printed out fifty-five copies of the letter (see Appendix A). I wrote a short covering letter and the envelopes were addressed. Linda drove to An Post's sorting office in Knockmitten, near Clondalkin, and handed in the letters after midnight. Most of the Council members received the document in the post the following day.

Once the letter was ready for posting, I phoned Pat Quigley to let him know my decision. However, the aforementioned leaking of information to the media led to Pat rapping me on the knuckles and letting me know what he thought of my lack of courtesy. Pat's reaction was understandable because he learned the news of my resignation from a journalist, who phoned him for a response. It was a night when I couldn't please everyone. All I could do was stick to my principles. If other people interfered and cocked up the situation, I shouldn't be held to account.

I had not made a statement to the press at this stage, but, of course, the media had knowledge of my impending resignation from Centime. Being first to the media with news was a priority for some of my supporters, and by doing this, they were leaving me with little room for manoeuvre. The *Irish Independent* had even got a copy of my resignation letter and I was front-page news the following morning. The final decision to resign was mine alone, with advice from Linda. I have no doubt that the decision was the correct one.

Being involved in the FAI was full of little idiosyncrasies. I had to travel to Zurich the following day with Pat Quigley, Des Casey and Bernard O'Byrne to attend a FIFA Congress. I bought the *Irish Independent* at the airport and saw that I was a front-page headline; I later heard that I had made it onto 'What it says in the papers' on RTÉ radio.

As I was departing, Linda asked how I could read the *Irish Independent* in front of people I was so strongly opposing. My response was that seeing as no one would be talking to me, then at least I had something interesting to read. My recollection is that Bernard, Des, Pat and I were separated on the plane, so the element of discomfort was reduced.

The FAI media machine, led by Gallagher and Kelly, was hard at work. I was painted as over-reacting, as being politically motivated. It was argued that my objections had no real substance. I had been rude by not telling the President that I intended to resign. This was untrue, but that never seemed to matter. I had signalled that I was considering my position and I had telephoned the President to formally tell him that I was resigning.

Being in mid-air makes it impossible to react. However, on landing I heard what was happening. My phone message box was overloaded, but I had forgotten how to access my voice messages from abroad. Linda phoned Eircell seeking help. She was told that my message box was full – there were thirty-three messages waiting to be listened to! She managed to access them in Ireland and provided me with a summary.

Linda kept me informed of events back home. Misinformation was being put out in the media. When I was in meetings in Zurich, I diverted my mobile to the house phone back in Ireland and Linda handled all calls. Linda in turn diverted the house phone to her mobile when she went out. So, when a journalist phoned expecting to get me they got Linda. Thank God for modern technology and a very patient wife!

As an aside to all this, during one phone conversation with Linda, John Delaney told her that John O'Brien, of *The Sunday Times* was finding that I was not very forthcoming with information and that maybe she would have a word in my ear! He said O'Brien would phone later. It makes life so much easier for a journalist, if they can get someone to turn on the tap of information. Bingo! They have their story from one source. Sorry, but my prime duty was not to make life easy for journalists.

As the morning wore on, Linda got a tip-off from a journalist that FAI headquarters had issued a statement criticising me. The journalist sent her a copy of it and she relayed it to me. Most of this had happened while I was in mid-air with Bernard O'Byrne, Pat Quigley and Des Casey.

The situation in the hotel in Zurich was ludicrous. Every time Bernard's phone rang, he excused himself and went off to speak with a journalist out of earshot. The same held for me. I am sure that, at one time, we were doing simultaneous radio interviews with different stations in different corridors, just off the main lobby of the hotel. Eircom Park had become big news and this would remain the case until the final curtain some eight months later.

I later got a phone call from Linda saying that I needed to respond to what was being put out back home. So I did. I drafted a statement and got Linda to issue it to all the media. She phoned the RTÉ Sports Desk, just as the Angelus bell was ringing. She was greeted like a long-lost relative. They had been trying to get me all day. She prevailed on them the urgency and importance of the situation, and they squeezed my statement in before the end of the evening news bulletin.

As a closing note, the formal response I got from Centime was curt, simply acknowledging my resignation. So much for my in-depth analysis! Brendan Menton had resigned and I suspect that Bernard saw this as a positive. He could now push on with Eircom Park, without questions being raised at the Centime Board. He was confident that he could hold his support at the FAI Board. I was now 'out of his hair' to some extent.

By autumn 2000, the expenditure limit of IR£3 million set by the FAI Board had been exceeded by at least IR£300,000, partly due to the non-refund of VAT. The FAI Board put an embargo on any more expenditure. Bernard O'Byrne then informed the Board that all the consultants would now be working on a *'pro bono'*[2] basis, until planning permission was achieved. What the FAI Board understood by this was that the consultants would work for nothing. I came to believe that what the consultants understood by this was that they would not submit invoices until the final planning decision was made. These were two very different things. This *'pro bono'* commitment allowed the project to continue.

I spoke to the Association's accountants, Deloitte Touche, about this in November 2000. They had not been asked to continue to work on the project on a *pro bono* basis. It had been suggested to them that they should delay issuing invoices for their work on the project until planning permission had been finally determined. There is a huge difference between working for nothing and delaying receipt of payment. The effect of this was that the FAI would not receive new invoices for costs on the project and, hence, it would appear that no expenditure was occurring. It actually worsened the position, as we would not even know what debts were building up for the Association.

---

2.   *Pro bono* denotes work undertaken without charge.

Despite a pledge at the FAI AGM that I would have access to any information I required, I was still finding it very hard to get details of the box and seat sales. Part of my decision to resign from Centime was the lack of this information. IMG were saying that I couldn't be trusted with the information, despite the fact that I was a signatory on the trust fund in which the money raised was kept. In August 2000, I had a resolution approved at the FAI Board, stating that I had to be given the information required. This did not work either. Every excuse was used: people were away; the figures had to be checked; the figures had already been supplied. At the September Board meeting the Chief Executive, Bernard O'Byrne, was instructed to pursue IMG on the matter of contracts for seats and boxes, with a view to achieving the resolution that had been passed by the Board in August. Who was running the show? In my view, IMG were ignoring the demands of the people who were writing the cheques for their Dublin office.

Michael Hyland tendered his resignation from Centime at this September meeting. He gave no reason for his decision and could not be persuaded to change his mind. A proposal that the FAI Board of Management should take over responsibility for the project was defeated by ten votes to seven. When things got really bad, the FAI directors needed someone to point the finger at. After my resignation, it had been decided that additional directors would be appointed to Centime. In September, Fergus McArdle, Ollie Byrne and Noel Heavey were asked to become directors. I believe that Noel Heavey, who had an expert knowledge of development projects, subsequently declined to become a director.

The row over Eircom Park was poisoning the Association. Nothing could be discussed or decided without acrimony. There was a complete breakdown of trust. Around this time, it was discovered that Umbro had been paid IR£30,000 in compensation for the early changeover of the national team sponsorship from Opel to Eircom. Umbro had a lot of Opel-branded products in stock, which were now unsaleable. In addition, Eircom were demanding changes to the position of logos. When challenged on who authorised this payment,

Bernard denied any knowledge of it. It had been offered in a letter from IMG to Umbro. Had IMG offered IR£30,000 of the Association's money to Umbro, without anyone in the FAI knowing of it? If so, things were really getting out of control. Who was running the Association? It latter transpired that Bernard had told IMG to finalise the deal, without, it seems, mentioning money; however, this 'instruction' led to the payment of the money.

By November 2000, I still had not received the information on seat and box sales from IMG, four months after the pledge at the AGM and three months after the Board resolution. The main row on Eircom Park during this period focused on IMG's performance in selling boxes and seats. I knew that IMG were overstating the figures. I had access to copies of the seat contracts in the FAI and knew how much money was in the trust account. The figures simply did not tally.

At November's Board meeting, I demanded a direct answer from the President as to whether the information had been made available to the Association. When I received a negative response, I stated that I would be sending a solicitor's letter to the Association and withdrew from the meeting. My memory is that this again was a spur of the moment decision. It was unprecedented, even for the FAI. The meeting then disintegrated. Five other anti–Eircom Park directors left the meeting after making statements. One remained and provided us with information on what transpired after we had departed.

There was a decision that the information be supplied in writing to all directors within ten days. The meeting was adjourned shortly afterwards. This all happened under discussion of the previous meeting's minutes and before any of the agenda had been dealt with. Football was not mentioned that day.

This withdrawal from a Board meeting caused consternation within the Association and, indeed, led to calls for my resignation as Honorary Treasurer. One FAI director approached Linda very late one night at a function, saying that my position was untenable. She simply said that time would explain why I left the meeting. However, no one tried to organise a putsch against me. The numbers were in my favour, as I would get the vast majority of the Eircom League club votes at National Council. This lack of response to my actions illustrates one of the main problems with the FAI Board. Many members saw their role as simply that of being football politicians.

I had my solicitor write to the Association demanding the information. Here, we had one of the FAI's senior officers threatening to take legal action against the Association because he could not get access to information to which he and, indeed, all other directors were entitled. The letter pointed out that I, as Honorary Treasurer, owed a duty to the FAI, the members and creditors and was obliged to look after and protect the interests of the Association. It also pointed out the Association's obligations, under the Companies Act, to keep proper books of account and to correctly record and explain transactions. A company is also required to make such documentation available to be inspected by the officers of the company. An ultimatum was given that, unless the information was produced, I would take legal action to force the issue.

This led to yet another FAI Board meeting in late November 2000 to discuss my solicitor's letter. IMG had written to the Association stating that they believed the issue had been dealt with at a presentation to the Board in early November. They gave a slick presentation but had provided no actual figures. They claimed that they were some 400 per cent ahead of target, but again they did not tell us what the target was. After a long and acrimonious meeting, a deadline was set that the information requested must be provided by 11 December. I thought that that was what we agreed in August.

The Board also decided that a special meeting would be held on 22 January 2001 to discuss Eircom Park. At this meeting, a revised business plan would be available. Progress was being made at last, but Bernard's delaying tactics were also working. If the appeal to An Bord Pleanála went in the FAI's favour, then there would be no turning back. The final decision was due in May 2001.

I got my information before the deadline. Success at last! It confirmed my knowledge from other sources. Just over 1,300 seats and 15 boxes had been sold. Many of these were tied in with sponsorship contracts, such as the deal with Eircom on the stadium-naming rights. IMG's previous figures had been smoke and mirrors, but no substance.

There was a National Council (the supreme body) meeting of the Association on 11 December. I made a detailed presentation. Appendix B provides extracts from this presentation and is a good summary of the overall situation with regard to Eircom Park and my stance on the issue.

In this presentation, I put the cost of the project at IR£130 million. With the construction cost alone running at IR£100 million, this would result in a debt of at least IR£70 million. I did not see this debt being financed by the banking system, despite Deutsche Bank's contrary view.

The revised business plan was worked on in the last months of 2000 and presented to the FAI Board at a meeting in the City West Hotel on Monday, 22 January 2001. The total costs were estimated at IR£130 million. What a coincidence! Even I had been too low in my estimate of the stadium construction cost, which alone was now IR£109 million – this for a much less grandiose stadium than originally planned.

Of course, revenue was also increased in this new business plan, a fact crucial to maintaining the possibility that the stadium was viable. The fact that IMG's sales of corporate boxes and seats had been very poor to date had no impact on this upward revision. Prices of boxes and ten-year tickets would be increased, thereby generating even more revenue. Realism went out the window.

Excluding the IR£16.7 million cost of the land, the gap between cost and income was now projected at IR£41 million; including the land it was IR£57.7 million. This was far higher than the projected debt of IR£30 million, the figure Deutsche Bank had told me they believed the project could sustain. If only we had been dealing with realistic financial projections from the start, we would have avoided most of the rows about the stadium, saved the FAI millions of pounds and could, perhaps, have achieved a lot more.

This January meeting of the Board of Management was seminal for the project. All the project partners – including the project manager, Deutsche Bank, IMG, RHWL, Deloitte Touche and the project's aviation expert – made presentations. However, the key issue was the revised business plan from Deloitte Touche. For the first time, the debate was based on realistic figures and the number of sceptics on the Board increased. Many still wanted a stadium for Irish football, but for the first time they realised that it was not going to be as easy as they had been led to believe. The FAI nor, indeed, the project itself could not sustain the estimated level of debt.

At the January Board meeting, I announced that I intended to meet with the Taoiseach to discuss Stadium Ireland. Attempts were made to stop me, but I refused to capitulate. I was the Honorary Treasurer of the Association, and I was determined to act in what I thought were the best interests of the Association. If the members did not like what I did, then they could vote me out at the National Council or the AGM. The official FAI stance was that I was meeting Bertie Ahern as a private citizen. What a load of nonsense!

Bernard's last card was an equity partner. He had always claimed that there were three parties interested in taking an equity stake in Eircom Park. He was instructed by the Board to bring forward any proposals in a last attempt to save the project. At the January Board meeting, Bernard had a letter from Davy Hickey Properties, expressing an interest in the project. How opportune! Davy Hickey Properties, the owners of the City West site on which the stadium was to be built and the adjacent technology park, were the only 'equity' partners to look at the project. A four-man delegation was mandated to negotiate with Davy Hickey Properties. This comprised Bernard O'Byrne; Fergus McArdle, one of the new directors of Centime; Laurence St John and me.

The first thing Davy Hickey Properties did was to re-estimate the cost of the stadium. They calculated a construction cost of IR£104 million (remember the IR£65 million cast in stone). Adding in the cost of the land, professional fees and the required infrastructure to be funded by the FAI under their planning permission would bring the total cost to between IR£130 million and IR£135 million.

Davy Hickey Properties are a serious company. Their shareholders include many of Ireland's wealthiest people, who use the company as a property investment vehicle. It was reported in the media that investors in the Davy Hickey Properties company (Place Properties Ltd), who owned the City West site and technology park, included Martin Naughton of Glen Dimplex, Sean Mulryan of Ballymore Homes, Paul Coulson of Ardagh and some partners of Davy Hickey's stockbrokers. Money was not an issue to these people.

Yes, Davy Hickey had a formula, under which they were prepared to underwrite the project. However, as is the case with all investors, they were not going to do this out of the goodness of their hearts. They required a serious financial return on their investment, and they wanted this guaranteed. Furthermore, they wanted first call on all the revenues: Davy Hickey Properties would be the preferential creditors, meaning they would get paid first out of any revenue generated. This was not an equity investment, as I understand the term. They identified the FAI's crown jewels as being the television revenue, and this was also tied into their repayment.

Davy Hickey Properties estimated the debt on the project at IR£35 million, excluding the cost of the land of IR£16.7 million. This IR£35 million debt level assumed that IMG would raise close to IR£80 million, which I think would have been impossible. Davy Hickey Properties would put up IR£18 million of this money by way of a guarantee to a bank, and the FAI/Centime would have to borrow IR£17 million under their own name. I am not sure that any bank would have lent IR£17 million to the FAI in any circumstances. The key issue was how the Davy Hickey Properties' loan was to be repaid.

It was not simply a matter of repaying the IR£18 million with interest.

The land was another vital issue in all this. The FAI's option to acquire the land had expired at the end of December 2000, as full planning permission for the development had not been received. Davy Hickey Properties activated this clause. The FAI no longer had any rights over the site. As part of the proposed new deal, the land would be purchased at the end of ten years.

The remuneration to Davy Hickey Properties was to last for fifty years. After ten years, the resale of boxes and seats would have raised significant revenue. The first IR£68 million of this was to go to Davy Hickey to repay the loan and to purchase the site. In ten years' time, the price of the land would be approximately IR£30 million.

After Davy Hickey had been repaid their debt and the cost of the site by this IR£68 million, the next IR£17 million could go to the FAI to allow their share of the debt to be repaid. Note that Davy Hickey Properties got their IR£68 million before the FAI got a penny. Any additional revenue raised over and above these amounts would be divided up as follows: 60 per cent to Davy Hickey Properties and 40 per cent to the FAI. And I thought 'equity' partners were treated equally in terms of returns and risk! It did not end there. In twenty years' time, Davy Hickey Properties would receive 50 per cent of the revenue raised from box and seat sales, and this would continue on a declining percentage basis for the next fifty years.

Hickey Properties were to receive a similar share of annual profits from the project. The figures were defined to include the FAI's television revenue, which would be raised from the televising of Ireland's international matches at the stadium. The revenues from TV rights are the FAI's financial crown jewels and are used to fund the Association's basic development activities. The FAI were to be put in hock. On the land sale and a loan of IR£18 million, Davy Hickey Properties could have generated a return over fifty years of somewhere around IR£300 million.

My initial reaction was that this proposal was a joke. It was so outlandish, I believed it was designed to force the FAI to cancel the Eircom Park project. However, Bernard was intent on building the stadium and he claimed that it was good deal for the Association. It certainly did have the possibility of enabling Eircom Park to be built, but the cost to the Association was phenomenal and endangered our primary function of administering and developing football in Ireland. We would have a IR£17 million debt, and our television income would be restrained for the next fifty years to meet the needs of the project and to remunerate Davy Hickey Properties. The FAI would get ownership of the stadium after ten years, but would be paying Davy Hickey Properties for a further forty.

I do not want to become too cynical about this, but the life of a stadium is about fifty years. The FAI would cease paying for Eircom Park just as it would need major modernisation. Would we have to start all over again? I was appalled by this proposal. In my view, the FAI's primary role is to develop the game of football, not to be property developers or stadium operators or, indeed, concert promoters. Bernard saw the proposal as rescuing the project and, hence, supported it, despite its cost to football.

There was one additional significant factor to the proposed deal. The FAI would have to bear all the costs of getting the project through the planning process. An Bord Pleanála had just announced that there would be an oral hearing on the planning appeals. This would use up the last of the Association's cash.

Davy Hickey Properties had some other conditions on their support. First, they wanted to assure themselves that the stadium could be constructed at a cost of IR£104 million. Second, they wanted to be convinced that IMG would achieve net revenue of IR£69 million – 100 per cent of their target from boxes, seats and sponsorships. The first target may have been achievable, but I doubt if the second would have been. Davy Hickey Properties also wanted the proposal to have strong support from within the FAI; they wanted an end to the rows. I guessed this was aimed specifically at me.

I met with the Taoiseach on Monday, 29 January 2001. My discussion with Bertie Ahern and the Minister for Sport, Jim McDaid, was perfunctory; we did not discuss the FAI using the National Stadium in any detail. We all knew that the fact the meeting had taken place was in itself sufficient to change the nature of the relationship between the FAI and the government on the stadium issue. The FAI's attitude was that my meeting with the Taoiseach had nothing to do with them. However, the door had been opened and there was no closing it again.

The number of meetings of the FAI Board increased in February. Normally, the Board meets once a month, but it had two meetings in the first week of February. The first meeting occurred on 5 February in Jury's Hotel, Ballsbridge. No firm decisions were taken at this meeting, as it was the first time the Board members were briefed on the Davy Hickey Property proposal. It was agreed to meet again on the Friday (9 February), when clarification of some issues would be provided.

At this stage, I was convinced that the project was dead, but given the nature of the decision-making processes in the FAI, I thought it would die slowly. I was very happy that, for the first time in two years, the debate was based on realistic estimates. However, I was still meeting opposition in getting Stadium Ireland on the agenda. It would be the simplest of solutions for all involved if the merits and demerits of both proposals for the Association were compared. But the proponents of Eircom Park were fighting hard to prevent this.

One of the interesting things that emerged during one of our meetings with Davy Hickey Properties was that they revealed that they intended to meet with the government to discuss the stadium issue. There was no way a company such as Davy Hickey Properties was going to antagonise the government in order to bail out the FAI.

The anti–Eircom Park group on the Board decided to push matters in advance of the Friday (9 February) meeting. At a meeting of the management committee of the League of Ireland on the Thursday evening, it was agreed that the following resolutions would be put forward to the FAI Board the following day. As most club delegates to the league were now opposed to Eircom Park, it was easy to achieve these resolutions.

- The FAI Board of Management should immediately appoint independent technical and financial advisors to review the Eircom Park project for the FAI.

- The planning process for Eircom Park should be processed fully through An Bord Pleanála, but at reasonable cost and subject to the independent expert advice.

- The FAI must immediately enter into substantive talks with the government to establish the basis for use of the proposed National Stadium, as a possible alternative to Eircom Park.

If all the league delegates to the FAI Board had opposed the continuation of the planning process, it would have spelt the end of Eircom Park. A key element of the league resolutions was that they had the support of three directors who had not opposed Eircom Park to date. For the first time, the anti–Eircom Park group would have a majority on the Board. Even if the resolution did not kill off Eircom Park, it was another very large nail in its coffin. It also forced Bernard O'Byrne to agree to meet the Taoiseach. As always with the FAI, this resolution was not put to a formal vote, but was agreed to by consent. It could in fact be considered a unanimous decision as no one objected to it.

It is interesting to note Bernard O'Byrne's quotes in the newspaper the day after the Board meeting. When asked if this was a setback for him, he responded:

Timing is essential in negotiations and you have to know when you are holding the strongest hand. I certainly urged various members of the Board to vote in favour of this. I would regard a setback for me as missing a two-foot putt on the eighteenth green on Saturday.

Thus, after the Board meeting of 9 February, the FAI set out on a twin-track strategy of continuing to negotiate with Davy Hickey Properties and talking to the government about Stadium Ireland. The Davy Hickey Properties deal was a take it or leave it one. Davy Hickey

Properties were carrying out their own internal evaluation of the project to see if it met the criteria they required. From Bernard's point of view, the only good news in all this was that the project could still proceed to the planning appeal.

Bernard had to write to the Taoiseach, seeking a meeting, which took place on Friday, 23 February. As usual, the FAI delegation was large, as all the officers insisted on attending. The post-meeting press statement was brief and uninformative, to the effect that the Taoiseach had outlined a government proposal for negotiations with the FAI on Stadium Ireland. The government also undertook to have a detailed proposal prepared for discussion at a further meeting between the two sides on 5 March. The two sides agreed not to comment further.

The outline proposals for FAI use of Stadium Ireland were much more favourable than the existing agreement with the IRFU over the use of Lansdowne Road. There was also mention of increased grant funding for the Association. Paddy Teahon, Chairman of Campus and Stadium Ireland Development Ltd[3], was designated by Bertie Ahern to have detailed discussions with the Association.

A number of meetings took place with Paddy Teahon. On 6 March 2001, the Taoiseach sent a detailed proposal to FAI President Pat Quigley. This, at last, provided the basis for FAI use of Stadium Ireland, with which we could compare the financial projections and risks for Eircom Park.

It was an unfair contest. The government's deal guaranteed a minimum income of IR£40 million from the sale of boxes and seats for FAI events. This money would be available for development, rather than paying for the stadium. The maximum rent was to be 17 per cent of gate receipts, which was slightly higher than at Lansdowne Road. However, the prospect existed of a significantly lower rental figure, depending on the number of major sports events (football, rugby and GAA) played at the stadium. The FAI would have

---

3. CSI Development Ltd was the company set up to develop Abbotstown.

a clean stadium[4] for their games. This was excellent news, as it meant the FAI could sell advertising at Ireland games, without paying a commission to the owner. The FAI would also have full control over television rights. All in all, this was an excellent deal. The share of the total revenue the FAI would receive from a match at Stadium Ireland would be well ahead of Lansdowne Road and also ahead of Eircom Park. It certainly beat the Davy Hickey Properties deal hands down. The larger-capacity stadium would also provide potentially higher attendances and, thereby, greater revenue.

There was even better news on the grant front. The government would increase capital grants allocated to football from the existing level of IR£6 million to IR£15 million. There was to be a partial offset from the future income from box and seat sales, but no matter which way it was analysed there would be significantly more money for football. In spite of all the evidence, Bernard's public stance remained that Eircom Park was the best solution for football.

Right in the middle of these discussions, on 4 March, the *Sunday Tribune* broke a story that Bernard had used his FAI Visa card to pay personal expenses. This was to be a key factor in Bernard's ultimate departure from the Association in April 2001. Very few people within the Association knew about this. It had been discussed with some officers in the summer of 2000 and dealt with in an inconclusive fashion. Let me state categorically that I did not leak the story. I had informed nobody of the situation, other than some of the officers.

The fact that the story was given to Paul Howard of the *Sunday Tribune* proves that the leak did not come from me. I seldom spoke to this journalist. In my view, his treatment of the FAI had been consistently unfair.

I have little doubt that the Visa card story was leaked from within the anti–Eircom Park camp. How they found out about it, I can only surmise. I agree with the journalist Philip Quinn's designation of it as a side issue in the Eircom Park debate. It served no useful purpose

---

4. A clean stadium means that there is no advertising in place and, hence, the event organisers can sell the advertising space at their events.

and was a stupid move. It only muddied the waters, at a time when we were finally getting clarity on the Eircom Park versus Stadium Ireland debate.

The Board sensibly shelved the issue for the short term, by setting up a Finance Subcommittee to investigate it. Normally, as Honorary Treasurer, I would have been Chairman or at least a member of such a committee. However, given the situation that prevailed, it was absolutely correct that I would not sit on it. I will deal with the fallout from the credit card issue later in this chapter.

Behind the scenes, the tide was turning against Eircom Park. The clubs of the Eircom League were not going to refuse the government offer. Many of the other affiliates were at last changing their position. The final decision was to be taken at meetings of the FAI Board of Management and National Council in the Green Isle Hotel on Friday, 9 March. This was exactly five years and one day after the Merriongate meeting.

On the Thursday evening, there was a meeting of the league clubs, at which the tide turned firmly in favour of Stadium Ireland. On the morning of the meeting, Paul Lennon, writing in *The Star* newspaper, estimated that of the fifty-five members of National Council, thirty-nine were in favour of Stadium Ireland, six were die-hards in favour of Eircom Park, with ten unknown.

Even Bernard's main political bases within football, the Leinster Football Association and the Munster Football Association, had both decided unanimously in favour of the government's proposal. The Board had decided to recommend that the Council accept the government proposal. The result was a foregone conclusion. Eircom Park was dead. The vote in the end was unanimous at 55–0. The patina of unity in the FAI was important.

The main controversy at the Board meeting had to do with the credit card issue. It was also decided that a further Board meeting would be held the following Friday to review the complete management of the Eircom Park project.

Bernard put a brave face on the Association's decision. He spoke of how a 'golden egg' had just been laid, of unbelievable new horizons stretching out before the Association, with levels of financing unheard of previously. He described it as a stunning offer from the government. In the aftermath of defeat, the two main proponents of Eircom Park, Bernard O'Byrne and Pat Quigley, embraced the new reality with enthusiasm. It was a red-letter day.

When we see the money being put into facilities all around the country, it will be considered a good day for the Association.

The figures being put on the value of the government deal varied greatly. I noticed that I was quoted as saying that we could generate IR£125 million for the Association over ten years. I don't think this figure was unrealistic, taking into account the increased direct government grants, the sales of corporate boxes and seats, increased ticket income from higher attendances and higher prices and the very generous commercial and TV deals available to us at Stadium Ireland. My greatest disappointment in football was that the full impact of the grants was only felt for one year. Two and a half years later, the other benefits still await a final government decision on Stadium Ireland.

My reaction to the vote was one of relief. The next morning, Linda asked me how I felt. My response to her was that I was energised. The right decision for football had been made. The stupidity of the previous eighteen months was finally over. By not conducting their business properly, the Association had needlessly tied themselves in knots with internal dissension. The FAI had been badly damaged and would remain very divided. It was not a moment for anyone involved in football to be proud of. However, there were some positives ahead, if we could reorganise and maximise the impact of the new deal.

After the obituaries for the project in the Sunday newspapers, Eircom Park quickly dropped out of the media headlines. However, this was not the case for the Association, as Bernard's credit card issue remained alive. John O'Brien also immediately launched attacks on me in *The Sunday Times.* According to O'Brien, I had lacked .

leadership in the Eircom Park debate and should not be appointed as Chief Executive in the event of Bernard's departure. Now, I am not stupid. John O'Brien was one of John Delaney's main media mouthpieces – in O'Brien's view, Delaney was the white knight of the Association. On 12 March, just three days after the demise of Eircom Park, Delaney was quoted in the Examiner:

> *I shudder to think what might have happened had John Byrne[5] and myself not put our efforts into this.*

I had become a non-entity. From support and erstwhile friendship to back-stabbing in just a few weeks! I can do without such friendship. The attacks on me by O'Brien did not surprise me. He was annoyed because I had not made his job easy by providing him with inside information during the Eircom Park saga.

Bernard came under attack from some quarters, particularly the Eircom League. They league would put a formal motion to the Board of Management on Friday, 16 March. The league clubs would insist on a full investigation of Bernard's handling of the Eircom Park project. If this was open and thorough, I have little doubt that it have would caused many difficulties for Bernard. The possibility of his suspension during this investigation was high on the agenda.

As always with the FAI, the officers saw the problems looming and tried to take action to avert crisis and controversy. They met with Bernard prior to the Board meeting, on 16 March, and suggested to him that he take leave of absence during the investigation. Later that day, President Pat Quigley denied that the suggestion to take leave had anything to do with the investigations. Why else would leave be required? After an initial period when I thought he would accede, Bernard decided to hang on. In fairness to Bernard, this was probably the best decision for him, if he wanted to stay as Chief Executive of the Association, which he obviously did. He knew that once he vacated the Chief Executive's office, there would be no way

---

5.   John Byrne was a prominent member of the anti–Eircom Park group on the FAI Board. John was the Galway United representative to the FAI and a director of the Association.

back. The lack of unity among the officers that day certainly helped him.

Irish football is very much divided between the Eircom League and the junior game. It is all about political power. Bernard was from the junior game, while the opposition to Eircom Park was concentrated among, but not exclusive to, the league. Many Council and Board members, who had abandoned Bernard on the Stadium Ireland vote the previous week, would back him politically now to ensure that the junior football camp remained in the ascendancy. It had nothing to do with right and wrong or with the overall interests of the Association. Bernard probably believed that, given time, he could muster sufficient political support to survive. Let me say that, while I disagreed with him on many issues, I had some admiration for his doggedness.

However, Bernard's problems were mounting. The remit of the Finance Subcommittee was extended to review Bernard's management of the Eircom Park project. In addition, a new row erupted at this Board meeting, which was held in the Aisling Hotel. (The reason the FAI was meeting in so many different locations was that it was very difficult to book suitable rooms in Dublin at short notice and we were having emergency meeting after emergency meeting.) IMG were demanding payment of commission and fees for all the work they had done in connection with Eircom Park. For a long time, we had been told that IMG were working on a success (no foal, no fee) basis. However, the memorandum of understanding, which Bernard had signed with IMG without bringing it to the Finance Committee or Board, was that IMG would be paid IR£60,000 a month from January 2000 and 15 per cent of the commission of all deals negotiated by the Association, not just those to do with Eircom Park.

Bernard should not have committed the Association to such an agreement without Board approval. We had already seriously breached the IR£3 million expenditure ceiling and now we were faced with another large bill. The IMG problem, which could have been a bill of IR£5 million, was added to the issues to be investigated.

Football took over for a while, as in April the FAI decamped to Cyprus and Barcelona for two World Cup qualification games against Cyprus and Andorra. Bernard was a lonely and isolated figure during the five days in Cyprus, spending most of his time on his own. During this period, the Finance Subcommittee concluded its investigations and reported to the FAI Board on Monday, 23 April. Bernard was not giving up; strong supportive comments from both Mick McCarthy and Brian Kerr appeared in the media.

When the report was presented to the officers, Finance Committee and Board at successive meetings that Monday, Bernard was left with little room for manoeuvre. The first meeting on that day took place between Bernard and the officers at 10 am in the Forte Posthouse Hotel at Dublin Airport. Bernard had been provided with a copy of the report in advance. He was asked to consider his position in light of the report on the credit card usage, but again stood his ground and refused to resign or discuss a severance package. He preferred to face the Board of Management that afternoon in Merrion Square. The Board meeting was surreal. The first two hours were taken up for a change with football business, while every director knew that there was really only one item of importance that day.

The FAI were receiving legal opinion on how to deal with the situation, as was Bernard. Bernard's problem was that if the report was formally put to a Board of Management vote, he would be removed as Chief Executive. The numbers were against him, if only just. The report of the subcommittee was unanimous and its membership included some of Bernard's political allies. The meeting was adjourned on a number of occasions to allow side discussions with Bernard to take place. Pat Quigley and Michael Hyland, two of Bernard's friends, participated in these with the other officers on standby.

As Neil O'Riordan reported in the following day's *Sun*, the outcome was another FAI fudge. Bernard's position had become untenable and, in the end, he recognised that. After being approached by friends among the Officer Board, he agreed to request a voluntary retirement package. The details were not discussed that Monday, but Bernard's reign as Chief Executive of the FAI was over. Yes, this was a fudge, but why not? The overwhelming majority of the Board approved the request. While I had fought bitterly with Bernard over many issues, particularly Eircom Park, I believe that there was no need to be vindictive in such a situation. Life goes on. I know some FAI directors would not agree with such a sentiment and would consider me weak for not publicising the credit card issue earlier. Nonetheless, I believe that I was correct in not divulging the information to a wider audience than some of the officers.

The FAI statement issued was as follows:

> *The Board of Management of the FAI met this afternoon to consider the report of the Finance Subcommittee on its enquiries into the use by the Chief Executive, Bernard O'Byrne, of the Association's credit cards and related matters. The report had already been adopted by the Finance Committee and the Officer Board and a copy given to Bernard. He was informed by the officers that they had taken legal opinion on the matter.*
>
> *Bernard himself sought legal advice and, following a number of exchanges between some of the Association's officers, he put forward the following proposal: 'With the conflict of legal opinion between us and the immense stress on himself and his family, he asked the Association to discuss a confidential voluntary retirement package. These discussions would take place over the coming days.'*
>
> *The Board discussed the matter at some length and agreed by an overwhelming majority to authorise the officers to negotiate such a package.*

As reported in the media, Bernard drove away from Merrion Square at 7.47 pm, in effect, no longer Chief Executive of the Association.

Again, I am not going to detail the agreement reached with Bernard. It was supposed to be confidential, but there is no such thing within the FAI. The details were published in the media. The agreement put Bernard's official departure date at 30 April. For the week after the Board meeting, he came into Merrion Square and acted as Chief Executive. During his last week in Merrion Square, Bernard wrote to Deutsche Bank, agreeing to pay them the second part of their fee for Eircom Park. Needless to say, Deutsche Bank did not receive any of this money.

The last piece of Eircom Park business was to disentangle the Association from their obligations to the numerous business partners for Eircom Park. The work was done by me, first as Honorary Treasurer and later as General Secretary, and the FAI's financial executive, with John Delaney becoming involved when he was elected Honorary Treasurer at the Association's AGM in July.

Dealing with most of the business partners involved in the Eircom Park project was straightforward enough. We negotiated significant discounts on the fees invoiced. The percentage discount varied from firm to firm. Remember, the FAI had been told that the firms were working on a *pro bono* basis from September 2000. One or two small firms insisted on payment in full, but these were not significant in the overall scheme of things. We managed to save about IR£300,000, but the total bill still came to IR£3.7 million excluding the payments to IMG.

Unsurprisingly, the most contentious negotiations in the aftermath of Eircom Park were with IMG. Relationships had totally broken down between the FAI and IMG, and I, as the General Secretary, wanted rid of them. However, they had a memorandum of understanding signed by Bernard O'Byrne, which appointed them as commercial agents for the Association on all activities for five years, with a cast-iron option to renew for a further five. IMG were demanding IR£5 million for work they claimed they had done on Eircom Park, money the FAI did not have.

The meetings to try and resolve this impasse were very acrimonious. Legal people were involved on both sides. However, in the end reality of a sort triumphed. IMG had no future in Ireland, and given that most of the major FAI commercials deals had been locked up for years to come – Eircom was contracted as main sponsor to 2012 and Umbro to 2006 – there were not many fat pickings left. IMG received an additional payment of just under IR£1.5 million and their contract with the FAI was terminated.

If the memorandum of understanding with IMG had been brought to the attention of the FAI Board in January 1999, when it was negotiated, I doubt that it would have been approved. I could never see how IMG could add value to the commercial activities of the Association, if they were taking a 15 per cent commission. I believe that the main deal IMG transacted for the Association, the ten-year sponsorship with Eircom for IR£5 million, badly undervalued the value of sponsorship of the Irish team.

All in all, the cost to the Association of Eircom Park was around IR£5.5 million. This was crippling for an Association that had financial assets and total assets of IR£3.8 million and IR£5.8 million, respectively, on their balance sheet in March 1999. The Association was just about breaking even on its day-to-day operating costs. This financially weak organisation was going to underwrite and manage a IR£130 million project!

I have no regrets over Eircom Park. While it would be great if Irish football had its own stadium that made a profit, Eircom Park was never viable. It took me nine months to realise this and much longer to bring this reality to the Board. I am not even sure that I ever succeeded in that. It was the lure of government money that changed the votes.

Speaking on *Prime Time* in February 2003, Bernard O'Byrne stated that the reason Eircom Park collapsed was that the Association ran out of money. The penny had finally dropped. My biggest disappointment, but not surprise, was the way the project was managed within the Association. It became the personal goal of a few individuals, rather than the goal of the Association. In my opinion, the Association were badly misled on a number of important issues; this delayed the demise of the project and cost the Association a lot of money. I am disappointed that so many FAI directors saw the rows as internal politics and never looked at the reality of the project, as was their responsibility. I am disappointed that so many sat on the fence, especially those with some business knowledge and experience.

Eircom Park would have been a millstone round the Association's neck for years to come, especially under the Davy Hickey Properties proposal. It would never have contributed funds to the development of the game; in reality, it would have diverted funds away.

I did what I thought was right for the Association. In the end, expert opinion proved my financial assessment to be correct. I can assure the reader that I had no ulterior motivation. I was accused of doing what I did because of a friendship between my late father and the Taoiseach. I can tell the reader that, when I sat down in the quiet of my own home during the Christmas of 1999, there were no external pressures or influences. The death of the project was based on business and financial realities. I had nothing to gain personally. In fact, I had all to lose as I trod, albeit softly in the beginning, on people's dreams. But that is all they were: pipe dreams.

Bernard's departure from the Association provided me with an opportunity to again apply for the position of General Secretary of the Association; this time I succeeded. With hindsight, I wonder if that was the correct decision for me. By and large, I had enjoyed being Honorary Treasurer of the Association, despite the hassles of Eircom Park. I could perform this role in a non-political way, even if many FAI people might not see that. Being General Secretary makes you a target for the politicians in the Association. It is simply a matter of power for many of them. If you do what the politicians want, you will survive in the role. If you don't agree with them, you will be undermined, whether you are right or wrong. The FAI were bitterly divided and old scores were waiting to be settled. I was probably naive to think that I could unify the Association. That is an impossibility. I was being undermined from a number of quarters from day one.

*****

Appendix A

Mr Pat Quigley,
Chairman,
Centime Ltd,
80 Merrion Square,
Dublin 2.
2 August 2000

Dear Pat,

I am tendering my resignation as a director of Centime Ltd forthwith. I find it very difficult to act as a director in an environment where key information has been withheld from the Board.

At the meeting between some of the officers and professional partners today, I learned that the basis on which Eircom Park is based is totally different from what I had presumed. I was never aware that the budget for the construction of the stadium was 'capped' at £68 million (the construction costs of £65 million plus the £3 million contingency). As a director I should have been made aware of this information at the earliest date. The change from a 'maximum price' to a 'maximum budget' represents a fundamental change. Clear communication of this change would have been in the best interests of the Association.

I know that serious questions as to costs were raised with the project manager and the Chief Executive approximately one year ago in a letter from Ascon (HBG's subsidiary in Ireland) to the project manager. Obviously, the decision to cap the budget was made at that time. This letter and the consequent decision to cap the budget were never brought to Centime for discussion and decision.

I accept that the project manager provided assurances that the project could be built from green-field site to completed project within the £68 million budget. However, the inflationary impact of the delay and the exclusion of site preparation from the original budget must have an impact on the design and construction. The potential infrastructure costs are also a significant variable factor. The fact that it is not intended to build the ancillary aspects of the stadium (retail space, etc.) within the current business plan was not disclosed.

As you are aware, I have tried to gain access to additional information on the project, particularly the research carried out by Deloitte and Touche and specific information on the number of boxes and seats sold. I have been thwarted in this and have been informed that I need a formal resolution of the Board to gain access to this information. This I will bring before the next Board of Management meeting of the Association. I find this difficulty in getting access to standard information unacceptable and it makes it impossible for me to carry out my duties as a company director.

In particular, the insinuation by a professional partner that I could not be trusted with the information was insulting and I reject it utterly. I am entitled to this information as a director of Centime, as a signatory of the trust deeds and as Honorary Treasurer of the Association. It is the directors of the Association who control the business of the Association, and it is not for professional partners to withhold information from us.

I will outline in detail all my concerns about the project to the next Board of Management meeting.

I trust you understand my decision to resign as a director of Centime. I will continue to serve the Association as Honorary Treasurer, a position I am very proud to hold.

Please inform the Companies Office of my resignation as director of Centime Ltd.

Yours Sincerely,

Brendan Menton
Director

*****

Appendix B

Extracts from Presentation to FAI National Council
11 December 2000

Eircom Park has proved to be a controversial and divisive issue for the Association. I am concerned that the project is not viable and if we proceed, based on emotion and optimism rather than on financial realism, the longer-term implications for our ability to develop soccer in Ireland are very adverse.

I have asked a lot questions. Unfortunately, in many cases, I have not received satisfactory answers. This has put me in an impossible position with regard to protecting the assets of the Association.

What I find most disconcerting is that my analysis and questions have not been answered. Rather my motives for asking questions about Eircom Park have been impugned. This only strengthens my belief that a serious reappraisal of the project is long overdue.

I believe that the project has been seriously misrepresented to the Association. The negatives have been concealed or downplayed. The positives have been overstated. This is not the way to assess a £130 million project. Meanwhile we have spent £3.3 million on professional partners.

I believe that the revised business plan produced in May this year is fundamentally flawed. It seriously underestimates the costs and overstates the potential revenues. As these two components diverge, the funding gap multiplies. We have quickly gone from a fully funded project, to firstly debt of £30 million and, in the current review, to debt, in my opinion, of at least £70 million.

On the cost side:

- The original estimate from HGB, the builders, assumed that the project would be completed by the end of 2001. It is now at least 21 months behind that schedule. The £65 million cost estimated by HBG in December 1998 was not 'cast in stone' but at best can be described as a very preliminary estimate.

- The original cost estimate did not include site preparation work such as levelling and piling, which is usually between 5 per cent and 8 per cent of construction costs.
- The sterling exchange rate used in calculating the December 1998 estimate was 89 pence. Today it is 77 pence.
- The budget for infrastructure costs at £3 million was always inadequate. It was always going to be a multiple of the amount in the business plan. The planning conditions imposed by South Dublin County Council confirm this.

On the income side:

- I have serious difficulty in believing that we can hold nine home international matches every two years, each with a full attendance of 43,000 paying spectators. For example, only 20,000 tickets were sold for the recent match against Finland. The average ticket price received was £18, as compared to a projected average of £29 in Eircom Park.
- In my view the number of non-football events planned and their attendances are very ambitious.

The project still faces severe planning difficulties, particularly on aviation safety and transport management.

The Chief Executive's statement of May this year that the Air Corps had 'no operational or safety issues' with Eircom Park has proved to be incorrect and their official report advises the strongest possible objection.

Many of the conditions laid down by South Dublin County Council have to do with transport management. Getting 45,000 people in and out of Eircom Park, most of them on a park-and-ride system, will be very difficult. The need to secure long-term leases on the park-and-ride locations will be difficult and expensive.

I have consistently raised these points, firstly by writing to the President, Chief Executive and other directors of Centime. In later months, I have raised these points at the Board of Management. I have found it difficult to extract adequate information and answers.

I have also been concerned that the project was using all the cash resources of the Association, without a realistic chance of being successful at planning or being financially viable if planning is achieved. We had started out estimating that the planning and development costs would be about £1 million (May 1999). We then raised it to £2.5 million (Sept 1999) and finally, this time last year, to a cap of £3 million (Dec 1999) to see the project fully through the planning process (including An Bord Pleanála).

The budget allocation has proved to be inadequate. We have spent £3.3 million to date and need another £500,000 to fund the appeal to An Bord Pleanála and possibly a further £1 million to complete the development plans. We have spent £3.3 million of the £3.8 million reserves we had accumulated in March 1999. We have an operating deficit of £500,000 to fund this year and our cash will be exhausted by the end of the financial year. Prudent financial management is a must.

We need outside funding to move the project forward. We are told that there are a number of equity partners anxious to invest in the project. It is urgent that the conditions on which these people become involved be finalised without delay. If we do not have outside funding for An Bord Pleanála, we cannot proceed.

Hopefully, from the points made above, National Council will accept that I have being asking genuine questions about the project. It was only with my recent action of writing a solicitor's letter to the Association that the information began to become available. As Honorary Treasurer, taking such action was a very difficult decision to make.

Last Friday, I received the information on sales of boxes and seats by IMG, which was promised five months ago. This information shows that the revenue generated has been greatly overstated. We have pursued the project, spending large amounts of our scarce resources, based on false premises.

I now want to explain my reasons for resigning from the Board of Centime. I had been expressing serious reservations about the financial viability of the Eircom Park project, both at Board meetings and in writing to the other directors since December 1999. I accept that the other directors did not share my views. Conscious of the fact that I believed that the project was not viable and of my duty as a director of Centime Ltd, I believed that it was in both the Association's and my best interest to resign as a director.

I believe that the Ascon letter of August 1999 should have been brought to the attention of both the Board of Centime and the Board of Management. A fundamental reappraisal of the project should have taken place in September 1999. This could have saved the Association £2.5 million.

I now want to comment on my reasons for leaving the Board of Management meeting of the 10 November 2000 and subsequently having my solicitor write to the Association demanding information. At the Board meeting of 11 August 2000, I proposed a resolution to the Board that detailed information on the box and seat sales for Eircom Park by IMG would be made available.

At the Board of Management meeting of 10 November, I asked if the Board resolution had been complied with. I was informed by the Chief Executive that it had not. At this point, I stated that I had been requesting this information for nearly five months and that I was entitled to it as a director. I then stated that I was withdrawing from the meeting on the specific issue of non-compliance with the Board resolution.

The advice provided to the Association by its own solicitor, A & L Goodbody, is that directors are entitled to be provided with all relevant information as soon as it is available. If I may quote:

> a director is entitled to the information necessary to enable him to discharge his statutory and fiduciary duties... a company would need to show significant justification for any refusal to disclose information to a director.

There is a history of overly optimistic assumptions about projected future attendances for large projects. Look at the Millennium Dome in London and Expo 2000 in Frankfurt. Wrong projections resulted in catastrophic losses for both projects. Look at Wembley. The FA has rowed back on Wembley before their commitment became too large. The international banks led by Chase Manhattan did not want to fund Wembley. What do we know that is different?

I believe that at all times I have acted in the best interests of the Association and carried out my duties as Honorary Treasurer to the best of my ability.

We are competing for the hearts and minds of a generation of underage players. We have made tremendous progress since Euro 1988. We have tripled our playing membership and are now the most played sport in Ireland, particularly with young people. We must build on this achievement. It is unthinkable that our young players will be togging-out in converted containers, in cars or at the side of pitches in 2010. If we have no money to develop the game this will be the reality. We cannot afford to gamble with the future of our young players.

Brendan Menton

Honorary Treasurer

3

World Cup Qualification

At the draw for the qualification of the 2002 World Cup, Ireland was a third-ranked team in UEFA's list. One place higher in UEFA's list and we would have been one of the second-ranked teams. We had lost three consecutive play-offs, in 1996, 1998 and 2000. This was Mick McCarthy's last chance. He had been given a new two-year contract in September 1999, when we looked assured of qualification for Euro 2000, but the last-minute defeat to Macedonia in Skopje and the subsequent play-off defeat to Turkey had changed all that. We had now failed to qualify for three European finals and one World Cup. Mick had been in charge for two of them.

In September 1999, I was Honorary Treasurer of the FAI, having been elected for a four-year term in November 1996. I supported the reappointment of Mick McCarthy. He had done a good job in building a totally new team, with a lot of young players. More new players would come through the ranks from Brian Kerr's European Youth and U17 Champions of 1998. I was confident that things would get better and believed that Mick deserved a further opportunity to manage Ireland to the World Cup finals.

The final whistle of that match in Skopje was one of the worst moments I can remember in all my time following the Irish team, as a fan or as an FAI official. It was even worse than the defeat to Switzerland at Lansdowne Road in October 2002. Within a few seconds of the final whistle, we had gone from top of the group and automatic qualification to a play-off position. We knew exactly what was happening in Belgrade between Yugoslavia and Croatia by telephone, as we waited for the final whistle to blow.

As a football administrator, you are not supposed to know anything about football, even if you have been involved in it all your life. You haven't played at the highest level, so please keep your thoughts to yourself. However, I believe that the tactical substitutions made by Mick allowed the Macedonians to attack us for the last fifteen minutes. We switched to a one-man attack in Keith O'Neill, having taken off Mark Kennedy, who had the ability to hold up the ball for periods. As soon as we cleared our lines, the ball was coming straight back. We were barely surviving when disaster struck from a corner in the ninety-third minute. Mick had turned from a hero into a villain, and despite the subsequent achievements of his team, Mick was henceforth a target for elements of the media.

The draw for the qualification groups for 2002 put us up against Portugal and Holland as the first and second seeds respectively. Given the pedigree of these teams, we were written off before the matches started. However, despite dropping to a third seed within Europe, the team was now a lot stronger than six, four or two years previously. The only connections with the Jack Charlton era were the four 'senior' players in Steve Staunton, Alan Kelly, Niall Quinn and Roy Keane and the two surviving members of the original 'three amigos' of 1994, Gary Kelly and Jason McAteer. Phil Babb had fallen by the wayside since his infamous night out in Dublin with Mark Kennedy in August 2000. Seventeen of the usual twenty-three-man squad had earned their first caps under Mick McCarthy. In addition, there was more strength in depth and more cover. A few withdrawals would not undermine the team. We would never again face a situation such as that against the Netherlands in Anfield in November 1995, when Jack Charlton had to field four full backs (Gary Kelly, Dennis Irwin, Jeff Kenna and Terry Phelan) in his starting line up.

There are two key factors in the draw for a qualification group. One is the football strength of your opponents and your chances of finishing ahead of them. The other, which is equally important from the point of view of the Association, is the commercial potential afforded by the group. TV revenue is the crucial factor here. Both Portugal and Holland are reasonable television markets and would provide good income. The commercial revenue would be way ahead of our previous group of Yugoslavia, Croatia, Macedonia and Lithuania. However, they would be far behind the multi-million pound TV revenue available from the German, Spanish, Italian and UK markets. We had not drawn one of these teams since drawing England in the qualification for Sweden 1992 and Spain in the qualification for USA 1994, and this was before TV revenue had exploded.

I often looked with envious eyes to our colleagues in the North, who have had little success on the field, but have an uncommon knack of drawing one of the commercially rewarding countries. During the group draw for Euro 2004 in Oporto, I was sitting beside the Icelandics (we were arranged in alphabetical order). Iceland had already been drawn in Group 1. The first seeds were drawn last. When Germany came out of the hat, they cheered wildly. The Icelandic Football Association's financial stability had been secured for the next few years.

*****

I am not going to give a blow-by-blow account of the qualifying matches for World Cup 2002, as that material has been covered in great detail elsewhere. However, there are a number of off-the-field issues I believe merit detailed comment. Some of these have been elevated into the lore of Irish football and deserve to be challenged.

Dealing with them in chronological order brings us to the 'cheese sandwich' issue in Amsterdam. The Irish team were staying in the Hilton Hotel, one of Amsterdam's finest. Since I have been involved with the FAI, the Irish team have always stayed in the best hotels available. The days of poor accommodation pre-dates the Jack Charlton era, although the choice of hotel in Orlando in 1994 left a lot to be desired. I spent one night in it, when trying to collect tickets for the round-of-sixteen match against Holland and it was way below the standard that I have seen subsequently.

At every hotel, the team has a reserved dining-room. FAI officials do not eat with the team and, even as General Secretary, I was reluctant to intrude on this sanctuary without good reason. Every type of food is available. Eddie Corcoran, who is the team liaison officer, always visited the hotels in advance and arranged the food. We brought our own chef and food when required. Different players have different dietary requirements and Eddie ensured that a range of foods was available to meet all needs. Let me tell you that this was an expensive exercise for the FAI, catering for a party of thirty-five players and staff in five-star hotels in Europe's main cities. It is, however, worth the investment.

The FAI officers and the six Council members who were entitled to travel with the team as a perk were an additional cost to the Association. I have no difficulty with the FAI having a travel rota for Council members. These people give substantial voluntary time to administrating the game at different levels. Football in Ireland could not be run without them. If the pay-back is a trip away with the international team once every two to three years, then I support it.

Roy Keane has used the 'cheese sandwich' issue as a prime example of his unhappiness with team arrangements. It appears that he went to the team dining-room looking for food and all he found were some cheese sandwiches. Let me explain the arrangements made by Ray Treacy and Eddie Corcoran for the players in Amsterdam. The team itinerary the day before the game was the normal one:

- Breakfast from 8 am to 10 am, buffet style and of five-star standard. (Any food the players required was available to them.)
- Player training in mid-morning.
- Lunch at 1 pm; a full five-course lunch with all the food required available.
- Bed in the afternoon.
- Training in the stadium in the evening.

- Prior to training, Eddie Corcoran asked the hotel staff to leave out in the players' lounge tea and mixed open sandwiches including lettuce, chicken, tomato and cheese. This was in addition to the normal fare available in the lounge. Some players had them and some did not bother.

- After arriving back from training at 7 pm, the players showered and had dinner at 7.30 pm, again a full five-star meal with a very wide variety of food available.

- Tea and biscuits were available in the players' lounge before bed.

If Roy Keane had to order a pizza to his room after all that, he must have been very hungry that day. I know that if Roy had asked Eddie Corcoran to organise other food for him, then this would have been done. Eddie does not leave the team hotel when the players are there. He is present to respond to their every need. Roy made accusations, not caring who got hurt.

The FAI do not bring a dietician with the team, but on occasion when we are travelling to the more exotic locations, we do bring a chef. The players are highly paid professionals and get all their expert advice on diet from their clubs.

The second myth I would like to debunk concerns the travel arrangements. The FAI always travel to away games by charter flight, out of Dublin. Usually a 150–180-seater plane is used. However, on occasion a larger Airbus has been used. The two teams (senior and U21), with the technical staff and the FAI official party use about sixty-five to seventy seats. The remainder are sold to a very identifiable set of fans and to the media in order to defray the costs of the charter. There has never been a problem with these arrangements. Charter flights to any destination in Europe cost at least €80,000. The problem with a charter is that the plane has to travel two legs empty of passengers and this greatly increases the cost. When Aer Lingus was the Association's travel sponsors, this was less of an issue.

The recommendation in the Genesis Report that the Association use charter flights but not recoup the cost by selling seats to the media or fans is ridiculous. This is a solution for a rich Association. In the first place, the Association have been using charter flights for years and, in the second, the Association cannot afford to forgo the revenue from selling the seats. The price of each away trip would be equivalent to the annual cost of employing, perhaps, two regional development officers. Given the choice, I would always opt for recouping the revenue where possible. I am sure that most of the players would also support this. I have no doubt that the vast majority of the Irish players have no difficulty with the current travel arrangements. Is it any different with the English Premiership clubs? In fact, the current Irish travel arrangements are superior to those of other countries Genesis visited for comparison. The only problem I can see with the arrangements is that it frequently delays the return flight, as the plane has to wait for the media to file their reports and photographs for the following day's papers.

Let me come to the famous flight to Cyprus in 2001, which features large in Keane's litany of complaints against the Association. This was the first occasion when the FAI had use of a plane with a separate business-class area. I believe that it was the first time that Aer Lingus was flying the team under the new sponsorship arrangement. Prior to this, the plane had always been a standard Boeing 137 or its equivalent, with no difference in the seats throughout the plane. The first row on the right was always occupied by Mick McCarthy, Ian Evans and the team doctor, Martin Walsh. The first row on the left was occupied by the General Secretary, President and either another FAI officer or one of their spouses, if they were travelling. The team were seated in a group together in the first half of the plane and separated by team security from the fans and the media. They were always left alone on the flight.

For the flight to Cyprus, Aer Lingus provided an Airbus, which has twenty-four business-class seats. The first I knew that things were different was when I boarded the plane and had, as Honorary Treasurer, been allocated a business-class seat. It was embarrassing. However, at that stage, it was too late to change the seating arrangements. But the policy decision never to allow it to happen again was quickly taken. I do not know who made the seating arrangements for this trip. However, I do know that there were animated discussions at the check-in prior to departure between the then General Secretary, Bernard O'Byrne, and Aer Lingus check-in staff.

On the second leg of that trip, from Cyprus to Barcelona (to play Andorra), a different charter was used. It probably originated in Cyprus to control costs. I was not on this part of the trip, having returned to Dublin directly from Cyprus. The reports were that the plane was 'old'. However, when the Aer Lingus Airbus arrived in Barcelona for the final leg home, the team were allocated the business-class seats. Roy chose to make his complaint, about FAI officials sitting in business class, directly to the media. This was after the FAI had decided that business-class seats, when available, would be allocated to the players.

From then on, the team always got preference with regard to seats. However, the one trip to Cyprus when the situation was messed up has been used to create the impression that the officials always take precedence over the players and that it was only player pressure that changed this. As I have said, this has become part of the lore surrounding the FAI and the team.

Let me refer to one other incident before returning to the game in Cyprus. On the trip to Russia in September 2002, Mick had allocated the seats. There are twenty-four business-class seats on the Airbus. The twenty-two players got seats. Mick McCarthy is a gentleman and he had allocated the remaining two to Milo Corcoran, the President of the Association, and me, the General Secretary. This was embarrassing and there was a lot of discussion before Mick agreed that he and Ian Evans would use the seats. Neither Milo nor I would have been the least bit comfortable with the arrangement, and I have no doubt that if we had sat with the players we would have been slagged off by sections of the media.

Roy Keane had other criticisms of the trip to Cyprus and here, for once, I can agree with him. After the game in Cyprus, in which Roy

Keane was magnificent – indeed I believe that this was one of his best games in the qualification campaign – Mick McCarthy returned to England, as his father had died. He rejoined the team in Barcelona on the Monday. The team went out on the Saturday night and I believe that curfews were broken. As the Genesis Report points out, most teams have a small celebration after a game, but the effects of an all-night binge take a long time to remove from the system. I watched the match against Andorra in Quinn's Pub in Drumcondra. We were awful. Was this the lingering effects of the long night out?

*****

Having beaten Cyprus and Andorra away and drawing with both Portugal and Holland, we had gained eight points from our four away games, more than anyone had originally predicted. The two real tests facing the Irish team were the home games against Portugal in June 2001 and Holland the following September. The game against Portugal would be my first home international fixture in charge as General Secretary and event manager, as we did not have one during my stint as Acting General Secretary in 1996.

We had major rows with the Portuguese over tickets. Each visiting team is entitled to a minimum of 10 per cent of the stadium's capacity. This was approximately 3,300 tickets in Lansdowne Road. The Havelock Square Terrace was completely reserved for the Portuguese, together with a small number of premium seats in the West Lower Stand. Having just 30,000 tickets for Irish supporters for this match was totally inadequate. From day one, there was a mad scramble for tickets.

As soon as we issued their tickets to the Portuguese Association, they began to appear on the black market in London. The FAI bought some of these tickets to confirm this. When we contacted the Portuguese Association, they stated that only Portuguese supporters had access to the tickets. This was a major issue for the FAI as we had responsibility for the security at Lansdowne Road and this included proper segregation of supporters. There were furious rows between the two Associations. When the media reported on the story, the

Portuguese Football Association President had a fit of pique and refused to attend or to allow his officials to attend the pre-match function. This is unheard of in football, as these events are where friendships are developed and relationships between Associations strengthened. I believe that the non-attendance of a delegation at such a function is without precedence in football. In an interview in the *Irish Independent*, the President also complained that we had only provided him with a top-of-the-range Opel rather than a Mercedes.

The Portuguese were also upset over the suspension of their captain, Fernando Couto, for using the banned substance Nandrolone at his club Lazio in Italy. The FAI was even accused by the Portuguese Association of conspiring to have the player banned. The ban was endorsed two days before the game. While the FAI was having difficulties with the Portuguese officials, particularly their President, Mick was having a run-in with their manager, Oliviera.

Our security people had to make contingency plans to segregate the Havelock Square end seating. It was not that we were afraid of problems, but the FIFA match delegate, who attends and reports on all issues that arise, could submit a negative report leading to a fine for the FAI. As the gates opened and the fans filed into the Havelock Square section, about 50 per cent of the supporters were wearing green and 50 per cent the maroon of Portugal. Trust the Irish fans to get tickets from any source. Irish supporters were put to the right and Portuguese to the left. The allocated seating by ticket went out the window. However, the plan worked well and a high level of fan segregation was achieved. The fans cooperated fully.

As the fans initially came in, I was standing in the committee box at Lansdowne Road with Antonio Sequira, who is a gentleman and was then General Secretary of the Portuguese Association. He threw his eyes to heaven when he saw the large number of Irish fans in the section reserved for the Portuguese. In the end, the FIFA delegate, who was well aware of the row over the tickets, was satisfied with the way the problem was handled and no action was taken by FIFA.

Held on a brilliant, warm June day, the match against Portugal was excellent. At times the Portuguese were on top and at other times we dominated. In the sixty-sixth minute, we went ahead through a goal by Roy Keane. At this late stage, the question was whether we could hold out and beat the Portuguese. A win would make us favourites to win the group and gain automatic qualification. This was what we wanted, even if the Association thereby missed out on lucrative revenue from a play-off. Portugal had to come at us and they did. Mick began to make changes. He took Niall Quinn off, replacing him with Matt Holland and reverting to a 4–3–3 formation, but with the Portuguese pressure, it quickly became a 4–5–1 formation. There were shades of Macedonia in my mind as we conceded large tracts of the pitch to the Portuguese, who piled on the pressure. Too much of the game was being played in our last third of the pitch. Then Figo headed the equaliser with twelve minutes remaining. It was now very much a case of damage limitation. Could we hang on for a draw? Mick made another substitution, bringing on Gary Doherty for Mark Kinsella and reverting to a 4–4–2 formation. This restored a better balance to the team and the match ended in a draw. As the Portuguese had beaten the Dutch in Lisbon, we were now favourites to finish second. All we needed was to avoid defeat against the Dutch in Dublin in September. We were too far behind the Portuguese on goal difference to have any realistic hope of finishing ahead of them. This was presuming that we would beat Estonia in Tallinn the following Wednesday.

Estonia had a new stadium, which at best could be described as three-quarters built. The pitch was a nightmare. The Dutch had struggled to beat Estonia the previous Saturday, requiring two late goals to come from behind. The FAI decided not to make any formal protest over the state of the stadium and pitch and the UEFA match delegate appreciated this. Estonia were a fairly new football nation and were trying their best to improve their facilities. If only the FAI had a new stadium! Despite Roy Keane's suspension for two yellow cards, the players got on with the task in hand of beating Estonia, and once Richard Dunne scored in a goalmouth mêlée in the eighth minute, we were on our way. Matt Holland increased the lead in the thirty-eighth minute. The Estonians had one very good player, Stepanov, who moved from centre half to centre forward late in the game and caused us some anxious moments.

My other two memories from Estonia were seeing Stephen Reid play for Ireland for the first time in the U21 match, and a mad-cap spontaneous football match in the old town square on the night before the game. Stephen's striking of the ball and his pace were a class apart. We had found another star. The old town square in Tallinn is beautiful. But on the Tuesday evening, it was the venue of an impromptu 100-a-side football match between Irish and Estonian supporters. I'm sure the old square had never seen its like.

*****

There are excellent relationships between the Dutch and Irish Football Associations, going back to Gelsenkirken in 1988. They had beaten us then and again in Orlando in 1994 and Liverpool in 1995 (the one-match play-off for qualification for Euro 1996). They were extremely confident that they would do so again, despite our achievement in drawing with them in Amsterdam. I think that result surprised everyone in football and merits being called an achievement.

There would be no issues with tickets with the Dutch supporters. They wanted the tickets for themselves and would turn up in numbers. It is interesting to note that the Dutch football officials stayed in the Merrion Hotel in Dublin, the most expensive hotel in town at that time, while their players were in the St Helens Radisson. This would never happen with the FAI. I wonder if their officials get stick from the media and fans over such policies.

I only occasionally attended Mick's pre-match press conferences in Dublin. This partly reflected the divide between Mick's football responsibilities and the FAI's other responsibilities. Mick felt more comfortable being on his own or with Brendan McKenna, the FAI media officer, sitting with him at the top table. However, I was in the City West Hotel when Mick gave his press conference on the Friday before the Dutch game and I called into it. Mick was asked a question about the role of Holland's Patrick Kluivert as a slightly withdrawn centre forward setting up other players. Mick responded by saying that Berkamp, who had retired from international football, was the best exponent in the world of that position. What a subtle put-down of Kluivert and the Dutch team. Despite the importance of the occasion and the attending pressures, I felt that Mick was fully in control and quietly confident.

*****

One innovation we introduced for the Dutch game was touchline seating. This has always existed for rugby internationals, but had never before been used at soccer internationals. We converted the terraces at Lansdowne Road into seated areas by installing bucket seats on scaffolding, even though such seats did not fully comply with FIFA requirements. Peter Buckley and I decided to introduce the touchline seats without seeking permission from UEFA or FIFA, and, indeed, without discussing the matter widely within the FAI. We increased the capacity from 33,500 to nearly 35,000, thus making close to an additional 1,500 seats available for Irish fans.

There was no reaction from UEFA after the match. I doubt if the match delegate realised we had made this significant change. There were no problems, so the delegate had nothing to report. We decided to charge premium prices for these seats, even though they are relatively cheap seats at rugby internationals. There were no complaints from the fans, who were delighted to get the tickets. The FAI use a different configuration of touchline seats from the IRFU in order to maintain the number of wheelchair places. No issues have ever been raised about the installation of these extra seats and they continue to be used at competitive matches.

*****

We needed a draw from the match; the Dutch needed to win. We were playing for second place in the group and a play-off position. We had a very shaky start and nearly conceded a couple of times early on. That the scoreline remained 0–0 was down to bad finishing by the Dutch. We then steadied a bit, but the Dutch were frequently pushing us back. Overmars was causing Gary Kelly problems, which lead to Gary getting booked early on. We reached half-time with no score and were probably lucky to do so. This was a very satisfactory scoreline from our perspective.

At half-time we put on a match between two Special Olympic teams, managed by Brian Kerr and Noel O'Reilly. We had to ensure that the FIFA delegate was downstairs having his cup of tea, as FIFA do not approve of such events at half-time. We also had to ensure that all evidence was removed before the delegate reappeared. I was very disappointed that no one from the presidential box (Association officials, politicians and guests), other than Linda and myself, remained to watch the match. At the end of the game, the FIFA delegate told me that he was aware of what had happened at half-time and was disappointed I hadn't invited him to stay and watch the game. He felt that FIFA should fully support such events. One of my undying memories of the occasion is of a player doing his own lap of honour at the end of the game and celebrating as if he had scored the winner in the World Cup final. The crowd responded with a standing ovation. It was a beautiful moment and it lifted my heart.

The second forty-five minutes of the Dutch game would decide whether Ireland had a realistic chance of going to Japan and Korea for the World Cup. The atmosphere in the FAI committee box was every bit as tense as anywhere else in the ground. We are fans, first and foremost.

Things started badly as Overmars again went past Gary Kelly, leading to a second yellow card and the mandatory red one in the fifty-seventh minute. Ireland were down to ten men with over half an hour to go; it was 'backs to the wall' to preserve a nil–all draw. I can't believe that at this stage anyone was contemplating victory. This includes Mick, as he took off Robbie Keane and brought on Steve Finnan in the right full back position. The Dutch nearly scored when a Steve Staunton headed pass to Shay Given went astray and put Van Nistelrooy in. Having watched it on replay, I would have had no complaint if the referee had awarded a penalty against Shay. Whether the Dutch now felt that their work was largely done or whether it was a renewed determination by the Irish team, the balance of the match incredibly turned in our favour. Our goal came in the sixty-seventh minute from Jason McAteer. The Dutch defence went missing on a cross by Stephen Finnan and Jason took the goal brilliantly. One up, needing only a draw and with twenty-three minutes left, we were now in control.

The Dutch panicked. They needed two to win; nothing less would do. They made it easy for us. The Dutch manager, Louis Van Gaal made a series of 'crazy' substitutions. He took off Overmars and Zenden, the two wide players who had been causing us difficulty. The Dutch ended up playing with four world-class centre forwards in Hasselbaink, Kluivert, Van Nistelrooy and Van Hooijdonk. They reverted to high balls into our box from distance, which were easily dealt with by our central defenders. We held out for a famous victory without too much difficulty. Our destiny was now in our own hands, with just the home game against Cyprus to come. Only an imponderable set of results would see us finishing other than in second place.

The Dutch officials were aghast at the result and could not believe that their team of stars would not be going to the World Cup. However, as true sportsmen, they still remain excellent friends with us. Shortly after the game, I was in the corridor outside the dressing-rooms. Having been suspended by the Italian FA for a drug offence and excluded from the Dutch squad, Edgar Davids was sitting alone on a chair outside the dressing-room. He was disconsolate, head in hands. One of the world's best players realised that he was not going to the World Cup.

*****

Our last qualification match was against Cyprus in Dublin on 6 October. The Cypriots don't normally travel well, despite putting up some good home performances. Portugal were playing Cyprus away in early October and this was the last chance for a slip up by the

Portuguese. At half-time, with Cyprus winning by 1–0, my hopes rose, but three second-half goals by the Portuguese put the result beyond doubt. The Portuguese were not going to slip up in their last match against Estonia in Lisbon.

Our match against Cyprus went off without a hitch in front of another full house at Lansdowne Road. Once we had taken the lead in the second minute through a free kick by Ian Harte and had added a second in the eighth minute from Niall Quinn, we were there. The result was never in doubt. The score ended up 4–0 to us, with second-half goals by David Connolly and Roy Keane. Portugal had their expected easy victory against Estonia and we were once again in the play-offs.

*****

We beat Cyprus on Wednesday, 6 October; the play-offs were scheduled for 10 and 15 November. We would be facing an Asian team. The second match would take place on the Thursday rather than the Wednesday due to the significant distance involved. If the play-off had been with a team from the Far East – and Uzbekistan were still a possibility – then I believe it would have been logistically impossible for the games to go ahead on those dates, given the distance and jet lag issues. FIFA need to re-examine this issue for the future.

As we knew that we would more than likely be involved in a play-off, we had done a lot of the advance planning. We knew we were drawn against the Asian qualifiers, but it was still far from clear who our opposition would be. FIFA had made the draw just before the Dutch game in September. They made the draw without reference to the potential participants.

Prior to the draw, the availability of Lansdowne Road was a potential major issue. The rugby team had scheduled a home fixture against the New Zealand All Blacks for Saturday, 17 November. If we were drawn at home in the second leg on 15 November, we would have a serious problem. There was no way that the seating we were forced to install for competitive fixtures could be removed and the stadium made safe between the Thursday and the Saturday. We might have to stage the game with a reduced capacity of just 23,000, closing off all the terraced areas. Even reconverting the stadium to its rugby format within a week was faster than had ever been done before. We discreetly signalled to FIFA that we could have a problem, but their decision was to wait until the draw was made.

We got what Mick wanted in the draw. We were drawn against the Asian qualifiers but more importantly, we were drawn at home first. The stadium problem had evaporated through the luck of the draw. There was a huge sigh of relief. However, at this stage it was still very unclear which team we would be playing, as the final Asian group matches had yet to be played and the second-placed teams in the two groups had then to complete a play-off. China would win one group, with either Saudi or, more likely, Iran taking the other. Other possible opponents included Bahrain and the UAE, but Iraq were unlikely. Uzbekistan had an outside chance of making it.

Iran lost away to Bahrain, which changed the picture. They finished behind Saudi Arabia and qualified for the play-off against UAE, which they duly won. The final match was not played until 31 October and hence it was just ten days before the home leg when we finally knew who our opponents would be. However, this sequence of matches allowed Mick and Ian Evans to visit the Middle East and observe our potential opponents.

The draw against the Asian qualifier had a further complication. The US invaded Afghanistan in early October and this brought a huge element of uncertainty and additional security concerns. Media speculation was rife, but it was impossible to achieve any clarity on this issue. We communicated our concerns to FIFA on this issue but their decision was to adopt a 'wait and see' approach.

We met and discussed the issue with Michel Zen-Ruffinan, FIFA's General Secretary, in Prague on the occasion of the FIFA congress. In the end, the Afghanistan situation had no impact on the match.

Ireland had never played an Asian team in a senior international match. We had no idea what to expect. How easy would it be to get visas? What would be the standard of the hotel? Did our contract with Aer Lingus include a charter flight for a play-off match? How many Iranian supporters would travel to Dublin? We had little time to prepare. However, the Iranian Embassy in Dublin were most helpful and facilitated us in every way possible. They insisted that they would allocate the tickets to the Iranian fans. This created its own difficulty as we needed prompt payment for the tickets. Three thousand tickets at an average of €20 was not a figure to be lightly dismissed. I reckon that it will be the one and only time that the residents of Mount Merrion Avenue (where the Iranian Embassy is located), one of Dublin's most exclusive roads, will have witnessed a queue of football fans waiting to buy tickets on its secluded tree-lined avenue.

The pre-match function with the Iranians took place upstairs in McGrattans, off Baggot Street, on the evening before the game, as in this instance there was no U21 fixture. These functions can be good fun, especially when meeting friends from other European countries. But they are also formal events, with speeches and an exchange of gifts between the Associations. The FIFA match delegate and referees delegate also attend. Our friends from Iran were strict in their observance of no alcohol. Very few had any English, and suffice to say we had no Farsi (the language of Iran). The idea is to have the function over quite quickly, but, for whatever reason, the meal took an age to serve. This was the most excruciating function I have attended, at home or away. The one in Tehran, five days later was much more enjoyable.

The evening in McGrattans was also the evening that we put the renewal of the kit sponsorship with Umbro to bed. The kit sponsorship deal was the last thing that our commercial agents IMG were involved with for the Association. We parted company with them shortly after that. As always, IMG's involvement complicated the process and slowed it down. It was impossible for them to add enough value to the deal to equate with their 15 per cent commission. There were only three possible players in the contest for kit sponsor of the Irish team: Umbro, Adidas and Nike. Adidas quickly signalled that they would not be bidding. Nike were sniffing around the contract, but it was impossible to get a firm commitment from them. They wanted more time. They wanted information on the number of jerseys sold under the previous contract, information that in my view was confidential to Umbro.

Umbro had been great sponsors of the Association since 1996. I put them up there with the main sponsors (Opel and Eircom) in terms of value delivered to the Association. They pay a substantial monetary amount, and in addition supply unlimited quantities of gear to all our international teams for up to 100 international games a year. They had offered us a generous increase on the previous terms. We made the commercial decision to go with Umbro again, without waiting for a formal response from Nike. Our information on Nike was that, while the monetary terms could be attractive, it would be very difficult to get additional gear from them above the amounts specified in a contract. This had never been an issue with Umbro.

I was also aware of the negative publicity Nike had received as regards their exploitation of workers in developing countries. During my one meeting with Nike, they jumped to defend the company before I could even raise the issue. Obviously, it was having its impact on them. FIFA have a standard regarding the manufacture of sports gear and the conditions of employees. I had been visited by SIPTU on this issue. All in all, Umbro were by far the better option.

John Courtenay of Umbro Ireland joined us at the pre-match function to shake hands on the deal. Eddie Cox had done all the negotiations with Umbro and had achieved a very good deal. However, it was John Delaney and I who met with John Courtenay. Delaney, as Honorary Treasurer, wanted the Finance Department to get involved in commercial matters, an area in which Eddie Cox had performed well for the Association since 1996. It was a matter of power and control, rather than performance.

During our meeting with Courtenay, Delaney upped the ante one last time. In my view everything had been pre-agreed. However, the

Association were facing a cost of about $40,000[1] for their share of the charter flight to Iran. Aer Lingus would provide the charter, but the contract specified free charters only for group qualifying matches. Delaney asked Courtenay for a contribution of €30,000 towards the cost of the charter as a final sweetener on the kit deal. Courtenay was astounded, but as a great supporter of Irish football, he agreed, despite being very annoyed. This illustrates the different ways of doing deals within the FAI. I believed that developing long-term partnerships with our sponsors was important.

*****

The home match with Iran resulted in a good victory. We were struggling to break through when one of their defenders gave away a silly penalty just before half-time, by tripping Jason McAteer just inside the box. Ian Harte converted comfortably. One–nil up at half-time was a satisfactory start. Before the match, I felt a 2–0 scoreline would be a great result. Conceding no goals to Iran at Lansdowne Road was very important for us. They were unlikely to score three against us in Tehran, given our defensive record. An away goal for us in Tehran would make their task impossible.

Robbie Keane scored our second, early in the second half. We survived a few heart-stopping moments as Iran pressed forward for a vital away goal. The difference between a 2–0 victory and a 2–1 victory would have been vast. Shay Given made a couple of brilliant stops, which earned him the Man of the Match Award. At the final whistle, we were quietly confident that we were going to the World Cup.

Of course, Roy's absence from the second leg was to become part of the saga of Saipan. I do not know, nor at this stage care, what was agreed between Mick, Roy and Alex Ferguson. I do not know who telephoned who. I will, however, quote from Roy's interview with Tom Humphries on his departure from the team hotel after the first leg:

---

1. International charter flights are always priced in dollars.

The lads were having a warm down. They were in their rooms.
It's not my scene. If I passed someone in the corridor, I'd say
goodbye.

We were treated royally in Iran. (Sorry, that is certainly the wrong adjective to use for Iran.) We made it through the airport formalities in twenty minutes, an event unheard of in Tehran. Even Roy Keane might have been impressed! Usually it takes at least ninety minutes, even for diplomats. The trick was that we had organised deluxe treatment for the Iranians on their arrival at Dublin airport. We had learned that if you did something positive for the Iranians, they would make sure that they did it better in return. If you created a problem for them, then you would have severe difficulties. Funny how when the FAI get something right, it doesn't make media headlines.

The hotel in Tehran was just OK. It had been taken over by the state after the revolution and had probably not seen much investment in fifteen years. The food was poor. I know of FAI officials who went hungry. We had brought our own chef to cater for the players, but even the best efforts of Simon Doyle of the Holiday Inn could not provide the usual standard. Basic ingredients, apart from those we had brought with us for the players, were not available. If Roy had been in Tehran, then he might have something to complain about, rather than cheese sandwiches and pizza in the Hilton in Amsterdam.

Tehran was bedlam – one long, continuous traffic jam on four-lane highways. All the cars were battered and bent. The only positive was that the traffic did not go fast enough to do any serious damage.

The key issue in Tehran was tickets for our fans. How many would be there? The FAI had to buy the tickets from the Iranian Football Association in advance, with no returns. Indeed, they wanted the Irish Embassy to distribute the tickets, as the Iranian Embassy had done in Dublin. We settled on 800 tickets. This was my decision and I overestimated the number of travelling fans. Peter Buckley advised 500 and he was closer to the correct figure. This cost the Association about $8,000 in unused tickets. The Irish Embassy had to go guarantor for the Association on the money for the tickets. There was a meeting in the Iranian Association's offices where the Irish commercial attaché had to provide a written guarantee that the Embassy would pay the money if we didn't. We had demanded money up front in Dublin, so we couldn't complain.

As usual, we had a number of female fans with us. We were assured that they would be allowed to attend the match, but there was always an element of doubt. It was interesting that the Iranian media officer was female and she could go to the match as she was working. However, she could not be a spectator. Women could watch women's sport, at which male spectators were forbidden. The likelihood of problems increased when we were told that the women, of which there were about five, would be escorted separately to the match. However, the Irish female fans got on the main fan buses and everyone got to the stadium with a lot of difficulty. Women spectators were a first for a sporting event in Iran. I know that a lot of abuse was hurled at our fans, especially the women, and that they were exposed to a very hostile environment.

*****

One of Ireland's greatest ever fans was Tony Booth, Secretary of the UK Irish Supporters Club. Tony was born in England, but had family roots in Killarney. I first met Tony in Cyprus in 1998, when we were both supporting the Irish youth team. Tony had travelled to Cyprus with his son. I came across the two of them at the most unlikely venues. As a true fan, Tony attended every U21 match. Tony was in the fans' hotel in Tehran. He was far from well. He had been suffering from a serious cancer complaint for some time and had discharged himself from hospital to come to Iran. He had travelled via Istanbul.

I meant to offer Tony a return seat on our charter to Dublin, but I did not see him again after the match. Unfortunately, we were never to meet again. Brendan McKenna and I travelled to Killarney to pay our respects at his funeral. Tony died on 16 January 2002 and is buried in the beautiful location of the Aghadoe Cemetery above the Lakes of Killarney. I know Tony was delighted that Ireland had again qualified for the World Cup. I am saddened that he did not survive to enjoy Japan and Korea.

*****

On the Tuesday evening, we visited the Irish Ambassador to Iran at his residence. As is well known, alcohol is banned in Iran. I doubt the claims of some fans that they found locations where it was served. The Ambassador's residence was an exception to the no-alcohol rule and the FAI party were able to imbibe a few cans of beer, which was well below the usual intake. These receptions with Embassy staff are part of being with the Irish team. I know that some FAI officials avoid them if at all possible, and on occasions it is necessary to round up enough bodies to be polite. At the reception, we met some of the small number of Irish people who live in Tehran. Despite our preconceptions about the country, the Irish living in Iran were enjoying life. For women, coping with the outdoor code of dress and behaviour was the most difficult aspect.

*****

One small incident in Tehran illustrates the fraught relationship between some of the players and the media. There was a daily press conference after training. Mick always kept the press waiting. This was a show of power. Training had run late. Mick had planned to shower and have lunch before the press conference. This was still the plan; the media could wait. It is the same after the matches at Lansdowne Road. Mick always spent time with the players and had a shower before speaking to the press. In Tehran, I felt that he could have got the press conference out of the way and then enjoyed his lunch. But no, the media could wait.

The press conference was uneventful; not even Roy Keane's absence was an issue. By the time the press conference was over, the players had retired to their rooms for the statutory afternoon rest. The media expected to have an opportunity to speak to some players to fill out their stories. FAI media officer Brendan McKenna had gone to the players' floor, but had been turned away by our FAI security, as the players were not to be disturbed. Suddenly, I had a media crisis on my hands.

I was told that Robbie Keane would speak to the media, but not if Paul Hyland of the *Evening Herald* was present, as he had written negatively about Robbie. I eventually persuaded Robbie to give an interview. I told him that I would deflect any negative questions. The interview went excellently. Paul Hyland sat in the front row and never opened his mouth. He just smiled sweetly at Robbie. He knew exactly what had happened. He already had his story and again wrote negatively about Robbie and his reluctance to talk to the media if he was there.

*****

We arrived into the stadium in Tehran, as usual, about ninety minutes before kick-off, with a heavy security escort. We were brought in through a back entrance and travelled through acres and acres of facilities, pitches, sport halls, mini-stadia and gymnasia. This was a developing country! What would we give for a fraction of these facilities? I have never seen as much security. If there were over 100,000 people at the match, there must have been close to 20,000 security personnel in and around the stadium.

As soon as we reached the dressing-room area, Mick instructed the players to get out onto the pitch as quickly as possible to get used to the atmosphere. Even at this early stage, the stadium was virtually full. The intensity of the barrage that greeted the players was unprecedented. It was pure abuse and it was continuous. By the time the match started, our players were mostly attuned to it. One funny incident happened during the pre-match formalities. In Iran, an Islamic hymn is sung before the match – an impressive sound when sung by over 100,000 people. Our players mistook it for the Iranian national anthem and, when it finished, moved to shake hands with their opponents in the normal pre-match protocol. They had to reassemble when the real Iranian national anthem started.

In one of my few football conversations with Mick, he had indicated that he saw the only threat from the Iranians coming through the centre. Their star player, Karimi, wore the No. 10 shirt and operated just behind the front runners. Their other good players, Ali Daei and Bagheri, also play in central positions. Mick was prepared to concede space out wide to protect the centre. He wasn't worried about crosses coming in, as he felt our defence would cope with them easily. As always in such a situation, the key issue was the balance between defending the two-goal lead and getting a precious away goal. Our emphasis was on defence in the first half. We had relatively few crisis moments, which Shay Given dealt with adequately.

At half-time, many of the Iranian dignitaries repaired to a prayer room at the back of the VIP area, where mats, facing Mecca, were laid out on the floor. Their prayers did little to improve the chances of their team. Early in the second half, David Connolly missed our best chance. That would have eased the tension. With about fifteen minutes to go, we knew we had qualified. The crowd began to barrack their own team. Iranian flags, which previously had been flown high, were now being burned. Suddenly there were thousands of such fires all around the stadium. Missiles began to rain down from above. Some of the FAI official party, who were sitting below the presidential box, had to retreat to a higher area where there was some cover. As the match moved into injury time, the Iranians were awarded a free kick close to our left corner flag. The ball was centred and Golmohammadi scored; it was too little too late. The match had just restarted when the final whistle blew. We had done it. We were again in the World Cup finals.

*****

From there on, everything was chaos. Mick was down on the pitch celebrating with his players. Thousands of people, security and media were on the pitch. The Iranians wanted to hold the official press conference immediately. Mick couldn't get to the dressing-room to congratulate the players. He was, in effect, escorted by numerous security people to a large room behind the VIP area. A significant number of Irish journalists could not gain entry. The press conference had to be held in three languages, with every word interpreted.

Mick eventually escaped after about twenty minutes and made it to the dressing-room. It was only on special occasions that FAI officials entered the dressing-room, and then only with Mick's permission. This was one of these occasions. Celebrations were in full swing. There was a media scrum outside, as the journalists waited for the players to emerge to get their reactions. Inside, Dave Maher, a photographer from Sportsfile, had been allowed in. The camera crew from FAI Productions had been refused entry by our own FAI security people. I managed to get the camera in for the tail-end of the celebrations. Dave Maher certainly got some exclusive photographs that night.

Our travel plans were to go straight back to the airport after the game, with take off to Dublin as early as possible. The players would be arriving into Dublin early on a Friday morning, having travelled overnight, and needed to get back to their clubs as quickly as possible to prepare for the weekend matches. As we left the stadium in a convoy of coaches with a large escort, we noted that the three-lane carriageway was completely covered with broken glass. The protests at defeat had continued after the game. As the cars were stuck in traffic jams around the stadium, gangs of youths had smashed every window in every car, thereby creating a ten-kilometre carpet of glass. Protests are not allowed in Iran, but football matches are one situation where large crowds can congregate. Whether the protest was political or merely sporting, I do not know.

Our main problems in Iran occurred trying to leave the country. We got to the airport ahead of schedule. The Aer Lingus Airbus was on the tarmac waiting for us, having spent the intervening period in Dubai. It took quite a while for the media to join us at the airport. However, there was no way that the Iranians were going to allow us to leave early. We spent about four hours waiting at the airport with all kinds of discussions going on. There is nothing as deflating as waiting at an airport. Our euphoria at qualifying for the World Cup was rapidly turning into annoyance. In such situations, there is little or nothing that you can do, but wait it out.

Eventually we took off for the five-hour flight to Dublin. When we were out of Iranian airspace, we had a celebratory drink. Dublin airport closes in the middle of the night and there is little point in arriving there before 6 am. Even then, you have to wait for the luggage handlers to come on shift.

On the ground everyone was celebrating. Quite a number of people had gathered to welcome the team and congratulate them on their performance. However, the players were all taking the earliest flights back to their clubs in Britain. Overall the arrival home was quite muted.

4

Saipan

The first I knew about Roy Keane's difficulties in Saipan and his intention to leave the World Cup squad was at about 5 pm on Tuesday, 21 May. FAI commercial manager Eddie Cox came to my office in Merrion Square to tell me that he had received a phone call from Umbro, our kit sponsors, informing him that they had been urgently requested to produce a new No. 6 jersey, with the name Healy on the back. The request presumably had come from John Fallon, who works for Umbro and who was with the team in Saipan. Umbro had been asked to keep the request for the new jersey confidential. At least someone in Umbro had the commonsense to realise the significance of Keane's replacement in the squad and telephoned Eddie Cox. Ireland's captain was returning home from the World Cup and the FAI was not to be told – incredible! We were supposed to learn about it from the media the following morning and manage the situation as best we could. The FAI staff and officials in Saipan had been sworn to secrecy by Mick McCarthy and, in their wisdom, had agreed to keep their employers in Dublin in the dark.

This was our first experience of the problems of operating in two very different time zones, a situation that caused us great difficulties throughout the World Cup. It was 5 pm on Tuesday in Dublin, but by then it was 2 am on Wednesday in Saipan. Everyone was asleep, and the hotel refused to page anyone. Unless the person you wanted was in their room, they were out of communication. In fact, Mick McCarthy had his telephone off the hook until 7.45 am Saipan time the following morning and even then was not answering his calls.

The problem with Keane had obviously arisen many hours previously, but there had been no communication with the Association in Dublin. I still do not understand why Mick McCarthy chose to manage the matter in this way or why there was no communication from Mick, FAI President Milo Corcoran or the FAI staff in Saipan back to the Association in Dublin. Had we not found out, I dread to think of the shambles that would have ensued the following day. Early morning phone calls from the media would have been met with the reaction that the FAI knew nothing about the story!

I sometimes wonder what the result would have been if Mick had phoned me and told me that Roy Keane was coming home. He might have persuaded me that it was for personal reasons and that Roy was carrying an injury. Mick had the final say on team matters, and if he had told me not to interfere then, in all likelihood, I would have done nothing to change the situation, once my conversation with Mick was over. However, the lack of communication from Saipan created a vacuum and vacuums always cause problems.

The first reaction to the news from Umbro was one of disbelief: surely someone was playing a practical joke. Peter Buckley of the Finance Department was also in my office when Eddie Cox informed me of the call from Umbro. When disbelief had quickly turned into grave concern, I decided that we needed to ascertain the truth of the situation. I rang Chris Ryan at her hotel bedroom in Saipan, at 2 am her time. Chris is manager of the FAI International Department and was the senior FAI staff member in Saipan. Her responsibilities included the logistical arrangements for the team. My first difficulty was in getting past the hotel switchboard – they had been instructed to refuse all calls. Eventually, I persuaded the hotel staff to put the phone call through to Chris. I asked Chris if anything was happening. She assured me that everything was OK. I told her that we were hearing rumours that there was a problem with Roy Keane. She assured me that there wasn't. End of conversation.

Eddie Cox was confident that his information from Umbro was correct, but it was in direct conflict with the response I had from Saipan. What were we to do? Mick McCarthy had left strict instructions with the hotel in Saipan that he was not to be disturbed and was, therefore, not contactable.

The urgency of the situation was compounded by the fact that midnight that night, Tuesday, 21 May 2002, was the deadline for submitting to FIFA the official list of twenty-three players and their numbers for participating in the World Cup. Every player was allocated a specific number from 1 to 23 and had to wear that jersey with his name on the back throughout the World Cup. We had submitted our list the previous week, when Mick had selected the final squad prior to the Niall Quinn testimonial game in Sunderland. However, unbeknownst to me and the Association in Dublin, Mick had requested Chris Ryan to send a fax to FIFA in Zurich, replacing Roy Keane in the squad with Colin Healy. Chris had done as Mick requested. Roy Keane had been officially withdrawn from the Irish World Cup squad.

There were fewer than seven hours in which to influence matters, and we were still without accurate information. As was to be proven later, when we tried to reinstate Colin Healy, it was impossible to make changes to the official squad line-up after the deadline.

Eddie Cox rechecked with Umbro and received the same information. I decided to talk to Chris Ryan again. This time I got the truth. Roy Keane had approached Mick McCarthy and asked to be allowed to withdraw from the squad for personal reasons. Mick had agreed and had called Colin Healy into the squad to replace Keane. A new No. 6 jersey had been ordered from Umbro in Dublin. Mick had put a strict embargo on anyone communicating this information. Mick controlled the senior international team and his decisions were law, seemingly even among my staff.

I instructed Chris to contact Mick at 7 am Saipan time. This gave us just one hour to rectify the situation before midnight Swiss time, 8 am Saipan time and 11 pm Irish time. It was getting complicated, but my initial view was that the deadline had to be midnight in Switzerland. I told Chris that I would be discussing the situation with people in Dublin and the UK and that I believed everything should be done to try and reverse the situation in the interests of the team, despite Mick's acceptance of Roy Keane's request.

I telephoned Michael Kennedy – Roy Keane's solicitor, agent and advisor – and appraised him of the situation. He was aghast and had no inkling of Roy's request. He stated that he would speak with Roy's wife, Theresa, and with Alex Ferguson and try to find out exactly what had happened. He agreed to work to reverse the situation. Certainly from my initial telephone conversation with him, Michael saw the withdrawal as being hugely detrimental to Roy.

I next telephoned Liam Gaskin (Mick McCarthy's agent and adviser) and told him of the situation. He had heard nothing from Mick. He agreed to speak to Mick as early as possible on Wednesday morning in Saipan, late Tuesday in Dublin, and to try to persuade him to reverse the situation if at all possible. I then briefed the FAI officers in Ireland, Des Casey, Michael Hyland, David Blood and John Delaney. They were all shocked by the news and supportive of all approaches to reverse Keane's withdrawal. Delaney was the only one who became actively involved.

A series of phone calls between Gaskin, Kennedy, Delaney and me ensued. We were all agreed that the situation should be reversed. This obviously annoyed Mick when he found out about it the next morning, but his lack of communication to us from Saipan left us with no alternative. Kennedy would urge Roy Keane's wife and Alex Ferguson to persuade Roy to remain with the squad, as he would himself. Liam Gaskin would ring Mick and urge him to accept Roy back into the squad if Roy changed his mind. By 7.30 pm all the pieces were in place and there was nothing we could do until 10 pm Irish time – 7 am Saipan time – when the Pacific island would awake.

I had arranged to meet friends that evening. It was a brief meeting. Gerry and Mary had travelled to Germany, Italy and the US with me as fans and Gerry was again going to the World Cup. We wanted to exchange travel itineraries and contact arrangements. As I entered the Foxhunter pub in Lucan, both Gerry and Linda immediately knew that something was wrong. I was described as 'ashen-faced'. I admitted that the FAI had a serious problem. Being astute people, they quickly realised that Roy Keane was at its epicentre.

I got home at about 9.30 pm, in time for the final round of phone calls. I had my son, Ronan, answering the phone, as I feared media involvement at this delicate stage. I told him to say I was unavailable. This resulted in my missing a critical phone call from Michael Kennedy, who then telephoned John Delaney to give him the news that Roy would be urged to change his decision. I rang Chris at 11 pm Irish time and briefed her on what was happening on this side of the globe. I again instructed her to go to Mick's room and advise him that the Association wanted the position reversed if at all possible. I told her to involve FAI President, Milo Corcoran, in the matter. Contacting people in Saipan was next to impossible; as well as the hotel being instructed not to put through phone calls for the official party, they had a policy of not paging people. It was Paradise Island after all! At one critical moment, I got lucky trying to contact Chris, who was no longer in her room. A member of the support staff was passing the front desk and I was able to give him a message to ask Chris to contact me urgently.

Despite the short window of opportunity before the FIFA deadline at 8 am Saipan time, our efforts were successful and Roy Keane was back in the squad for the World Cup. I cannot be precise as to what actually transpired in Saipan during that hour, but by 8 am (or to be more precise shortly afterwards) another fax was on its way from Saipan to FIFA headquarters in Zurich, reinstating Roy Keane in the official Irish squad for World Cup 2002. Mick McCarthy's version in his *World Cup Diary* and Roy Keane's comments in his autobiography are the only written records of events in the hotel in Saipan on that Wednesday morning. Mick's account is his personal one. I suspect that all the main players will have their own version of events. With Mick's permission I quote the relevant paragraphs from his book:

The morning after the night before.

I am awoken at 7.45 am by a knock on my bedroom door from one of the hotel staff. They have spent the night shielding calls on my behalf and they would be grateful if I could place the phone back on the hook now. The porter explains that the switchboard has been hopping all night, even though I kept Roy Keane's decision to quit within a very tight group. So much for confidentiality!

My phone goes into overdrive as soon as the handset is functional again. I ignore the calls. I know what they are about and I want some time to myself to think the day through. The one certainty is that we are going to have an eventful few hours ahead of us.

Mick Byrne is in the room now. He is concerned for me and the team in the wake of Roy's decision to go home. He is taking calls for me and as soon as the first journalist gets through, we know the proverbial has hit the fan.

FAI President, Milo Corcoran, pops his head around the door and asks if he can do anything. The FAI have been on the case all night with a succession of phone conversations involving their General Secretary, Brendan Menton, Treasurer John Delaney and Roy's solicitor, Michael Kennedy. They all want a bit of this and Milo's information is that Roy now wants to stay.

It's news to me. Roy has not been down to tell me, nor has he sent any message through to my room. Why has he left it so late? I can count the minutes to the FIFA deadline on two hands and I have still heard nothing from my captain about this alleged change of mind.

I send Mick Byrne up to Roy's room for one last check. Is he in or is he out?

The fax has already gone to FIFA with Colin Healy's name on it by the time Mick comes back and confirms the Roy Keane U-turn. If it wasn't for Mick going to his room, I would never have known that Roy wants to stay.

Panic stations. A new fax is sent to FIFA but there is no guarantee that it will make Switzerland in time to confirm the latest twist in the game of musical chairs. We have no choice but to wait on that score.

Once Roy had decided he wanted to stay and Mick had agreed to it, the crisis was getting the fax to FIFA before the deadline of midnight on Tuesday, 21 May. I had dictated the contents to Chris and she duly sent it off. As it was some minutes after 8 am, it was technically after the deadline. I decided therefore to send another fax from my home in Ireland, confirming Roy Keane's reinstatement. This fax was sent at 11.40 pm Irish time, as Ireland at that time of year was one hour behind Switzerland. I believed that we could always argue, if FIFA disputed the timing of the fax from Saipan, that they had been informed prior to midnight Irish time.

In any event, FIFA accepted Roy Keane's reinstatement in the official squad. Problem solved; we could all relax. If only we knew what lay in store just two days later. My only regret is for Colin Healy. Colin was unlucky to lose out in the original squad. He was called in at the eleventh hour, but requested to stand aside less than twelve hours later. Colin was a true professional in the manner in which he accepted this.

The fact that I had faxed FIFA as a fail-safe mechanism prior to midnight Irish time was later used to undermine my relationship with Mick McCarthy. I quote from Mick's book:

Then I discover that a fax had been sent by the FAI half an hour earlier with Roy back in the squad, before I even knew he was staying. I am livid when I hear this news.

This is incorrect. There is no way that I would interfere to that extent in team affairs. They are absolutely a matter for the manager. Having said that, I accept that we did intervene to reverse the first Keane decision. However, that was the limit to which we would go and the reinstatement only happened when Mick agreed to it. My fax was sent from Dublin at least thirty minutes after Chris Ryan's fax from Saipan. However, Mick McCarthy was told by someone that I had pre-empted his decision to re-admit Roy Keane to the squad and had faxed FIFA to this purpose in advance. There can be only two explanations for this. Either this person does not understand international time zones, which is entirely possible, or more likely he saw an opportunity to sow rancour and dissent. This is part and parcel of the FAI. The pre-emptive fax story also appeared in the media, fed, I believe, by an officer of the Association. This again is an example of the media being fed a titbit and using it without checking its accuracy with the people directly involved. It was only months later that I became aware that Mick had been misled in regard to the fax and I could sort it out with him. I have no doubt that my relationship with Mick McCarthy ended up on a good footing, despite a stream of stories planted in the media from within the FAI that I had a poor working relationship with him.

*****

Why did the Irish team management choose Saipan as their preparatory base? The pre–World Cup strategy proposed by Mick McCarthy was to get to the Far East as early as possible, in order to maximise the time available for acclimatisation and adjustment of the body clocks. Japan was eight hours ahead of Ireland, and from first-hand experience it takes a long time to adjust to this. Being unable to sleep at three and four o'clock in the morning is the least of it. The players were unable to take any body clock adjustment medication, because of the very strict FIFA doping control regulations.

Mick wanted a long acclimatisation period, but did not want to work the players too hard too early, particularly after a long season, which had ended only the previous week for some players. The strategy was, therefore, to have a week of easy work, relaxation and acclimatisation in Saipan, before transferring to Izumo in Japan where the intensive preparations would take place.

Let me quote the relevant paragraphs from the Genesis Report:

> The overall quality of fixtures chosen for the build-up was appropriate for Ireland, especially given the group for the first stage of the World Cup.
>
> Training for the competition was not on the agenda, as Saipan was planned to be a week of relaxation, acclimatisation and light training.
>
> Saipan was a good choice of venue for acclimatisation and relaxation, but it added a disproportionately large complexity to logistics management.

Although they did not include it in their report, the Genesis consultants stated that other countries they visited when compiling the report were envious of the Irish team's acclimatisation. It was based on sound scientific grounds. Throughout the World Cup, the Irish players consistently stated that Saipan was an excellent location for acclimatisation and attributed their ability to finish the stronger team in all their matches to the week spent there.

> The preparation and planning done for the Irish team in Korea and Japan were excellent.
>
> Excellent facilities were provided and excellent thought and preparation went into making sure that everyone was accommodated.

The only negative factor of Saipan as a geographical location was the long (twenty-three hours) journey one day after playing the friendly match against Nigeria in Dublin, and the additional four-hour travel time past Tokyo. Genesis' opinion was that travelling such a distance so soon after the game against Nigeria could have caused more physical problems for the players than actually occurred.

Quotes from the players praising the training facilities were included in the Genesis Report:

> The hotels and training facilities were regarded as excellent, with the exception of the training pitch in Saipan. The training facilities in Japan were world class and of a consistent standard:

'The best I have ever seen.'

'The lads' eyes were out on stalks.'

The attention to detail made the difference – it helped the players relax together. Izumo was a good choice – away from the main cities – and the facilities there and at Chiba were really appreciated by the players.

FAI travel agent Ray Treacy, who was instrumental in making the arrangements for Saipan, has absolutely no regrets about the choice of location. He has given me permission to quote him:

One year on, if doing the same arrangements for the World Cup, I would not change a thing. We obviously got something right because we were the fittest team in Japan. Our preparations were perfect. We were so well acclimatised that we outran every other team in the last twenty minutes. Some players loved Saipan so much that they would have liked to have been based there and travelled to the games from there.

Let me say it again, Genesis reported that other teams were envious of Ireland's acclimatisation when they saw how the team performed.

The only other negative views on the selection of Saipan were from a number of well-meaning people who wrote to me describing Saipan as the sin island of the Pacific, with prostitution rife. They were concerned for the moral well-being of our players.

One of the ironies of the situation was that the FAI paid for Saipan, while the host towns for the training camps (Izumo and Chiba) met all our expenses while we were there. The two and a half weeks in Japan did not cost the Association a penny, not even the infamous €20,000 bar bill after the Germany game. If we had gone straight to Izumo (rather than Saipan), the town would have been delighted and met all our costs. Indeed, they paid for a charter plane that flew the team directly from Saipan to Izumo on Friday, 24 May. They were disappointed that we only spent a week with them. They were so thrilled to host our training camp that Mayor Masahiro Nishio came with the charter plane to Saipan to accompany the team on the trip to his town.

So what went wrong? There were probably just three factors:

1. The Saipan training pitch.

2. The arrival of the kit in Saipan one day after the players.

3. Roy Keane and the lack of communication to him by Mick McCarthy of the objectives of the week in Saipan.

Even Genesis concludes that the pitch and skip incidents became hugely more damaging than the technical impact they would ever have had on the team's performance in the World Cup – they were the tip of the iceberg for some. I think they meant one – Roy Keane!

Within the FAI, there was a clear division in our minds between the week in Saipan and the training and preparation based in Japan that would commence a week later. The key decisions on where and when the team went were made by Mick, with the advice of Ray Treacy (FAI travel agent) and Eddie Corcoran (team liaison officer), and endorsed by the professional staff of the FAI. We saw our role as delivering what Mick wanted for the team. However, we did visit each of the training sites in Japan and inspected all the facilities. We met with the officials from the host towns and made arrangements that ensured that the FAI could function efficiently, that security arrangements were adequate and that the media could operate effectively from our bases – a vital requirement by FIFA. In both Izumo and Chiba, there were well-equipped media centres arranged by the FAI, which included press conference rooms, interview rooms, work desks, e-mail facilities and ISDN lines. The good behind-the-scenes work we did never got mentioned. From the day we landed in Japan to the day we left Korea, nearly everything worked like clockwork. Some minor issues arose which are detailed in the chapter on the World Cup. The only negativity was the legacy of Saipan and Roy Keane, which was a continuous black cloud.

FAI staff personnel visited each training centre in Japan, but they did not visit Saipan. Ray Treacy (twice), Mick McCarthy and Eddie Corcoran visited Saipan and were enthusiastic about it for the first week of acclimatisation. It was hotter and more humid than Japan and it was one hour further ahead. Therefore, it would accelerate the players' acclimatisation. This proved to be the case. Let me repeat the Genesis Report conclusions: Saipan was a good choice of venue for acclimatisation and relaxation. In my opinion, these were the objectives of the first week. The FAI simply made the arrangements to get the players and equipment to Saipan. We presumed that the facilities, hotel and training were good, as Mick and our two senior travel and venue people had visited the island.

The one mistake made by Mick McCarthy was the training pitch. Saipan is an American protectorate and its game is baseball. Little or no football is played on the island. As part of the deal for the Irish team going to Saipan, the hotel agreed with Mick during his visit in early February to construct a training pitch. Only Eddie Corcoran from the FAI subsequently visited Saipan, and he gave no negative feedback on the pitch. No one from the FAI professional staff visited Saipan. This was probably a mistake. We relied on the reports from the technical support personnel to the team. I can imagine the reaction within the FAI and particularly from the Finance Committee, who in fact control most decisions in the Association through the purse strings, if I had suggested sending someone to Saipan. I probably should have just done it and taken the criticism, but that was not my style.

The timing of the arrival of the skips containing the team's equipment only became an issue because of other events. Chris Ryan, as manager of the International Department, had de facto responsibility for the World Cup logistics. However, Eddie Cox, the FAI commercial manager, had responsibility for the relationships with sponsors, including Umbro and DHL. This lack of clarity about internal roles and responsibilities and poor working relationships between staff members did not help matters, nor did the fact that most staff members with previous experience of World Cup logistics had been casualties of the Merriongate saga of 1996. The twenty-five FAI staff in Merrion Square were fractured into three or four different cliques. If an issue arose between the different camps, I was told about it and had to get involved, rather than it being sorted out directly on a one-to-one basis.

At the outset, I want to state categorically that DHL were in no way responsible for the 'late' arrival of the skips. The skips arrived in Saipan within the time frame guaranteed to us by DHL. They arrived into Saipan airport at 2 am on the Monday morning before the players and media had gone to bed.

The task of getting the skips together ready for transportation was Eddie's. He had to coordinate all the technical and support staff to do this, including the team doctor (Martin Walsh), the physiotherapists (Ciaran Murray and Mick Byrne), the kit man (Joe Walsh) and Umbro representative (John Fallon). The logistics were difficult, particularly as Saipan was not on DHL's direct destination list. The decision was taken to send the gear and equipment needed for Japan directly to Izumo (thirty skips weighing three tons) and to send only the eleven skips containing the training equipment needed for the first week to Saipan. Four skips accompanied the squad on their scheduled flight. I often wonder what these skips contained, if not training gear!

Eddie Cox met with the support personnel well in advance and told them what was required in terms of timing and paperwork. The paperwork was a nightmare. Importing stuff into Japan was difficult, especially when some of it was to be re-exported at the end of the tournament. In addition, some of the skips would contain drugs and medical equipment. Saipan is an American protectorate and, hence, was a second jurisdiction with separate regulations. There had to be a complete list of every item accompanying each container. Being connected with the World Cup did not reduce in any way the bureaucracy of Japan. The Japanese are great people, but they are governed by rules and regulations and have no flexibility in that regard.

When Eddie Cox checked with the technical staff close to the deadline, he found that different people had come away from the preparatory meeting with very different perspectives. We were behind deadline in getting the material together and the paperwork was not satisfactory. Eddie had to redo some of it. The last delivery of equipment to Eddie was at 4.30 pm on that Friday, 10 May. All this resulted in the skips departing from Dublin on 13 May, rather than 10 May – a Monday rather than the previous Friday. It was still six days before the team were due in Saipan. DHL committed to having the skips in Saipan on Monday morning, 20 May. This they achieved. My understanding is that the skips for Saipan had to take a very circuitous route, visiting London and Korea en route to Saipan.

The skips were not available for one training session on the Sunday. Quoting the Genesis report:

> *The training session on the first Sunday was a light stretching session which was added to the schedule by Mick McCarthy to help recovery from the flight. The players had equivalent kit with them, and the balls acquired for the session, although not the official World Cup balls, were more than adequate for light training.*

In any event, the players had with them the training kit that they had used in Sunderland and in Dublin during the previous week. The skips arrived on Monday morning in time for that day's training. This had been scheduled as the first training session.

Should the skips have gone out earlier? There were two constraining factors. First was the World Cup jerseys, with the players' names on the back. Mick did not want to disclose his final squad until very close to the team assembling in Sunderland for the Niall Quinn testimonial. Mick officially announced the squad on Tuesday, 7 May. This was reasonable, but it cut down on the time available for getting the match gear ready. Second was that we wanted FAI personnel on the ground in Saipan when the skips arrived. We did not want our World Cup equipment to go missing. Eddie Corcoran and Ray Treacy had arrived in Saipan on Friday, 17 May, and this, therefore, was our earliest target day. Our approach was to send everything at the same time – close to the arrival time of the squad to minimise other potential problems.

Let me react to some things written about these events in *Sunday Tribune* journalist Paul Howard's book, *The Gaffer.*

> *(Sunday) The players were forced to do a training session without footballs and in their casual wear.*

This is not true. The players had the appropriate training gear and they had footballs, albeit, not the Adidas Fevernov balls to be used in the World Cup. The Genesis Report confirms this.

> *(Monday) Training goes ahead in the afternoon. The skips containing the equipment still haven't arrived.*

This is also untrue. The skips had arrived by this time. Paul Howard was in Saipan. The correct facts were available to him. Why does a journalist get basic facts wrong and thereby perpetuate myths? Howard was very negative about Mick McCarthy and was also very anti the FAI. Anytime the *Tribune* writes on domestic football, which is seldom, it regularly has a negative slant.

We also had a problem when the skips were sent unaccompanied to Japan. Despite all the documentation, they were held up by Japanese custom officials in Osaka, across the country from Izumo, their destination. They would only be released when an FAI official presented him or herself to claim them. However, thanks to the intervention of Michael Gaffey of the Irish Embassy in Tokyo, Masahiro Nishio, Mayor of Izumo, and Paul Ennis, DHL's man in Tokyo, the skips were released and were in Izumo when the squad arrived. The team were arriving on the Friday and were due to play a match against Hiroshima on the Saturday. Can you imagine the reaction if there had been no strip!

Let me state categorically that the gear had to be shipped independently of the team, who were travelling business class on scheduled flights. The total amount of gear filled forty-five large skips, weighing perhaps 5 tons, enough to cater for all the needs of a trip that could last up to six weeks. The gear was of the highest quality. Players always carry their own footwear. The only issues were that isotonic drinks and footballs had to be acquired locally. The drinks were not the Gatorade recommended to the players and, as stated, the footballs were not the official World Cup footballs. The skips would not have been an issue but for other events.

*****

The first I knew about the problem with the arrival of the gear was a phone call from Eddie Cox on the Sunday evening. He had received a phone call from Mick McCarthy and they had exchanged words. Eddie firmly believed that the late departure of the gear was due to the slow collection of the items by the technical staff and the inadequate paperwork. However, the skips would arrive the following morning (Monday) and this would solve that problem. Mick was obviously annoyed, which suggested to me that someone had got onto him about it. There was only one candidate – Roy Keane.

If it hadn't been for Roy Keane, Saipan would never have become an issue. The training pitch was not ideal but the 'late' arrival of the skips was in reality a non-issue. Roy was the only one to make them an issue, but whether he used them as an excuse for other problems he was having or whether he was genuinely so upset that he could not, as Irish captain, stay with the team for the World Cup, we will never know. The issue became divisive from the outset and most people's views are based on whether they are pro-Roy or pro-Mick. There was certainly no one pro the FAI.

Let us review some of the history. This account is largely based on the contents of both Roy's and Mick's books. They had a row during a trip to the US in 1992, which never healed. As captain, Mick took Roy Keane to task in front of other players. This personal antipathy was compounded by Roy's late withdrawal from the squad for the US Cup in 1996. Mick had appointed Roy as captain. This was Mick's first trip as Irish manager and his main opportunity to build a team for the 1998 World Cup qualification campaign, commencing the following September.

Let me state, that in 1996, no one in Merrion Square was contacted by Roy Keane or his agent Michael Kennedy or Manchester United to alert them that Roy would not be travelling to the US Cup. This contradicts the statement in Roy's book which says:

> United informed the FAI of that decision.

The statement in Keane's book also contradicts the account in the *Irish Independent* of 30 May 1996, quoting a statement from Roy Keane in which he claims that he left a message with the FAI. I was acting FAI General Secretary at the time and I fully checked for any communication. There was none. To the best of my knowledge, Mick McCarthy received no communication from Roy, his adviser or his club. Perhaps Roy could clarify this, as it certainly caused a further deterioration in the relationship between him and Mick. At that time, I took the decision for the FAI to say nothing, being of the view that anything said would only exacerbate the situation. If the FAI took the blame, perhaps the rift between Mick and Roy could be more easily repaired. I lived in cloud cuckoo land on this issue. I also took this line during much of the World Cup, a decision I now regret. Roy was a hero, Mick was a hero and the FAI was the anti-hero.

There is a very clear procedure about notifying players of international call-ups. The club is notified in writing of the call-up and asked to inform the player of the arrangements and reporting time. Perhaps the FAI should introduce a procedure for withdrawals. It is done by telephone communication by either the player or his club to the international manager. Seldom are the FAI informed in writing. This is important, as history repeated itself just prior to the World Cup in 2002, when Roy Keane withdrew from the squad for the Niall Quinn testimonial game. It appears that Roy may have communicated his withdrawal to a member of Mick's technical staff, but not to Mick or officially to the FAI. This became an issue for the media. Mick knew Roy would join the squad in Dublin on the Wednesday. This meant he missed the first official gathering of the World Cup squad on Monday 13 May in Sunderland. The Irish team gathered without its captain and without clear knowledge of why he wasn't there. The first seeds of dissension between Roy and some of the senior players had been sown.

Roy's absence from Sunderland had a further important impact on future events. On the Monday evening in Sunderland, Mick briefed the players on the plans for the World Cup, including the purpose of the week in Saipan. I believe that Roy was not briefed when he joined the squad in Dublin on the Wednesday. Thus Roy arrived in Saipan with a totally different set of expectations from the rest of the squad. Roy wanted to train and prepare at his usual 110 per cent, while the rest of the squad were in a much more relaxed mood and were prepared to take things easy, have a barbecue and play golf.

It is now obvious that Roy had a number of issues. The Genesis Report states with regard to Roy that:

He possibly felt that he should not have gone at all – he had a
bad feeling in advance and was carrying a long-term hip injury.

Roy had, in my opinion, one of his poorest ever performances for Ireland in the match against Nigeria, the day before departure from Dublin. I believe he has to take a large share of the responsibility for Nigeria's winning goal from a corner.

The next day, Roy became upset at the airport. Previously, the Irish team had been permitted to do a group check-in at Dublin airport, but after 11 September, regulations had changed and individual check-ins became mandatory. Aer Rianta had reserved one row of desks for the use of the players, cordoned off the desks and had adequate security. The team bus pulled up to a door close by the check-in desks. Of course, there were fans there to see the team off, but these were mainly kids and were well-behaved. They had made an effort to support their team. After check-in, the players had to walk about ten yards from the end of the check-in desk to stairs leading to the private function room that had been reserved for them. They did this with the protection of FAI and airport security personnel. I cannot envisage that Manchester United could move through an airport with less difficulty. If you want to complain, you will always find something to complain about.

There were a good few people in the reserved function room on the first floor of the airport, as has been the case in the past. They included FAI officials and staff, some sponsors, well-wishers and media, including broadcast media wanting pictures and interviews for the evening news. The Japanese and Korean ambassadors were also there. It was not overcrowded and everyone respected the wishes of those players who wanted to be left alone. It was election day and Taoiseach Bertie Ahern joined us to see the team off and, of course, to have his photograph taken for the evening papers and the TV news. Bertie moved around the players wishing them well. Roy was sitting on the floor leaning against a pillar, close to the windows. When Bertie came to Roy, everyone wanted a photograph of it. Roy didn't stand or sit up to facilitate the photograph. Bertie had to kneel down beside him so that the photograph could be taken.

Obviously, the Irish captain was not a happy person prior to his departure for Saipan. He himself admits that he had a go at members of the media at the wait over in Amsterdam airport, over his treatment in the Sunderland no-show story.

In Amsterdam, the players were cordoned from the public in a private area of a business lounge. The FAI were not asked by the team manager to segregate the team during the wait at Dublin airport. If we had been asked, we would have done so. This is probably at the core of the problem. The FAI did what we were asked to do by the team management. Mick McCarthy accepted that fans and sponsors were part of the Irish team and that departures and homecomings would happen. Roy had a different attitude. From an FAI perspective, we depend on the fans and sponsors for our financial survival and more importantly to have the resources to spend on developing the next generation of players. We would be committing financial suicide if we totally ignored them. In this, we are no different from any professional club. Sometimes I think that Roy Keane would only be totally happy playing football in a team of ten other players of similar ilk, managed by Alex Ferguson and with no fans present. No mistakes would happen then, would they?

*****

One of the key issues in Saipan was the presence of the media. Mick McCarthy and I discussed banning them, but this was impossible. They would go to Saipan in any event. The media were not going to miss seven days on a tropical island. The easiest course was to allow them to travel with the team as was the usual practice. We could not stop them booking seats on the commercial airlines we were using. Only a proportion of the journalists going to the World Cup travelled to Saipan. They knew what Saipan was about and had been told that there would only be press briefings with Mick and the players every second day. They were happy with this, as long as they could generate news, views and stories to carry over two days' demands from their editors. The newspapers and other media wanted value for the money they were spending on sending journalists to Saipan.

The travelling party to Saipan consisted of the team and technical staff of thirty-five people. (Only one technical support person, Ian Rogers, a computer video analysis expert from New Zealand, would join the technical staff in Japan.) There were about thirty media people. The travelling party was completed by FAI personnel, consisting of FAI President Milo Corcoran, media officer Brendan McKenna and manager of the International Department Chris Ryan. The only other person travelling to Saipan was John Givens, who represented the players with regard to sponsorship and media matters.

A key question is, should I as General Secretary have gone to Saipan? I am probably the first person in the history of Irish football to have passed up the opportunity to spend a 'blissful' week on a tropical Pacific island. Why didn't I go? The plan was to gear up our organisational capacity for the arrival of the team in Izumo. I didn't think that I would be needed. It was meant to be a week of relaxation for the team. In any event, we had three senior people, including the President, in Saipan. In addition, there were significant issues back home. Largest among them were what became known as the 'Paul Marney' affair and the question of who won the League of Ireland in the season 2001/02 (see page 5). If Shelbourne were not good enough to win on the field of play, then Ollie Byrne, their Chief Executive, was going to win in the committee room or in court.

I was conscious of a possible court injunction to prevent me travelling to the World Cup the following Thursday, as planned.

Ireland's World Cup participation would have to take second place to a petty domestic squabble.

Roy Dooney was about to resign as Commissioner of the Eircom League as a result of the 'Paul Marney' affair. We were in detailed discussions with solicitors. Many of the league clubs, led by Shelbourne, wanted him to go, but we had difficulty reaching a separation agreement as the clubs didn't want to bear the cost. Roy reported for work in the league that week on the instructions of his solicitors, although everyone knew that the end was close. I had met with Roy Dooney's solicitor, on Wednesday, the day before my departure to Japan, and I sent a briefing note to Des Casey on the Thursday morning, 23 May. Des, as Honorary Secretary, would take over the negotiations. It was typical of the league: they get themselves into a mess and then look to the FAI to solve it. Yet any suggestion that the FAI should run the league is always strenuously resisted.

If I had gone to Saipan, would I have made any difference? Not to Roy Keane going home. I would simply have been 'another hand at the pump as the ship sank'. The story was bigger than the FAI's capacity to handle it, no matter how many people and how much expertise we had there. Mick would not have consulted me before he acceded to Roy's initial request to go home for personal reasons. I may have been able to intercede earlier, but the same people – Michael Kennedy, Alex Ferguson and Liam Gaskin – would have to have become involved and spoken to Roy and Mick, respectively. The FAI did not get involved with players and team matters. We were the blazers and were to be kept at a distance. The President of the Association was in Saipan; he knew about Roy going home and accepted that it was in the best interests of the squad. Being in Saipan, I would have gained perhaps six hours and Roy's initial decision may have been reversed on the Monday evening in Saipan rather than the Tuesday morning. In the light of subsequent events, this would have made absolutely no difference.

*****

After Roy's change of heart, I had given Chris Ryan explicit instructions to keep me fully informed of all developments. I got the first inkling that the matter had not been fully resolved when Chris telephoned me on the Wednesday afternoon (22 May) stating that Roy had given interviews to Tom Humphries of *The Irish Times* and Paul Kimmage of the *Sunday Independent*. Alarm bells went off straight away, as I was aware that part of the 'settlement' between Mick and Roy was that neither would make any reference to the issue in the media. In his book, Humphries expressed his surprise at how easily Roy Keane agreed to the interview.

My information on that Wednesday was that Humphries' article would not appear until the Saturday, the normal day for his main column. This was also Mick McCarthy's view. Paul Kimmage could not publish until the Sunday because he wrote for the *Sunday Independent*. I hoped that there would be time to get to Japan and further paper over any cracks in the relationship between captain and manager, before Roy's interviews appeared in print. I did not know Roy at all well, as he kept an unbreachable wall between himself and most people, but I am a football fan and wanted him to play for Ireland in the World Cup.

However, Humphries and *The Irish Times* published the interview on the Thursday. Humphries could have had little doubt that the result would be another blow up between Mick and Roy. In fairness, Humphries checked the contents of the interview with Roy before publication. He knew his story was dynamite. Understandably, Humphries' first loyalty was to his employer, *The Irish Times*. The easy access of the media to the players did not help matters in Saipan, but if the FAI had barred access, they would have been cast as villains.

I was due to travel to Izumo in Japan on the Thursday/Friday, via Amsterdam and Tokyo. The departure time from Dublin was 11 am on Thursday, 23 May, arriving in Izumo at 3 pm on the Friday, 24 May. Allowing for the eight-hour time difference, the travel time was nearly twenty-two hours. As I sat on the plane at Dublin airport, Eddie Cox, who was travelling with me, received a phone call from Chris Ryan.

Chris wanted to speak to me urgently. I had my own phone switched off by this stage. It was 8 pm in Saipan and the face-off between Mick and Roy had already taken place. Mick was sending his captain home. He had received a copy of the Humphries article by fax and was aware of the interview before it hit the streets in Dublin on the Thursday morning.

*****

The Thursday morning was pandemonium in the Menton household. I was going to be away for at least three weeks and hopefully a lot longer. My family was travelling to the World Cup, but under its own steam. My eldest daughter, Aisling, had made all the arrangements on the Internet. My car had a puncture – a very regular occurrence thanks to the potholes on the roads of Meath. The panic in the Menton household had infected our dog Skippy, who bit the AA man; I kid you not! (I would like to thank that very understanding AA man.) Linda drove me to the airport, before going on to Merrion Square to deliver last minute documents and instructions from me to Des Casey regarding Roy Dooney.

Even before getting on the plane, I was being chased by the media in the form of the *Marion Finucane Show*, which was on air as I was checking in at the airport. After the publication of Humphries' interview, they wanted to know the latest developments. I refused to make a statement as I had heard nothing from Saipan. This did not best please the show's researcher. Ten minutes later, there was another phone call as I was saying goodbye to Linda and finalising meeting arrangements with her in Seoul for the following Monday. The *Finucane Show* was carrying out a telephone poll and most callers were supporting Keane. At this stage, nobody in Ireland was aware that Mick was sending Roy home. I made a derogatory comment about telephone polls in a situation where people were not fully aware of the issues involved. Of course, this got broadcast as a statement. Finding out the facts was unimportant, keeping the row going was – a prime example of tabloid radio.

Even in November 2002, when I did an interview with Marion Finucane the morning after my standing down from the FAI and the release of the Genesis Report, the only topic she was interested in was Saipan and the Roy Keane row.

*****

From my phone call with Chris, I learned that Roy Keane was going to be left behind in Saipan, when the rest of the Irish squad departed for Izumo the next day (Friday, 24 May). Chris and Ray Treacy were making travel arrangements for Roy to get him back to Manchester via Tokyo and Amsterdam, business class all the way. The story that we had abandoned Roy and made no arrangements for him was completely untrue. This was the version of events carried in Paul Howard's book. In contrast, Roy Keane, in his Tom Humphries interview, said that the initial breaking of the story of his going home could be attributed to the fact that the FAI had made travel arrangements for him.

I telephoned, FAI Honorary Secretary Des Casey and briefed him on what had happened. We discussed whether I should stay in Dublin or continue as planned to Izumo. Our joint decision was that I should travel, as I was needed more in Japan; Des and the other officers could hold the fort in Ireland. The problem was that this would take me out of the loop for nearly twenty-four hours.

By this stage, I had read the Humphries interview with Keane, having purchased *The Irish Times* at the airport. My reaction was that it was not as bad as I had feared, but there were five or six things that would have been better left unsaid. Rereading it some seventeen months later, my reaction hasn't changed. Roy's implied criticism of his team-mates was strange, as he was then staying in the squad. He seemed to suggest that they were content to be journeyman professionals and lacked real ambition. This is absolutely untrue. Most of them, particularly the younger players, are dedicated professionals and have achieved a lot, despite not having the talent of Keane.

Keane's criticisms of the World Cup arrangements and, hence, of Mick McCarthy were also uncalled for. They were a thinly veiled attack on Mick. Keane talked about his need to have good players and good people with him, people he could trust. The implication was that he didn't have good players or people he could trust in the Irish squad and management. I believe that Mick thought that they had an arrangement to avoid public comment on these issues until the World Cup was over. Hence, the publication of Roy Keane's interview caused Mick to call the meeting of the squad that Thursday evening (23 May).

Before Mick had a chance to say much at the meeting that Thursday evening, Keane launched into his astonishing tirade. It is worth repeating what Roy is reported to have said to illustrate that Mick had no alternative but to send him home.

> *Who the f*** do you think you are having meetings about me? You were a crap player and you are a crap manager. The only reason I have any dealings with you is that somehow you are the manager of my country and you are not even Irish, you English c***. You can stick it up your b*******.*

Roy Keane has talents as a footballer that entitle him to the label of world class. Not every player, even at international level, can achieve on the pitch what Roy has. It would be a strange world if they could. Many of the members of the Irish squad, with less talent than Roy, achieved what they did through dedication and professionalism. To, in effect, describe them as journeyman professionals on the eve of the World Cup, when Roy was officially back in the squad, can only be interpreted as saying, 'I want nothing to do with you'. No wonder Roy got little or no backing from the players in his face-off with Mick.

One of the ironies of my journey to Japan was that there were about twenty journalists on the plane, heading out to the World Cup. Many of them worked for English-based media. They were linking up with the Irish squad in Izumo and would remain with the squad for the duration. Most of the main Irish soccer journalists had travelled with the squad from the outset. At least the travelling media hadn't heard about the latest development before take-off, and I wasn't telling them.

On arrival at Amsterdam, I decided to get off the plane as quickly as possible and head for the business-class lounge, which we had use of, courtesy of KLM. As we taxied to the gate, I could hear mobile phone messages being received all over the plane as phones were switched on. There was little doubt that 99 per cent of the messages were about one topic.

I hadn't a hope of beating the media to a sanctuary, but at least I had been forewarned. I was approached by a number of them for comment before the plane had reached the terminal building. I told them that I was aware of the development, but wanted to make a number of phone calls to get the full facts before speaking to them. We had a two-hour wait over in Amsterdam and I said I would talk to them prior to departure for Japan. What I hadn't anticipated was that the journalists also had access to the business lounge, but in fairness to them, they gave me and the remainder of the FAI travelling party space. On that Thursday, I was travelling with Eddie Cox, FAI security officer Joe McGlue and three of his colleagues. The security people would work with FIFA on fans' issues in and around the stadium and would also augment the team's security, provided by Tony Hickey and two colleagues, in the hotels and at training. Trevor O'Rourke, a colleague of John Givens in Irish International Promotions (IIP), was also travelling. Trevor and John were the player's media advisors.

I again contacted Des Casey in Dublin. As Honorary Secretary of the Association, Des is in charge when the General Secretary is abroad. Bedlam had broken out and Merrion Square was under siege by the media and fans. They had called a press conference for lunchtime. They were in contact with Milo and Chris in Saipan and were briefing themselves on developments. The FAI were fire-fighting a crisis once again.

*****

At this point let me digress slightly. One of the criticisms in the Genesis Report was that the FAI had no crisis response prepared for things going wrong in the World Cup. This is rubbish. No, we had not anticipated Roy Keane walking out of the squad. Had anyone? Even if we had carried out an analysis of what could go wrong or what could cause a crisis, this would have been well off the radar. How could we have prepared for this and the biggest story of the World Cup that ensued? The Genesis criticism is an instance of being wise after the event. How many small organisations have the resources to carry out a crisis evaluation and the funds to hire people just in case something happens? Many of the comparisons in the Genesis Report were with Associations with much greater resources than the FAI.

I can imagine the response within the FAI if I had requested another six people to accompany the squad to Saipan. We were a relatively small organisation, with an administration staff at that time of twenty-five, three of whom worked in the International Department. The international team is vital for the FAI as a major source of funding, but it comprises only a small proportion of the work of the FAI, which is focused on administering the domestic game at all levels. Expanding the administration of the FAI was always resisted both on financial grounds and on 'political' grounds. For many FAI politicians, more people in Merrion Square equals less power for the committees and affiliates and less money to spend on football.

*****

While in Amsterdam, I again discussed with Des whether I should continue on to Japan or return to Dublin. The original decision was confirmed. I also spoke to Chris Ryan in Saipan to see if there were any further developments. There weren't. I spoke briefly to the accompanying journalists in the business lounge. By this stage they knew as much as I did, as Mick had met the press in Saipan and informed them of Roy's departure. I gave them my reaction, which was one of huge disappointment, particularly in the context of having succeeded in getting the original decision reversed. The decision was now made and I backed Mick McCarthy's judgement. The squad needed to move on, leave the issue behind and focus on the World Cup. The next phase, the real preparation in Japan, was commencing the following day.

I did back Mick McCarthy throughout the problem, despite attempts by some people in the FAI to drive a wedge between the two of us. Mick's two strongest supporters in the FAI were President Milo Corcoran and me. My belief is that the manager must have final say on team affairs. It is his job and he has the ultimate responsibility. That is what he gets paid for. We had interfered once in getting Roy to reverse his initial decision, but this was unlikely to happen again. My relationship with Mick was professional. We were not golfing or drinking buddies, but I believe we had a mutual respect. If Mick needed something done, he would contact me if required. We had a telephone conversation or meeting before each game or trip, but as the organisation of the FAI international team had became well developed over the years, there were seldom any issues. There was a group of support staff well versed in the different aspects of the international team and its logistics.

We took off from Amsterdam at 3 pm for the eleven-hour flight to Tokyo, landing at 7 am Japanese time. However, I would be out of contact for nearly twenty hours, as the earliest I could contact Dublin was 3 pm Japanese time, 7 am Dublin time, when I was due to arrive in Izumo.

Flying business class is certainly the way to travel long distance. The FAI had done a deal with KLM on the Amsterdam to Tokyo route, giving us access to business-class seats at a much discounted price. In any event, FIFA were funding the travelling cost for the official party of fifty-five at full business-class fares.

In Tokyo, we had a two-hour wait for the connection to Izumo. At this stage, I could not contact Chris Ryan as the squad were in transit from Saipan directly to Izumo. It was a case of having to sit and wait. I was largely unaware of what was happening in Dublin and of the reaction to the FAI press conference. On speaking to Linda, in the middle of the night, she told me that John Delaney had led the press conference and had done well. However, he had painted himself as the hero in getting Roy to change his mind initially and had airbrushed me out of the picture. I believe that it was my contact with Michael Kennedy and Liam Gaskin and, more importantly, their contact with Roy and Mick that was critical.

The country was totally split into pro-Mick and pro-Roy factions. Most people with real football knowledge, former managers and former players, were backing Mick. As I was out of the country for nearly the next four weeks, I never got to fully appreciate what was happening back in Ireland and the reaction to the story.

Just before take-off from Tokyo, I made contact with Chris Ryan. The squad had landed in Izumo to a tumultuous reception. There was to be an official welcoming ceremony at 3 pm in the Dome, a magnificent indoor circular arena. I would be met at the airport and brought straight to the Dome. Everything was positive with Mick and the squad. The trip from Saipan by charter had passed off without a hitch. All the skips were waiting for the team in Izumo. Everyone had moved on. Roy had been left behind in Saipan. FAI personnel had gone to Roy's room prior to departure but had received no response. Whether Roy was not in his room or chose not to answer the door, only he can explain. Roy was collected by private plane by Manchester United, who were moving to protect their valuable asset. The FAI had to be unfairly abused as part of this blame-game process.

Suddenly, I realised that there was a new dimension to the story. Roy Keane was captain of Manchester United. The Far East was United's most lucrative and rapidly expanding commercial market. A lot of the press coverage in the area was negative towards Roy and by extension towards Manchester United. I was later shown a copy of the front page of the *Bombay Times*, where Roy Keane was the lead story. I believe that at this point, the Manchester United PR department became heavily involved in handling the story from the Roy Keane perspective. I believe that every move in the 'will he, won't he' return circus, including the interview with Tommy Gorman and the final decision to remain in Manchester, was orchestrated to minimise the negative publicity for Roy Keane and Manchester United. I do not believe that at any stage Roy intended changing his mind again. It was a damage-limitation exercise, managed by experts of spin.

*****

My first contact with Mick and the squad was at the welcoming ceremony at the Dome in Izumo on Friday, 24 May. I had arrived straight from the airport and was in the Dome before the squad. As with everything Japanese, this was a formal ceremony, and I did not get the chance to speak with Mick before it started. My first impressions were from watching the players walk into the arena. They were smiling and seemed very relaxed. The mood was obviously upbeat. There were no obvious signs of tension or negativity. As the Mayor of Izumo welcomed us, Robbie Keane was making faces behind his back at the local kids. Given the formality of Japanese society, I doubt whether they had ever experienced such behaviour before. It seemed the crisis of Saipan was behind us.

My first opportunity to speak with Mick was in the hotel in Izumo. He felt that the matter was now closed and Roy Keane had gone. Mick had the full support of the players and technical staff and I assured him that he had the full support of the FAI and, for what it was worth, he also had my personal support. The meeting did not last long, as the issue was closed. I asked Mick about the training gear difficulties on the Sunday in Saipan, and he assured me that the players had more than sufficient top quality gear. Ciaran Murray, the team physiotherapist, assured me that he had had everything he needed, including isotonic drinks. We were back on track and the serious preparations for the World Cup would start the next day with the match against Hiroshima.

I communicated with Des Casey in Dublin, telling him of the conversation I had had with Mick. As far as we were concerned, the issue was closed. Des was travelling to the FIFA Congress in Seoul the following day (Saturday, 25 May), leaving three officers in Dublin:

John Delaney, Michael Hyland and David Blood. Despite the wishes of Mick McCarthy that the matter be left closed and despite my communications and judgement from Izumo supporting that view, John Delaney kept in contact with Michael Kennedy.

*****

Who was keeping the saga going? I have already referred to the reasons Manchester United and Roy Keane had for keeping the issue open. As Mick McCarthy and I agreed in Izumo, it was the blame game. If Roy Keane was not to blame then someone else must be responsible. Who would finally be held accountable in the court of public opinion? What people had not factored in was that there could only be losers. Roy Keane lost, Mick McCarthy lost, the FAI lost and I personally lost. The team may have lost. We will never know what Ireland, with a not-fully-fit Captain Keane, might have achieved. Would the rancour from Saipan have soured the squad if Roy had remained or returned? One thing is certain, nobody won!

John Delaney resurrected the issue without consulting me, Milo Corcoran or Des Casey, or perhaps the Dublin-based officers either. It was reported in the *Irish Independent* of 29 May that:

> Over the past week, since Keane was ordered home by the manager, Mr. Delaney has been trying to broker a deal with (Michael) Kennedy who liaised with Keane.

This contact was against the expressed wishes of Mick McCarthy. Remember that I had initiated the first successful attempt to get Roy to remain with the squad. Having spoken to Mick and met with the squad, I agreed totally with Mick. Indeed, senior players in the squad spoke to me and told me that Roy was not wanted back and if he did return it would cause massive tension. The players were united in this. It was hinted by one player, who felt so strongly against Roy after his attack on Mick in Saipan, that he would 'box' him if he returned.

As later became evident, Niall Quinn was also involved to some extent. Niall was a friend of Michael Kennedy, who also acted as his solicitor and adviser, and has admitted to being in contact with him. I refer the reader to the conversations between Mick and Niall Quinn on this matter in Mick's book and the blow-by-blow account given by Niall Quinn in his autobiography, co-written by Tom Humphries.

I am not going to quote from Niall's book, but I will make comment on some of the issues he raises. Niall criticises the FAI for not being involved in Izumo in the attempts to get Roy back. This is very unfair. The FAI, in the person of me, was getting a loud and clear message from both Mick McCarthy and the players: Mick did not want Roy back. The vast majority of players did not want Roy back. However, Mick did not place an embargo on Niall telephoning Michael Kennedy. Perhaps he should have.

What should the FAI do? Go behind the back of the manager and against the wishes of the players, as communicated to us. As Niall admits in his book, this could have provoked a walk-out by Mick. Niall was doing his own thing and, in fairness, seems to have informed Mick McCarthy of his actions. However, at no stage did Niall communicate with the FAI that he was trying to resolve the situation. Communication is a two-way exercise.

*****

The FIFA Congress was due to commence in Seoul on Tuesday, 28 May, with a pre-conference UEFA meeting on the Monday evening. It was customary for the President and General Secretary to represent the FAI at FIFA and UEFA congresses. They were very formal events, the equivalent of AGMs, and while one delegate and one Association would have very little impact, we were obliged to attend. Meeting and greeting people outside the formal meetings was as important as anything else. The main item on the agenda at the congress was the election of the President, where the incumbent, Sepp Blatter, was being challenged by Issa Hayatou from Cameroon. The contentious issue was the financial management of FIFA. Des Casey, as a Vice President of UEFA, was strongly anti-Blatter and Ireland was lined up to vote accordingly.

Milo and I decided to reschedule our flight from Izumo to Seoul from the Sunday to Monday. There was a small regional airport about two hours drive up the coast, which had occasional direct flights to

Seoul. Sunday was quiet in Izumo. The match with Hiroshima on Saturday had passed off well, with the exception of the ridiculous tackle by Hiroshima's Cameroonian centre-half on Jason McAteer. The resulting injury to Jason remained a factor throughout the World Cup campaign. The players trained for the first time at the magnificent facilities at the Dome. I wondered if even these facilities would have satisfied Roy Keane!

The communication with Dublin in the person of John Delaney was that all was quiet. The country remained divided, but the impression we were getting was that opinion was slowing swinging behind Mick. Roy had had another go in the Sunday papers in the Paul Kimmage article and also in one of the British tabloids. Roy had thereby further closed the door. Mick had also spoken to a British Sunday newspaper. Milo and I discussed whether we should both go to Seoul, which would remove us from Mick and the team. At this stage, we were firmly of the opinion that the issue of Roy Keane's participation in the World Cup was over. We decided that we would stick with our schedule and go to the congress on the Monday. What I believe we had not factored in was that Roy Keane and Manchester United were not going to let the issue lie while Roy was being perceived as being in the 'wrong'. Nor were we aware that John Delaney was communicating with Michael Kennedy. If I had been advised by the FAI in Dublin that talks were ongoing, then I would not have gone.

It has been reported in the media that I was advised not to travel to Seoul. I strongly refute this and on the Sunday and, indeed, as late as the Monday night in Seoul, I was informed by John Delaney that there was no chance of Roy returning to the squad. I refer to an article by John O'Brien in *The Sunday Times* of 23 June 2002, which stated:

> *As negotiations to resolve the [Keane] row were nearing the apex, Menton departed from Izumo to Seoul to attend the FIFA Congress, though at least one other senior official advised against it.*

This was not the situation. No official advised me not to go to Seoul. Nor were there any official negotiations underway that I was aware of as I departed Izumo for Seoul. O'Brien wrote the above in *The Sunday Times* without checking it. He certainly didn't talk to me about it. I believe that much of what O'Brien wrote about the FAI and me, personally, in *The Sunday Times* was inaccurate. When challenged legally on one aspect in early 2003, *The Sunday Times* were quick to issue a clarification and meet my legal costs.

On arrival in Seoul, I joined Des Casey, who was our third delegate and who had travelled directly from Dublin. We attended the UEFA pre-conference meeting where Des was vocal in his criticism of Sepp Blatter and the financial management of FIFA. After the meeting, there was a drinks reception, which Milo and I spent discussing Euro 2008 with our Scottish friends.

At about 10 pm Korean time, I retired to my room for the night. Linda had joined me, having travelled independently from Dublin. I wasn't in the room very long when I received two phone calls from the media, both asking whether there was any new movement on the Roy Keane issue. If I remember correctly, they were from Emmet Malone of *The Irish Times* and Roy Curtis of the *Daily Mirror*. The proximity of the phone calls suggested that something might be stirring, but if there was, nobody had thought to ring the President and General Secretary of the Association. I contacted Milo Corcoran, who joined me in my room. I telephoned John Delaney in Ireland to find out if there were any developments and was told that there weren't, thus confirming our communication of the previous day. I discussed the issue with Milo and particularly whether I should return to Izumo. As it was not possible to achieve anything that night, we decided to wait until the morning before making a final decision. Early morning in Korea was late evening in Ireland and there would be a window for communication.

Some hours later, about 3 am Korean time, I received a phone call from John Delaney informing me that the situation had changed; negotiations had recommenced and there was a chance that Roy would return to the squad. Furthermore, Roy was going on RTÉ television on that Monday (27 May) and it was likely that he would apologise. Everything had suddenly changed. As Milo and Des were leaving for the congress venue very early the next morning, I wrote them notes, summarising developments and telling them that I was returning to Izumo.

I would love to know when contacts recommenced between the FAI (John Delaney) and Michael Kennedy. The FAI officials in Japan and Korea were not being kept up to speed. In addition, I believe that there was no contact between the FAI in Dublin and Mick McCarthy on this re-opening of negotiations. The people involved in this were John Delaney, Michael Kennedy and, to a lesser extent, Niall Quinn. Mick McCarthy was not consulted, except by Niall, and neither Milo Corcoran nor I were either consulted or briefed. We had given our total backing to Mick and were not moving from this. This is reflected in Mick's book where he states:

> *Thankfully there has been no suggestion that the FAI would do that* [force Roy's return on me], *their support has been rock solid and much appreciated by me.*

At no stage was there any discussion within the FAI about re-opening negotiations. I did not believe Roy was coming back, but I was aware that he was mounting a media campaign.

The Roy Keane interview with Tommy Gorman was aired on RTÉ at 8 pm Irish time on Monday, 27 May. Having subsequently read a transcript and viewed part of it on tape, my one criticism of Tommy Gorman, who is a tremendous supporter of Irish football, is that he did not push the issue to a conclusion: 'Roy, are you apologising?' All the interview achieved was to repair some of the damage to Roy's image and to delay a final resolution for another day. Roy Keane was still impeding Ireland's preparation for the World Cup, from a distance of 10,000 miles.

First thing on the Tuesday morning, I contacted Chris Ryan, who got Ray Treacy to make the travel arrangements for me and Linda from Seoul to Izumo. It was a convoluted trip, Seoul to Osaka, a change of airport from one side of Osaka to the other (necessitating an hour-long taxi trip) and then Osaka to Izumo. I left the hotel in Seoul at 9 am and arrived in Izumo at 6 pm. Again I was out of contact for much of the time as the Japanese mobile system was not compatible with the Korean mobile system. Chris had informed me that a press conference with Mick had been scheduled for 3 pm. I got Chris to speak to Mick, and it was agreed that the press conference would be rescheduled for 8 pm, when I would be present. My fear was that Mick would blow any chance of reconciliation with Roy out of the water, especially in front of antagonistic journalists.

However, I learned from Chris that Mick had spoken to the press that morning and, on the basis of a possible apology from Roy had left the door ajar, despite the huge difficulties this would cause to Mick's managerial authority and the divisions within the squad. Deep down, I believed that the chances of Roy returning were small, but if Mick made the final call to exclude him, he would take the blame. The issue now was not whether Roy would play for Ireland in the World Cup, but rather who would take the major share of the blame for the rift between Roy and Mick. My information is that public opinion had turned against Keane in the media over the weekend, so a PR stunt was needed to redress this balance.

During this period, there had been many developments in Izumo. Not being there, I will rely on Mick's *World Cup Diary* to fill in this gap:

> *I ring Liam* [Gaskin] *when I get up and ask if there was any apology issued on RTÉ television while I slept... it seems that Roy Keane went close to an apology a few times, but never close enough to force me into a corner. The ball is, however, back in my court... A posse of journalists has camped on the steps of the hotel. They still have time to make the late editions back home and they deserve a reply to the interview. Brendan McKenna (FAI Media Officer) arranges an impromptu press conference outside the front door.*

The journalists suggest that Roy Keane has apologised, but my information tells a different tale, but I turn the tables anyway. I acknowledge that the door can still be open to Roy Keane, but only on my terms, which must include a phone call direct to me, not dialogue through interviews or intermediaries.

Back inside the hotel, I read the full transcript of Keane's TV interview, which has been faxed through from Dublin. It does not make for pretty reading and there is little sign of remorse...

The endless debate on the subject is working against the one thing we came out here to do. It is eating into our World Cup and it is time to call an end to it... I decided to call a meeting with the players before we go training. I need to put their minds at ease, as rumours sweep through the hotel, again, that Roy Keane is coming back. The suggestion that we are a one-man team, that he got us here on his own, needs to be put to bed as well. More than anything, I want to know where they stand now.

I sit down with the twenty-two players and the staff and tell it as it is. I explain that, having read his transcript and considered his interview, I realise he has not apologised and, it appears to me, he has no intention of doing so. As a result, I do not want Roy Keane back no matter what was said on the steps of the hotel this morning. If he comes back against my wishes I tell them that I may walk. I cannot look any player in the eye and tell them that he will not play because Roy Keane is coming back...

I tell them that I may find it impossible to work with Roy Keane even if he apologises. If the players feel otherwise, however, I will listen to them... if they tell me that we are better side with Roy Keane in the team, then fine, I will go with them. I may have to re-think my own situation after the World Cup finals if that is the case. I will do whatever they feel is best for Ireland...

And then I leave the room, taking the staff with me. All twenty-two players stay behind to decide exactly what they are going to do. Their meeting takes about twenty minutes, delaying the start of the training session.

We depart for the training ground and some of the players work on a statement for the media, down at the back of the bus. By the time we get to the ground, just five minutes up the road, they have a press release ready, which they ask me to approve. I am delighted and surprised by the statement, which reads:

'Regrettably the manner of Roy's behaviour prior to his departure from Saipan and the comments attributed to him since have left the staff and players in no doubt that the interests of the squad are best served without Roy's presence. The players bear no malice towards Roy on a personal level and we are looking forward to a successful World Cup with the complete support of our loyal supporters, both at home and abroad.'

The door which I had appeared to open to Roy Keane this morning is now, it appears, closing rapidly. The players also want to bring this to an end. They have backed me, shown the world that they are behind their manager on this. You have no idea how good this feels. I know the storm this hard-hitting statement will kick up but it is, I believe, indicative of how we all feel right now.

[after training] Of course the issue soon comes to life again. I have no idea when the players' statement will be released... the plan I believe is to release it after I update the media on my reaction to Roy Keane's television appearance, now that I have read the full transcript, but nothing goes to plan today. My press conference is delayed to allow Brendan Menton to get back from a FIFA meeting in Seoul in time to add his presence to the podium. I go back to the hotel as the players statement is released, prematurely, to the press. FAI media officer, Brendan McKenna, is left to carry the can as accusations of player power rain down on the top table...

Niall Quinn, well aware of the furore that the players' statement caused this morning, decides to face the media on behalf of the squad to explain the vote and the stance they have taken. More than anything, Niall wants to make it clear that the players acted in my defence. He outlines the timetable of events behind the statement and the level of support for me as manager that exists within the squad. Their statement was a public gesture of that support.

Quinny goes on to say that the squad want to do what is best for Ireland. If that means bringing an end to the conflict between Roy and me then, despite everything that has happened today, Niall would gladly act as a peace broker no matter what his former captain said about him over the last forty-eight hours...

Quinny has spent serious time on the phone with Michael Kennedy, his solicitor as well as Roy Keane's, and believes the two sides can be brought together if Roy Keane is prepared to apologise...

Big Niall and the players are prepared to back any plan that can benefit everyone, even Roy Keane, so long as it protects my tenure as manager. He spends forty-five minutes with me in the evening, to find some way to work things out to everyone's satisfaction. He has been on the phone constantly to Michael Kennedy since this morning's vote and still believes that a deal can be done for the good of the country...

He wants my blessing to make one last call to Kennedy to see what can be done. I tell him to make that phone call but remind him that Roy Keane must apologise. I can't see it working but it is worth his time making the effort. I will do anything now to try and end this.

The players had their own media advisers with them, Trevor O'Rourke and John Givens. O'Rourke and Givens seem to have played a passive role in the issuing of the players' statement and allowed Brendan McKenna to take the hot seat and the blame. This statement was issued prematurely. Remember that Niall Quinn was privy to the negotiations with Roy Keane, and was also party to the drafting and releasing of the players' statement.

This sets the scene for Izumo as I arrived back at about 6 pm. Mick, in his book, describes it as one of the worst days of his life. My first task was to try and prevent Mick from walking. I had assured Mick earlier that the FAI would not do anything without speaking to him and I assured him I would keep him fully informed. Now we had the situation where elements of the FAI had re-opened negotiations without reference to Mick, me or indeed the President of the Association.

I met Mick in the lobby of the hotel. He had been joined by his wife, Fiona, who had travelled from London to support him. It was a funereal atmosphere. The media were getting impatient due to the long delays over the press conference. However, time was not a factor, as it was early morning in Ireland and the critical deadlines for the media were still hours into the future. I told Mick that I needed to shower and change after the trip and that I would meet him in twenty minutes to discuss what was happening and to plan our strategy for what was going to be a difficult press conference.

I again contacted John Delaney and was informed that discussions with Roy Keane's advisers were still on-going and there was a possibility that he would return to the squad. Despite believing that this was simply a PR exercise, my strategy had to be to persuade Mick to once again leave the door open for Roy Keane.

Mick and I met for about twenty minutes before going to the press conference. A major objective was to convince him that neither I nor Milo Corcoran had known anything about any attempts to re-open the Roy Keane issue, that the first I heard about it was a phone call I had received in the middle of the night in Seoul. I knew that there was a danger that Mick could walk away if he felt his position was being undermined by the Association. I think the fact that I had been caught so far off-guard by the developments, being in Seoul, persuaded Mick that the official FAI were acting in good faith.

We spent about ten minutes planning for the press conference. I persuaded Mick that the door had to be left open. We were playing the blame game. If he closed the door on Roy, Mick would become the villain. Neither of us believed that Roy would return. I told Mick that the press conference would be short, that I would not let it last more than ten minutes. If it went on longer than that, then all the old rows would be dredged up and we could only lose. We agreed the bones of an opening statement which Mick would give. The media are nothing if not predictable. They simply wanted to feed the story and we wanted to avoid that if possible. The objective was to walk away with the door still seemingly open for Roy Keane's return.

Mick and I travelled to the press conference, with Ian Evans, Packie Bonner and Brendan McKenna for support. Unsurprisingly, it was a large press conference and the media, having waited all day, were impatient. When the press conference started, Mick made his opening statement, which left the door open for Roy. Once the questions started, things became difficult very quickly. Many of the media were openly pro-Mick or pro-Roy. The first few questions were fielded easily enough, but quickly some of the pro-Keane media wanted to re-open the war. This might be good for newspaper headlines the next day, but was not what was needed for the good of the Irish squad and for the possibility, however remote, of Roy's return.

I tried to close the press conference, as I had told Mick I would. I don't think that Mick really believed that I would walk out and bring him with me. He continued to answer the next question. However, the problem was resolved when Roy Curtis of the *Mirror* asked a question Mick didn't like. I believe that there was intense dislike between the two. I spoke privately to Mick and told him that we had to get out. This time he listened; I closed the press conference and we left. As we moved from the dais, I heard a last question from the back of the hall from, I think, Miriam Lord of the *Irish Independent*: 'Does this mean that the door is still open?' If this was the general response, we had achieved what we had set out to do.

That press conference met with a critical reaction from large segments of the press. From my point of view it was successful. This shows how the same event can elicit polar reactions. My objective was not to feed the media frenzy, but to protect the slim possibility that Roy might actually come back. However, it was more important not to fall into Keane's PR trap of casting Mick as the villain of the piece. I have been heavily criticised for that press conference, but with hindsight I would change nothing, except that I would insist that Mick walk out with me the first time.

Niall Quinn also has a go at me in his book over that press conference. Niall didn't attend this press conference, so I assume that the quotes used in his book are from his ghost writer Tom Humphries' notes. It is still beyond me how Niall can argue, at that delicate stage, that allowing Mick to 'reassert that he is in charge' in front of a hostile media that were only interested in keeping the row going could help the situation. Niall, from his own words, still believed that there was a chance that Michael Kennedy could get Roy to change his mind. I can only assume that this segment of Niall's book is more Humphries than Quinn.

In Humphries' own book, he states that, as Mick and I exited the press conference, Humphries was shouting questions as to who had said and written what and when. I was aware that Humphries and Roy Curtis of the *Mirror* – a strange alliance if there ever was one – were the most vociferous in shouting questions. However, I had no interest in answering them. It is not surprising that different people with opposite agendas can have very different memories of the same event. It is also not too surprising that it was a non-football journalist, who identified the key issue – whether the door was still open for Keane.

The Irish Times kept producing a picture of Mick looking aghast in my general direction at a press conference and captioning the photograph as 'the chaotic press conference at Izumo'. The photograph shows me in casual clothes, but I wore a suit at that press conference. I told Emmet Malone of *The Irish Times* on a number of occasions that this was the wrong photograph. Emmet checked and apologised to me personally, but that did not stop its continued use with the same caption by *The Irish Times*. The photograph was used in *The Irish Times* the day after I stood down as General Secretary of the FAI.

After the press conference, I went back to the hotel, where I spent about an hour and a half with Mick discussing strategy. The rumour mill was rife and I even heard that there were three private jets lined up at Dublin airport to bring Roy back. I thought one would have been sufficient, even for Roy Keane.

Mick's position at this stage, as is obvious from his book, was that if Roy apologised then he could come back. Telephone calls were made back and forth to Ireland. I was working through John Delaney, who was talking to Michael Kennedy, who I suppose was talking to Roy. At this stage, I was still unaware that Niall Quinn was also talking to Michael Kennedy. Eventually a formula was hammered out. Roy would ring Mick at 10 am Japanese time, 2 am Irish time, the following morning (Wednesday, 29 May). He would simply say that he wanted to play for Ireland in the World Cup and was sorry for his personal abuse of Mick. As I left Mick at 11 pm, I thought that the matter was finally settled. It was now Roy's decision. Did he really intend to play for Ireland or not?

I met a senior member of Mick's staff, who spoke very derogatorily of Roy. If Roy apologised and returned, that would create its own problems. The next morning would be telling.

I adjourned to the FAI office with Linda, where I had a brief meeting with Chris Ryan and Eddie Cox to catch up on other developments. After the meeting, I remained in the office to get some privacy, have some food and a drink after a long and taxing day. The office was across the corridor from the room Mick was using. He had been joined by his key staff. At times we could hear angry voices. Mick's decision to keep the door open for Roy's return was not being met with universal approval. Mick had no choice. It was against his instinct and he was angry that the matter was still interfering with the squad's World

Cup preparations. However, his position could quickly become untenable if he rebutted any olive branch offered by Roy's camp.

Perhaps the best illustration of the chaotic environment in the Royal Hotel in Izumo is the fact that there were two independent streams of communication occurring. I was speaking to John Delaney, who was in contact with Michael Kennedy, and I was keeping Mick informed. We agreed the formula for resolution through this channel. At the same time, Niall Quinn, from his conversations with Michael Kennedy, was promising Mick that the phone call from Roy would come. Niall criticises the FAI for not being involved. Yet my impression was that Niall's involvement had at best lukewarm support from Mick and only limited support from the rest of the squad. I accept that Niall's involvement was with the best of intentions. However, if, as I believe, Keane never had any intention of again changing his mind, then we were all being used in a PR exercise.

A phone call to my room from John Delaney at about 5 am Japanese time, finally resolving the matter. Surprise, surprise! Roy had decided not to return. If this was his final decision, why all the posturing? The only plausible answer is that it was to save his public relations image. Roy had been boxed into the corner of calling the final shot and he baulked at it. He never intended coming back. He used the players' statement as his final excuse. That was rubbish. Nothing had changed from the previous Thursday. He was aware of the mood among the players. If we want to pursue that line of reasoning, we have only to refer to his comments – insults – on some of the senior players in the media over the weekend. Was that setting the scene for a possible return?

Mick had requested not to be disturbed too early in the morning. His timing of the possible phone call for 10 am, 2 am Irish time, was a little imposition on Keane and perhaps a small show of managerial authority. If you are a member of a squad, you do what the manager wants at a time that suits him. I decided not to waken Mick. I wrote Mick a note, telling him the news – Roy was not coming back – and

Linda put it under his door. I thought it would be safer to get Linda to do it, as if I had been seen, I would have been subjected to a barrage of questions. As Mick said in his book, the nation expected two words from Roy – I'm sorry – but instead got 167 in a statement issued through RTÉ. Re-reading the statement after a long interval is instructive. Let me just quote two sentences:

> *I believe that the time has come when I should bring to a conclusion the continuing speculation with regard to my participation in the World Cup.*
>
> *I wish the team and the management all the best and they will have my full support throughout the competition.*

Word had filtered through to the players and other staff from the Irish media by breakfast time. There was relief all around. Roy was history, but there were only two days left in Izumo before the transfer to Niigata on Friday for the match against Cameroon.

On reflection, I sometimes regret that I ever interfered in the matter in the first place. What if I had never heard that Roy was coming home or, having heard from Eddie Cox through Umbro, I had left it alone on the basis that team affairs were Mick's responsibility? Roy would have left Saipan on the Wednesday, not have given the interviews to Tom Humphries and Paul Kimmage and the Thursday meeting of the full squad would not have happened. Colin Healy would have played in the World Cup. A lot of what subsequently transpired would have been avoided. One has only to read the respective accounts of Mick and Roy about what happened on the Wednesday morning in Saipan when Roy initially decided to stay. It only came about because of the influence of third parties on both of them. There was certainly no meeting of minds and no direct personal contact.

The other possible scenario is what would have happened if Mick McCarthy had telephoned me on the Tuesday and told me that Roy Keane had requested to go home for personal reasons. As team matters were Mick's responsibility, I would very easily have been persuaded by Mick not to intervene. I could not have gone against such a request without undermining his authority.

Roy Keane did not want to play in the World Cup for Ireland. His negativity can be traced back to the Eircom Awards function in February, when he rightfully received the Senior Player of the Year Award. He had been flown in on a private jet by the FAI, courtesy of Eircom, to be in time for the award. When asked by George Hamilton if he was looking forward to the World Cup, his reply was yes, if the facilities were good. Contrast this with the world's greatest midfield player, Zinadine Zidane, who couldn't play through injury and was bitterly disappointed. Let me tell you that the facilities in Korea available to World Champions, France, were well below the magnificent facilities enjoyed by the Irish squad in Japan. Roy never even got to see them.

*****

I at last got to visit my tropical island, Pangkor, off the coast of Malyasia. I put the final editing touches to this chapter, sitting on a beach of golden sand. Was Saipan as nice as this?

5

Korea & Japan 2002

Preparations

After Ireland's qualification for the World Cup, letters of congratulations poured into Merrion Square. Foremost among them were congratulations from FIFA, together with mountains of documentation to do with the World Cup. The most important document was a 300-page manual, full of instructions, regulations and guidelines. This was to be our bible for the preparations, and we adhered to it. The World Cup tournament belongs to FIFA and, if you qualify, you do what they tell you. There is no flexibility. The regulations cover everything from the size of the manufacturers' logos on the gear, to the financial contributions from FIFA, as well as all transport issues from day of arrival to day of departure, dealing with the media, disciplinary matters, customs regulations, ticketing, accreditation of players and officials and the time for confirmation of the official list of players. No matter what might happen in the World Cup, it was regulated for in the manual.

By the time of our actual qualification, we had only made some rudimentary preparations in case of qualification. My attitude had been not to assume that we would qualify. I don't know whether this was based on superstition or a fear of looking silly if we failed to qualify and had spent a lot of time and resources on unneeded preparations. We had sufficient time to make the necessary plans between December and June. Ray Treacy had been out to Japan and, indeed, Saipan, and Mick had been persuaded to consider Saipan as the first location. We knew that the Mayor of Izumo wanted us to use his town as our preparation camp and was prepared to underwrite the costs.

Brian Kerr had brought a youth team to an invitation tournament in Japan some months previously. However, Brian and Mick, as technical director and international team manager, respectively, did not see eye to eye and I doubt that there was much communication between them. We did not yet know whether we would be playing in Japan or Korea in the first phase. The draw for the groups would take place in Busan in South Korea on 1 December. That would give us a lot of direction.

The trip to Busan for the draw was my first trip to the Far East. The official party was made up of Milo Corcoran, Michael Hyland (as Chairman of the FAI International Committee), Mick McCarthy and me. Mick and Ray Treacy used the occasion to visit Saipan and Izumo before the draw, to assess the facilities. When they joined us in Busan, they were very pleased with both venues. Ray Treacy came to Busan because, in his role as FAI travel agent, he needed to be on the ground to finalise travel and hotel arrangements, once we knew where we were going. He was catering not only for the players, technical staff and officials, but also for very large numbers of media and fans.

There were more than fifty approved locations for training camps in Japan and Korea; each location was touting all participating countries for business, except Izumo which had focused on the Irish team. Many of the larger countries had spent a lot of time and resources scouting the various camps in advance, but this was difficult to justify for a small Association. We had been visited in Dublin by a Korean delegation from Nam Hae and were persuaded to visit their camp while in Busan. This we did the day before the draw. It was a three-and-a-half hour trip each way. The traffic was appalling, even on the motorways. When we got there, we had the mandatory meal with the local officials – plenty of raw fish, which was a special treat for the conservative FAI eaters. At least they provided us with a table and chairs, while they sat cross-legged on the floor.

The camp itself was on an island off the south coast of Korea, joined to the mainland by a causeway. It was a truly beautiful location and the training facilities were very good, if not quite up to the standard of those we would use in Japan. The problem was that the only hotel was still a construction site. We toured it in hard hats, trying to imagine what it might be like in a few months time. We had no way of being sure that it would be ready in time. This was a wasted journey for us, as we were never based in this part of Korea. It would only be useful for a preparatory camp, as it was too remote from the match stadia. I believe that the Danes used Nam Hae and were very happy with it.

Throughout our stay in Busan, we were inundated with presentations about the merits of the different training camps. We were joined by the Major of Izumo, Masahiro Nishio, to lend his support in the draw.

Did we want to be drawn in Korea or in Japan? We had no set view. Typical of FIFA and the World Cup Organising Committee, everything had to be treated the same in Korea and Japan. It was a matter of saving face. Even if costs were 50 per cent lower in parts of Korea than in Japan, you still received the same subvention from FIFA. In the end, having been in both countries, Japan was the better location in terms of facilities and organisation.

There is no such thing as an open draw for the World Cup. There were to be two European teams in most groups (fifteen European teams had to be spread across eight groups). The other two teams in each group would come from Asia, Africa or the Americas, but only one from each continent, or football confederation, as FIFA calls them. Different groups of teams are drawn from different pots. The showbiz element was paramount. As a football fan, I prefer these things to be kept simple: make the draw and put us out of our misery. In Busan, the draw was interrupted halfway through for entertainment.

I remember the draw for the US World Cup. Robin Williams turned it into a comedy routine. I still won't watch Robin Williams' films because of it. However, in Busan, Mick greatly enjoyed the 'half-time' singing by Anastacia.

Mick was happy with the result of the draw. We were in a group with Germany, Cameroon and Saudi Arabia. Germany would be difficult, but the Saudis were a good draw. Having beaten Iran, we should manage the Saudis. Cameroon were African champions and would be tough. Overall, we had a good chance of progressing. We would play against Cameroon in the first Japanese-based game of the tournament in Niigata on day two of the World Cup. It was probably the vital fixture for us.

Perhaps the best aspect of the draw was the location of the venues. We were in Japan, which was good, but Niigata, Ibaraki and Yokohama are all located fairly close together. We probably had the least internal travel of any World Cup participant. The draw confirmed that Izumo would be a good preparatory venue. If we got our plans right, we could perhaps need only one base when the tournament got underway. Ray Treacy quickly identified Chiba, just north of Tokyo and close to the airport, as an ideal location for us.

After the draw, we split up. Milo Corcoran and Mick returned home, Ray went to Niigata and I went to Izumo. We had predetermined that Izumo would be our preparatory camp if we were based in Japan. Mick and Ray had already been there and found the facilities to be first rate.

It was in Izumo that I found out how important food is to the Japanese. I was greeted by a large welcoming delegation at Matsue Airport on my arrival in mid-afternoon. Among the welcoming party was Estelle Smith from Dublin, a language graduate of DCU, who was working for the Shimane Prefecture, the local county, on an exchange programme. I was brought immediately to Izumo and a welcoming lunch. Japanese food is fantastic. Having had a very early start, I tucked in. I was then taken on a tour of the facilities: the Dome, the alternative training pitches, the stadium, the hospital and finally the hotel. Everything was first class. At the Dome, there was a large crowd of schoolchildren waving Irish and Japanese flags. I got presented with a bouquet of flowers. Even the hospital was bright and cheerful, with many people awaiting treatments, but no queues. Izumo is a town of 80,000 inhabitants, very small by Japanese standards, and located in a very rural area on the south-west coast. Nonetheless, I was assured that the hospital had all the most advanced facilities and treatments available.

My impression of the Japanese system is that the elected mayor carries out his programmes with very little red tape. He is more of an American-style mayor than an Irish one. It is a sort of paternalistic feudal system. The Major wanted to build a stadium, so it got built. He has to stand for re-election every four years. I was not surprised to receive a letter in June from Masahiro Nishio to tell me the good news that he got re-elected in early 2003.

I was left to my hotel by the Mayor at about 6 pm. He informed me that he would collect me at 6.30 pm for an official welcoming dinner. I had just finished a very large lunch. By 7 pm, I was sitting down facing another very large meal, with bottles of Guinness as the mandatory drink. Guinness is brewed in Shapiro on the northern Japanese island of Hokkaido. I quickly learned the art of pushing food around my plate and hiding it under lettuce leaves, as my capacity for consumption was well below that of my Japanese hosts. We had formal welcoming speeches, with Estelle translating. Izumo were delighted to welcome the Irish team and would do everything possible for us.

The next day, there was a formal press conference to announce Ireland's choice of Izumo as our preparatory camp location. The story made the national news, as did everything to do with the World Cup. I was accompanied by a second DCU graduate, Elie Tsu, for this day. Our announcement caught the Japanese World Cup Organising Committee (JAWOC) on the hop, as all such matters should have been pre-cleared with them. In fact, JAWOC allocated a liaison officer to each delegation, but ours was in Niigata with Ray, and they were unaware that I had travelled independently to Izumo. However, as Izumo were only interested in the Irish and the Irish were the only team looking at Izumo, there were no problems with our selection and, somewhat premature, announcement.

After the press conference, it was lunch in a very traditional Japanese restaurant. It was shoes off and into slippers at the entrance, which is traditional practice in every Japanese home. I believe that this signifies a clear separation of the home from external activities. I have the impression that, while the men may make the rules outside the home, the women are clearly in command within it. The table was set at knee height. I have an artificial hip, so luckily for me there was a foot well, which allowed me to sit as normal. The food was again delicious, especially the seafood. It was about the best I had ever eaten. There was plate after plate of wonderful food served to us by two geishas, who, Japanese-style, joined in the conversation.

After lunch I was brought on a tour of the sights of Izumo: the Shinto temple – home to 8 million gods – the beach and the golf course. My flight to Tokyo was due to take off at 4 pm. At 3 pm, I was taken to the local brewery for a farewell function. More food and drink had to be consumed. I do not believe I have ever eaten so much within a twenty-four hour period. We left Izumo for the airport, thirty minutes away, at 3.30 pm, for a 4 pm flight. However, I need not have worried. The Mayor had obviously instructed that the plane should not take off until I and my travelling companion, Mr Ito[1], had boarded the plane – such is the authority of the Mayor. It is the only occasion when a plane has been delayed for me. I don't expect that it will ever happen again. There was a large farewell gathering at the airport, with many people present whom I thought I had said goodbye to at the brewery. I suspect that we had gone the long way around, so that everyone would reach the airport before us.

We had already agreed some of the significant points with Izumo covering our stay with them. It was very simple. They would pay for

---

1. Mr Ito, a Japanese gentleman living in London, had introduced us to Izumo and had acted for the Mayor in persuading us to have our training camp there. He stayed with us throughout the World Cup as an unofficial liaison officer, and was very useful.

everything for as long as we stayed. The best hotel would be reserved solely for our use, even though we would use only one-third of the rooms. All food, drink, transport and facilities would be provided free of charge. This was great financial news for us. FIFA would provide a subvention of $450 a day per person for a party of forty-five for eight days before the World Cup and until two days after our exit. As we had no expenses during our week in Izumo, the Association would profit to the extent of approximately $140,000.

The news would get even better. Izumo would organise a match for us against J-League (the Japanese league) team Hiroshima Sanfrecce, to officially open the new stadium, for which we would receive a fee of ¥6 million (close to €60,000). In addition, at their expense, they would send a charter plane to bring the team from Saipan to Izumo. This would probably have cost at least €60,000. I have no idea how much the people of Izumo invested in total in the Irish team. They are brilliant people and earned our eternal gratitude for their generosity and hospitality.

As a small gesture in return, I offered to bring Brian Kerr with us to Izumo to hold coaching courses for the kids of the town. This offer was greatly appreciated. For reasons that will be obvious later, it was Noel O'Reilly who came with us to Izumo.

Tokyo has two airports, Hameda on the south side for domestic travel and Narita on the north side for international travel. When I arrived back in Tokyo, I was ambushed in Hameda by a delegation espousing the merits of a training camp close to Narita. I suspect that I had been set up by Mr Ito. Our plans were that if Chiba's facilities were adequate, then that would be our second base in Japan. It did not suit me to travel to Narita the following day, despite it being only a short distance away. However, it is difficult to turn down the Japanese, so I went. When I got there, the training facilities were reasonable but the hotels were very poor, being standard airport hotels. It was an absolute non-starter. Roy would rightly have been very upset if we had ended up there.

Chiba was excellent. We were met by a representative of the City Council, Tsatsumi Ono, who showed us all their facilities. Tsatsumi was to be available to us at all times until our departure from Chiba more than six months later. If Izumo's facilities were excellent, Chiba's were out of this world. They were situated just ten minutes from the New Otani, the best hotel that the FAI have ever used. There were fourteen restaurants in the New Otani. The indoor gymnasium was incredible, and included not only two indoor tennis courts, but also an indoor golf driving range. The magnificent facilities available to our players in Chiba were shown on RTÉ television. There was no decision to make. It was simply a matter of trying to manage the hotel costs. The hotel knew we wanted to stay there and were in no mood for bargaining. It was a matter of getting as much financial help as possible from the local Chiba City Council. We had initial talks with them and agreed we would discuss the details further when we returned in early February for the FIFA World Cup workshop.

In the end, Chiba City provided us with a budget of ¥21 million, which is about €200,000. They would cover all accommodation and meals in the hotel for the official party of fifty-five people. They would provide additional transport, both cars and minibuses, above that provided by the JAWOC. They would set up a media centre at the training grounds, equipped with modern communication channels. The swimming pool at the training centre would be refurbished and reserved exclusively for the players. The FAI would have an office at the training centre and there would be both a manager's office and a medical room. Again, anything we needed within an agreed list was provided free by Chiba City. We signed a formal agreement with Chiba when we visited the city in early February, while attending the FIFA workshop. The benefit of this to the Association was enormous, as we could pocket most of the FIFA subvention as profit for the Association. There were rumours that some of the major countries, such as Brazil, were being paid a fee to locate at a specific camp. However, between Izumo and Chiba, the Association did extraordinarily well from a financial perspective.

A delegation from Chiba visited Dublin in mid-March and walked in the St Patrick's Day parade behind Mick McCarthy, who was the Grand Marshall of the parade.

The other benefit of Chiba was that we could spend twelve days there without moving base. From Izumo, we would travel to Niigata on the day before the opening match and spend just one night there. We were obliged to be within one hour of the match venue on the day before each game. After the game, we would travel to Chiba and set up our permanent base for the duration of the first phase. We could travel from Chiba to both Ibaraki and Yokohama fairly easily. Every other team would be changing their base more frequently than this and with longer distances to travel.

Our major issue in finalising these arrangements was in persuading JAWOC to provide us with a charter flight to Tokyo after the first game in Niigata. They wanted the team to travel by the Bullet train. We won this battle by insisting that we needed three quality days to prepare for our second match against Germany; only by flying immediately after the first game could we achieve this. The threat of adverse publicity and unfair treatment turned the argument in our favour.

During our second visit to Chiba in early February, we measured the travelling time between the hotel in Chiba and the stadia in Ibaraki and Yokohama, to ensure that the travelling time was not too long for the players. Mick wanted a maximum travelling time of seventy-five minutes prior to a match. We believed that we had achieved an excellent itinerary for the team in Japan.

The Genesis Report described the preparations as excellent, although it was critical of the fact that we had not documented every decision. Sometimes getting things done is more important than writing about them. We had worked diligently through every aspect of the World Cup preparations, using the FIFA manual as our bible, meeting regularly as a working group with a set agenda on all the relevant areas. The people involved had set responsibilities, had experience, if not previously at World Cup level, and were competent. I will stand over our arrangements and facilities fully from the day we arrived in Izumo to the day we left Seoul.

By this stage, the main parts of the World Cup itinerary had been decided. What was left to be done was the detailed planning. The Genesis Report criticised our arrangements for not drawing on the experience of the officers who had gone to the World Cup in 1994. Did the Genesis consultants not read the Bastow Charlton report? They were given a copy. My view was that things should be done differently this time around. There had been major problems in 1994, not only with the ticket disaster that led to Merriongate in 1996. The hotels and training facilities were poor. Commercially, the tournament was a disaster for the Association.

I believe that a significant contributor to these problems was the lack of a clear distinction between the role of the officers and the role of the professional staff. I was going to rely on my full-time colleagues in Merrion Square. I know that this did not go down at all well with some of the officers. If they were not allowed to interfere, then I was undermining their authority. I thought that it was one of the ironies of the Genesis Report that they strongly advocated the development of a professional staff in the FAI, yet were critical of the FAI for adopting this route in the planning for Japan and Korea. Genesis' criticisms of our preparations were largely spurious.

*****

A key phase in the World Cup planning was the FIFA workshop in Tokyo in early February. The draw had been in Korea, so the workshop had to be in Japan. The biggest difficulty in the World Cup was the historic hostility between the Japanese and the Koreans. The cracks were papered over for the World Cup. Our only difficulty during the World Cup arose when we were transferring from Japan to Korea.

The workshop covered all aspects of the World Cup preparations. The travelling party included Mick McCarthy, as there was a half-day session for the managers; Martin Walsh for the medical seminar; Joe McGlue for security; Brendan McKenna for media; Peter Buckley for ticketing and Chris Ryan, who was co-ordinating the overall arrangements for the Association. It was three days well spent, as by the end we had a very clear idea of what was required. One of the biggest issues that came up was whether training sessions would be open to the public and the media. The big countries, with England as their spokesperson, wanted most sessions closed. In the end a compromise was reached. Traditionally, most of the Irish training sessions are open, so we did not have an issue with this. In any event, we were very much aware that our facilities and security at Chiba were top class and we did not anticipate any difficulties. We would be able to close off the training site if required.

During the World Cup workshop, we were introduced to our JAWOC liaison officers. There were four of them: Tsedui Sato was our main liaison officer (Ray Treacy very quickly nick-named him Dickie Rock because of his similarity in appearance); Hato was his assistant, and Kimi was our media liaison officer. She had previously worked for Disney World in Tokyo. We told her that she was therefore a very good choice for the Irish! We also had a security liaison officer, of whom we did not see much.

The Japanese people are great. However, everything must always be done absolutely by the rule book. They are not taught to be independent decision makers. Every time we wanted to change an arrangement, no matter how slightly, it caused consternation. Everything had to be discussed by everyone before any change could be made. We were always asked if we were sure we wanted to change. The decision had to be referred upwards to a superior authority. This approach is the polar opposite of that of the Irish. Despite this we got on very well with our liaison officers. By the end, they had got used to our way of doing things and began to understand the Irish sense of humour. We also had a good number of people allocated by the Izumo and Chiba Councils to help us. One thing we were not short of in Japan was local assistance.

It was during a coffee break in the workshop that I met the Nigerians and put in place Ireland's final warm-up fixture. I overheard them trying to arrange a fixture with another European country, but they were having difficulties. As they were drawn in a group that included both England and Sweden, they quickly agreed to come to Dublin. We played all four of our preparatory fixtures (Russia, Denmark, the US and Nigeria) at home, because it is financially rewarding to do so. We paid a fee to the visitors and met their access and accommodation costs while in Dublin. For each game, we could anticipate revenue from crowds of between 30,000 and 40,000, plus in some instances we could earn revenue from TV rights. These matches were lucrative for the Association. Most away matches are at best break-even, and frequently loss-making because of the high costs involved and the smaller attendances at most venues.

As Mick was only needed at the workshop for one day, he used the time to again visit Saipan and check on the arrangements there. Mick expressed himself happy. The rest of the group visited Chiba, where we signed the formal agreement to use their facilities and finalised the details of the financial and logistical support we would receive. While I was at the meeting in Chiba, Chris Ryan and Joe McGlue travelled from the hotel in Chiba to the stadium in Ibaraki and timed the run at fifty-eight minutes, well within the time specification set by Mick. We also visited the stadium at Yokohama, which was the venue for our match against Saudi Arabia and also the World Cup final. We could be the only team to play there twice!

The traffic between Tokyo and Yokohama is awful, despite a fantastic road network, consisting of a large number of motorways, sometimes operating at three different vertical levels. The volume of traffic is crazy. Tokyo is a large city and has invested heavily in road and transport infrastructure to allow it to function. It may not be aesthetically pleasing, but that is the compromise they have had to make to accommodate 13 million people.

It was during the trip to Yokohama in early February that we identified a potential difficulty in travelling from Chiba to Yokohama on match day. The distance was not far, but the duration of the trip was unpredictable, due to traffic. In addition, JAWOC could interfere and instruct the team to leave Chiba very early for the match. In the end, we solved this problem very simply. The team travelled to Yokohama on the morning of the match and had their pre-match meal and a rest in the Yokohama Sheraton Hotel. This cost the Association about $8,000, but it was worth it, as it removed any logistical difficulties on the day of the match and prevented us having to decamp entirely from Chiba.

After the workshop in Tokyo, we had a very clear view of what needed to be done. It was now a matter of putting it into place.

*****

Qualification for the World Cup provided a commercial opportunity for the Association. In both 1990 and 1994, the Association had got it badly wrong and had not made any money. According to the Bastow Charlton Report, the financial returns from these two tournaments were a loss of IR£132,000 from Italy and a profit of IR£176,000 from the US, roughly breaking even over the two tournaments. There were two problems. First, the players' and technical staffs' bonuses, which were set guaranteed figures, were too high. They were based on overly optimistic projected revenues from commercial opportunities. Second, the Association mismanaged their commercial opportunities and made little money from them. Putting it plainly, the players and support staff got virtually all the money from Italia 1990 and USA 1994. This could not be allowed to happen again.

In discussions with Peter Buckley, I developed the concept of a shared pool arrangement. All the money from commercial ventures by both the Association and players would be amalgamated into one fund and shared equally, after deductions of agreed expenses. Under this concept, both the players and the Association would benefit equally from the commercial opportunities available to them. This should guarantee the FAI a profit from the World Cup.

There was a lot of money due from FIFA, but not enough in my book. Apart from an initial grant of $100,000, FIFA met all our access transport costs at business fare rates from Dublin and provided a daily allowance of $450 per person, for forty-five people, from eight days before our first match to two days after the last. FIFA also paid the Association $1.5 million per match for the first phase, rising to $1.7 million for phase two and increasing thereafter, depending on how far the team advanced in the tournament. In addition, there were generous bonus payments from our gear sponsorship with Umbro, depending on the level of shirt and clothes sales. There was a lot of money available and it was vital that the Association should retain a substantial profit, rather than disperse it as bonuses. I hoped that a good profit would sustain the development of football in Ireland for a number of years.

Once the principle of a shared pool had been agreed with the players, the FAI side of it was managed by John Delaney and Peter Buckley. Steve Staunton, Niall Quinn and Roy Keane represented the players in the discussions. The players used Michael Kennedy as their main negotiator. Trevor O'Rourke and John Given of IIP would represent the players on the ground. Overall, the system worked quite well, even if the number of commercial deals brought in by the players was below expectations. They tried to focus on a select number of large deals, with only limited success.

The FAI had removed the players as competitors in sponsorship and commercial activities. Both sides benefited from this agreement. The biggest competitors now to the FAI in the market were Mick McCarthy and FIFA. Mick had his agent Liam Gaskin working hard and successfully on his behalf. Mick had the advantage of being a one-man show, which certainly eases the decision-making process. I expect that proposals got a very quick yes or no. The Irish team manager historically had a lot of commercial freedom, independently of the FAI, going back to Jack Charlton's days. The only stipulations were that he could not represent competitors of FAI sponsors. This worked reasonably well in the lead up to the World Cup, except for Mick's representation of Adidas Predator boots. This was the main factor in the delay in putting pen to paper on Mick's contract. This issue is dealt with in detail in Chapter 7, on Mick's resignation as Irish manager.

FIFA own the World Cup logo and all the rights to the World Cup event itself. These were to be exploited for the benefit of FIFA. The commercial revenue filters back to the Associations, under FIFA's Financial Assistance Programme, which grants each Association $250,000 a year for development. In addition, the profits from the UEFA Champions League and European Championships are used to support the Associations and clubs to a significant extent. One of the idiosyncrasies of the FIFA approach is that small Associations, such as the British Virgin Islands, get the same grant as Ireland or, indeed, Italy.

We were hauled over the coals by FIFA for using the World Cup logo unofficially. It appeared on the cover of the World Cup guide, which was produced on a franchise basis for us and made a reasonable contribution to our joint commercial pool. We were told by FIFA to withdraw the guide. We responded by saying that all copies had already been sold and that we would not use the logo on any reprint.

I had reached an agreement with the accountancy firm, Arthur Andersen, to get two people to assist us with our World Cup commercial activities. This was done on a semi-sponsorship basis and represented excellent value for the Association. We wanted to maximise our income. However, I was astounded to receive an instruction from John Delaney telling me that IIP would represent both the players and the FAI in all commercial dealings for the shared pool. This had been agreed in negotiations with the players. In my view, this was an attempt to sideline Eddie Cox from his role as commercial manager and also to sideline the expertise I had brought in from Arthur Andersen. It was also a horrific conflict of interest. The interests of the players and the FAI were different. There was no way I was handing over control of the FAI's commercial interests to outsiders, who also represented our main sponsors, Eircom. Luckily, I knew Trevor O'Rourke well and we quickly agreed a joint *modus operandi*, where all sides were kept fully informed and each concentrated on the deals they had going. At that stage, the FAI had about six commercial ventures in the frame, all of which turned out successfully.

One of the biggest commercial problems we had prior to the World Cup was the renegotiation of our contract with 7Up, one of our best sponsors in previous years. 7Up had focused on our underage game, sponsoring our All-Ireland schoolboy (SFAI) cups and our summer soccer clinics. Lucozade, who were represented by IIP, wanted to become our sports drink sponsor. However, there was serious competition between 7Up and Lucozade. John Givens of IIP approached John Delaney directly when Eddie Cox was reluctant to allow Lucozade in as a sponsor for fear of losing 7Up. The 7Up sponsorship was much more valuable to us than the proposal by Lucozade. John Delaney, in his capacity as Honorary Treasurer of the Association, agreed to the Lucozade sponsorship and pushed it through the FAI. This left Eddie Cox and me to sort out the resulting problems with 7Up.

The 7Up sponsorship was not due for renewal until after the World Cup. The argument was that soft drinks and energy drinks were two separate sponsorship categories. This is a reasonable argument on a product basis, but falls apart if the two brands compete directly with each other in some markets, as is the case with 7Up and Lucozade. The sports drink Gatorade is a 7Up product. The other problem was that Lucozade were promised branding and promotion opportunities that only much more valuable sponsors were entitled to. How could we look for more money from 7Up, if we could offer them less and were also promoting a rival product? In the end, 7Up decided to renew their sponsorship but on reduced commercial terms. 7Up are an excellent sponsor.

One of the ironies of all this is that the players use Gatorade, not Lucozade, as their isotonic sports drink. The drinks that were reported to have been missing on the Sunday in Saipan were Gatorade.

One further decision that was made at an officers' meeting early in 2002 was that there would be no staff World Cup bonuses, a fundamental change from the situation in both 1990 and 1994. The Association had made no money from either of these World Cups, and yet paid bonuses to everyone in the FAI. We planned to make a significant profit in 2002, but bonuses were banned. Fair enough, we needed the money to develop the game and to rebuild our financial reserves after the losses of the Eircom Park fiasco.

I was absent from an FAI Finance Committee meeting in September 2002, as I was in Geneva on Euro 2008 business. At this meeting, it was proposed and agreed that ticket office staff only would be paid a World Cup bonus. Staff matters are supposed to be the responsibility of the General Secretary, but this proposal was put forward and agreed to without my knowledge. I still do not know what scale of bonuses was proposed and whether they have been paid. Other staff members worked equally hard and successfully during the World Cup. This preferential treatment of some staff members by a subcommittee was hugely embarrassing for me, as I was the person who, on the instructions of the officers, had previously told the staff in general that there would be no World Cup bonuses. This was very disappointing, especially for the longer-serving staff members. It is yet another good example of how the FAI operate at times. It shows that there is not equal treatment by the FAI of their employees. If the voluntary committees make a decision and push it through their own committee structure, the professional staff can do nothing about it.

*****

One of the innovations that Mick introduced for the World Cup was video analysis of opponents. It was identified through a cold call to the Association from a company called Sports Tech International. Such systems had been in operation with some of the larger countries and in many of the English Premiership clubs for some time. The cost of the Apple Macintosh computer and the required software was about €25,000. In addition, there was the cost of bringing someone to Japan who knew how to operate the system. The basic premise of the system was that you input a match into the computer either directly from a (handheld) camera, which we purchased, or from a video feed from a television set.

The software was pre-programmed to instantly analyse key components of the game, looking at both ourselves and the opposition. Were the opposition attacking more from the right or the left? From where on the pitch did they tend to send in crosses? It could also instantly recall any piece of play, once the operator knew the time it occurred. The system was used for pre-match analysis. I know that Mick also obtained accurate data from the system on the Irish and opposition's performances before he did his post-match press interviews. I was allocated a budget of €50,000 by John Delaney to acquire the system and to meet the cost of bringing the analyst to the World Cup. Excluding the cost of the extra trip to Korea for phase two, the budget was largely achieved.

The analyst we acquired was a New Zealander called Ian Rogers, who joined Mick's technical team in Japan. I know the system was used extensively, with Ian watching and analysing the matches from a television feed in the stadium rather than watching it live. I also know that the system was used to video Jason McAteer in training, in order to check whether he had fully recovered from injury. Ian Rogers fitted in very well with the Irish squad and had a ball. Brian McCarthy, one of the FAI's regional development officers, has now been trained as the video analyst for Brian Kerr.

*****

FIFA introduced a new totally computerised ticketing system for the 2002 World Cup. The idea was that everyone who purchased a ticket would have their name printed on it. This was for security purposes, but it would also hopefully reduce black market sales, as all tickets would be traceable to the initial purchaser. Fans could buy tickets for the second and subsequent phases. They would be issued with a swipe card; the cards would be inserted into machines in Japan and Korea, which would then dispense the correct tickets. John Delaney and I attended a presentation on this system in Oporto in January 2002, during the draw for the Euro 2004 qualifiers. It looked superb on paper, or should I say, on audio visual presentation. If it worked, it would prevent a reoccurrence of the 1990 and 1994 FAI ticketing disasters. It would certainly cut out a lot of wheeling and dealing in tickets and would greatly reduce the role of the Associations in ticket purchase and distribution. From my perspective, it appeared to resolve a lot of potential problems for the FAI. Nonetheless, there was a lot of opposition to it from some countries, including Portugal.

Unfortunately, the World Cup was not the tournament to introduce a radical new ticketing system. It should have been tried out on a smaller tournament, so that the teething problems could be cleared up first. It had to deal with sixty-four matches in sixteen venues, with a possible attendance in excess of 3 million. In my view, the FIFA ticketing system, which was operated by an external agency, was not well enough resourced to cope with this volume of ticketing. Ironically enough, we included this system as part of our proposals for Euro 2008, arguing that it should be very efficient by that time. The ticketing system fell way behind its time schedule, and the tickets bought by fans through the FAI only arrived shortly before departure. The FAI ticket office recorded all the sales on our own system, which was a duplication of what the FIFA ticket system was doing. However, the FIFA system appeared to work well for people who bought tickets on the Internet. We were aware from reports that Irish fans were some of the largest purchasers of tickets online.

There was one problem we were going to avoid. This time, the FAI would not be the ticket agent for Irish fans. This was the practice that had caused the Merriongate scandal. Irish fans would get their own tickets from whatever source. In 1994, the FAI were expending a lot of resources and energy working as a ticket agent and achieving very little. Their impact was minuscule, despite the high profile of some officers of the time in chasing tickets. I was not going to allow this to be repeated.

The FAI bought their full allocation of tickets (8 per cent of each stadium) for the three first-phase matches. This was not on a speculative basis, as had been the case in 1990 and 1994. We were meeting specific orders, which had been fully paid for in advance. We were at no financial risk. As none of our opponents, Germany, Cameroon or Saudi, took up their full allocation, we were then entitled to purchase more tickets out of the quota allocated to them. Again, we had orders and payments for these tickets. In effect, we supplied tickets to everyone who had applied by the due application date, enclosing the full payment in advance. We purchased about 150 additional tickets for each Irish game to have in reserve. This, in the final analysis, cost the Association some money, but it was strictly limited. The only trading of tickets we did was to swap some of our complimentary entitlement for the group matches involving our direct opponents for their tickets for our games. It was a much more controlled system than in 1990 or 1994 and worked well. It was only when we qualified for the second phase that the officers took the decision that the FAI should purchase tickets for selling on to the fans. This had shades of 1994 in more ways that one, and did cost the Association money, as the tickets were on a non-return basis. As shall become evident later, there were other difficulties with the allocation of these tickets.

In 1994, the FAI bought nearly IR£300,000 worth of tickets for other (non-Ireland) games. This also was not going to be repeated. In 2002, we bought a small number of tickets for some games and for the quarter-finals through to the final. These were for selling on to FAI and football officials, sponsors and other individuals who might want to see these matches. This was done in a very small way, compared to 1994. However, it still cost the Association some money for two reasons. First, very few people wanted to see additional games and the Association were left with unsold tickets. Second, a number of tickets for games in the Tokyo area went missing while in Japan. It was later discovered that they had been given to an Irish fan by mistake, who had received them along with tickets for the England v. Argentina match in Sapporo. He only discovered them when he arrived at his destination. Their value had to be written off. This just proves that ticketing is a nightmare. Despite only purchasing a small reserve for the Irish games and a limited amount of other match tickets, each aspect cost the Association money. However, the amount was small and very far from the substantial ticket losses sustained in 1994.

*****

A few weeks before the World Cup, Brian Kerr came to me and said that he would prefer not to travel to the World Cup. As FAI technical director, he was entitled to be there. However, he felt that, given the duration of the tournament, he could be in the way of Mick McCarthy. Brian had no involvement in the senior team under Mick McCarthy. In addition, the U19 European Finals were taking place in Norway shortly after the World Cup ended, and Brian needed to be in Ireland to prepare the team (which eventually finished fourth and thus qualified for the FIFA U20 World Championship in Dubai). Brian also felt that Noel O'Reilly would handle the training sessions with the children in Izumo better, given the language barriers. Noel is an experienced child care worker, who has dealt with a lot of deaf children. Brian had a firm view on this, and so Noel O'Reilly was added to the FAI World Cup party in place of Brian. I understood all of Brian's reasons for this decision and believe that he was right.

It was suggested to me that I should bring a second doctor as part of the official party, given the age and health of some of the FAI officials travelling. Thus Dr Conal Hooper of UCD was added to the travelling party. I asked Conal to take charge of the doping control procedures for the Irish team after each match, as this would allow Martin Walsh to focus on dressing-room requirements. This worked well.

The final element of the World Cup preparation was the allocation of the official accreditation badges. Initially, FIFA decided that only forty would be allocated to each Association. Following representations at the World Cup workshop, this number was increased to forty-five. It was stated at the FIFA workshop that the senior officials of each Association would be entitled to VVIP tickets at the stadium and, as such, would not need accreditation. Genesis' criticism of the accreditation was mistaken. Rather than analysing the facts, they listened to the complaints of officers. The only difference between VVIP and accreditation was that accreditation gave you greater freedom in walking around the stadium.

The allocation of accreditation was one of the major rows between the officers of the Association and me during the World Cup. They were far from happy with being allocated VVIP tickets instead of accreditation and, of course, the story was inaccurately leaked by one of them to a number of Sunday newspapers. It was stated that the lack of accreditation for officers was an oversight on my part. This was not true. It was a deliberate decision. No country got more than forty-five accreditations. I would allocate them in the same way if I had to do it again, as I put the needs of the team and technical staff ahead of those of the officers of the Association.

Let me explain how I determined the allocation of the forty-five accreditations. There were twenty-three players in the squad. They had to come first. Next in line were Mick and his technical staff, which amounted to twelve[2] people. There were four FAI security people with us, led by Joe McGlue, the FAI chief security officer. They needed the freedom to be able to move around the stadium to do their job; this proved to be very important in a number of instances. This used thirty-nine of the forty-five available accreditations. The remaining accreditations, I allocated as follows: Milo Corcoran, President of the Association, as the head of our delegation to the World Cup; Ray Treacy, who was in charge of the travel arrangements for the team and the media and who needed to be able to move around the stadium; Brendan McKenna, FAI media officer, who had important roles at the media conferences after the matches; Chris Ryan and myself.

---

2. Mick McCarthy (manager), Ian Evan (assistant manager), Packie Bonner (goalkeeping coach), Martin Walsh (team doctor), Conal Hooper (team doctor with responsibility for doping control), Ciaran Murray (chartered physiotherapist), Mick Byrne (physiotherapist), Joe Walsh (kit man), John Fallon (Umbro kit), Ian Rogers (video analysist), Eddie Corcoran (team liaison officer) and Tony Hickey (team security). Other team security people remained at the team hotel.

The final accreditation I allocated to Mr Ito, who had been instrumental in bringing the Irish team to Izumo. He was also extremely helpful to us in finalising many of our arrangements in Japan. Having a native Japanese speaker as part of our group was a valuable asset to us. There was no way I could provide an additional four to the officers, who could not be included in the list, no matter how much they wanted it. Accreditation was of critical value at the stadia on match days. It was important that we had an effective operation there. This was my priority and I make no apologies to the officers.

The accreditation row became farcical in Japan. The officers expected to have accreditation and, hence, when three of them arrived in Niigata on the Thursday, 23 May, the day before the team arrived, they went to the FIFA centre seeking their accreditation. They were in fact accompanied there by an FAI staff member who had been at every World Cup planning meeting at which the accreditation was discussed and decided and who was therefore fully aware of the situation. In Japan, I had a meeting with the officers about every second day to keep them briefed on what was happening. They raised their lack of accreditation at the first meeting in Chiba on 4 June. They felt they needed accreditation, in their own words, to have free access in stadia for other (non-Ireland) matches they might like to attend, to be able to go out to the Irish fans at the stadia and allocate tickets (and I thought we had made a policy decision not to do this) and to have equal accreditation to other delegates (even though they had access to the same areas). Having a shiny piece of plastic on a chain around your neck seemed to be an important status symbol.

I should have anticipated this reaction. At the last officers' meeting before departure to Japan, I was informed that Michael Hyland would be in charge of transport for the World Cup. My interpretation of this was that it was to ensure that the officers had priority access to the official FIFA cars when they wanted them. Even though I explained that I had negotiated significant additional transport to be provided by Chiba City, this was not to their satisfaction. Michael Hyland would be transport officer. What impact would this have on our operations? That was not their concern. And this was the expertise Genesis rebuked me for not using!

I had to write to FIFA requesting additional accreditations. I told the officers that this would not be successful, as there was an absolute embargo on more than forty-five per Association. I got the anticipated rejection by return. I even offered the officers to change the accreditation allocation. By this stage, we had one spare one, as Roy Keane had gone home. Des Casey, as a UEFA Vice President, would be entitled to one in his own right. I asked Ray Treacy and Chris Ryan to forego their accreditation and they agreed, even though this would weaken our operation at the stadia. This would not satisfy the officers either. They preferred to play the role of 'martyrs' and have something to moan about, both within the FAI and to the media. I believe that this 'important' issue was discussed at all five meetings with the officers that were held in Japan and Korea. What a waste of time and energy.

The last issue to be resolved before departure was the remuneration of the technical support staff. In 1990 and 1994, they had been given the same bonuses as the players. We had changed the system and this level of bonus was not going to be available to them. If the players wanted to remunerate them from their part of the pool, then this was OK. We were setting a flat rate with the technical support staff, recognising that they would be away from home for at least a month and hopefully longer. An individual agreement had to be reached with everyone and it took some doing.

I know that one of the technical staff was upset with me because I spoke to him about it in a hotel corridor. I think he was more upset with the realisation that the FAI were not going to provide the guaranteed gravy train they had done in 1990 and 1994. Eventually by the Monday before the Sunderland match, all agreements had been reached, with everyone reasonably happy and the finances of the Association safeguarded. Incidentally, the officers of the Association and the General Secretary were allocated an allowance of €100 a day to meet their expenses while in the Far East.

*****

The squad, having been announced the previous Tuesday (7 May), gathered in Sunderland on Monday, 13 May, for the Niall Quinn testimonial game the following night. The only incident of note, apart from Roy Keane's absence, was the forced withdrawal of Mark Kennedy from the squad and the call-up of Stephen Reid. From Sunderland, it was back to Dublin for the match against Nigeria on the Thursday and the departure to Saipan on Friday, 17 May. I had a further six days in Dublin, much of it taken up with the 'Paul Marney' affair and Roy Dooney's departure from the post of league Commissioner, before setting out for Izumo on Thursday, 23 May. The events of Saipan, which dominated the first week, are dealt with in Chapter 4. Here I want to focus on the real action of the World Cup.

The World Cup

Izumo and Final Preparations

By the morning of Wednesday, 29 May, Roy Keane had decided he was not returning to the World Cup squad. Mick could finally focus on preparing the team for the match against Cameroon. Izumo was a perfect place for preparation. The training facilities were excellent and everything that Mick and the players wanted was provided. The Mayor and people of Izumo could not do enough for us. The Royal Hotel was for our exclusive use and the town provided superb security. The players had a large function area as their dining-room, recreation room and games room. The bedrooms were small, as is usual in Japan, so the players had a room to themselves rather than sharing.

Izumo is a small town by Japanese standards and is a mix of the urban and rural. Rice paddy fields are very common within the town boundary. It was part of Mick's plans to bring the players to different environments at different sages of the tournament to prevent boredom setting in. He certainly achieved this with Saipan, Izumo, Chiba and Seoul. Each location was very different from the others.

The people of Izumo were very supportive of the Irish team and turned out at all training sessions and functions in great numbers without ever intruding on the team's space. The Japanese are a very decorous people and are always anxious not to offend.

Noel O'Reilly's training sessions with the children of Izumo were hugely successful, and he has been back in Izumo since the World Cup as a guest of the town. There is a key difference between Irish kids and Japanese kids. The Japanese kids are very well disciplined. For example, they will wait until instructed before performing any task, even kicking a football. While this discipline probably has significant benefits in other areas of society, I wonder if it helps create the spontaneity required for a natural footballer. However, Noel has remarked on their ability to learn quickly.

There was some sort of a function every evening in Izumo. If there was no official function, we were brought out for a meal by the Mayor. As we were their guests, the Japanese felt obliged to entertain us and, given their generosity and hospitality, it was impossible to refuse. Functions started early and on time. Seven o'clock for dinner meant you were sitting down at seven o'clock. They also ended promptly. At ten o'clock, the function would be declared formally closed and everyone would leave. Between and even during the different courses, the guests would wander from table to table chatting to their acquaintances. This was all very different from an Irish function. Luckily, we were able to provide some Irish entertainment. Noel O'Reilly is an accomplished ballad singer and had brought his guitar. Linda performed some Irish dancing, to the tune of 'The Saints Go Marching In' played by Izumo's prize trumpeter. Our hosts favourite song was 'The Spirit of the Gael', which they adopted as their anthem for all official occasions.

On the Wednesday afternoon, Mick had allocated forty minutes of the players' time to coaching the children of Izumo in the Dome. They had put together twenty-three squads of twelve children, with one squad to be taken by each player. Packie Bonner filled in for the missing Roy Keane. I am sure that places on this session were like gold dust to the kids of Izumo. Again, everything was extremely well organised. Everything happened on the blast of a whistle. Each of the kids took their turn in an orderly fashion. There was no mobbing of the players. Overall, the football clinics by Noel O'Reilly and this session by the players were a huge PR success for the Association and Ireland with the people of Izumo. These occasions are the basis of sport. They are about sharing, learning, understanding and exchange.

It was on such occasions that we met lots of different people from the town. One of our interpreters at the main official dinner was Ayumi Mishiro, who was completing a doctorate in English at Bristol University. Interpreters sat behind the guests at the table and did not partake of the food. This took some getting used to. Ayumi has since visited Ireland with her parents and has become a friend of our family.

On one evening after a dinner, we were brought to the home of Nobby, one of the town's successful businessmen, who had donated the site for the Dome to the town. By Irish standards the house was modest, but it had its own ornamental garden. We were told that the garden was the best indication of the wealth and status of the house owner. Shoes were left at the front door. There was a Shinto shrine in the corner of the main room. The rooms were small and sparsely furnished by Irish standards. We were treated to a range of local delicacies, this after a large meal at a local restaurant. Everywhere we went, food played a very significant role. We had to sit cross-legged on cushions on the floor at a knee-high table. For me this is a physical impossibility.

One small incident in Izumo occurred in the Royal Hotel, when Robbie Keane was playing head tennis with Mayor Masahiro Nishio. Robbie misheaded the ball, and it hit a large crystal chandelier. The ball broke one of the glass fittings. When the hotel manager was alerted, he got Robbie to autograph the largest piece of broken glass. Robbie wrote 'sorry' and signed his name with a permanent marker.

The chandelier was repaired in such a way as to include this piece of glass. There is now a plaque on the wall, commemorating this incident; it has become a shrine to the stay by the Irish team in the Royal Hotel.

*****

One of the formalities of this week was a visit by FIFA personnel to inspect our gear. As I mentioned previously, FIFA had very strict regulations on the size and positioning of logos. Our gear had to be inspected to ensure that it complied. We did not expect any problems, as the gear had been manufactured to these specifications. The Irish team's gear was equal to the best available to any other squad. Umbro did us proud. Our inspectors were Pertti Alaja, from Finland, whom I knew well as he was heading up the Nordic bid for Euro 2008, and Marion Meyer from the FIFA administration. Everything was satisfactory, except that we had no goalkeeping gloves for Shay Given to show them. These gloves were being especially made by Sindaco, with a reduced logo to meet FIFA requirements, but they had not yet arrived in Izumo. This was the first I knew of the matter, but we assured the FIFA people that all was in order.

A pair of gloves arrived the next day by courier. However, the ones that arrived in Izumo belonged to David Seaman. Shay's gloves had been sent to the English camp in Sapporo. There was no way of rectifying this before the first game on Saturday. In any event, Shay would not use new gloves for the first time in a match. He would need to break them in during training for a few days first. Shay Given would have to play with 'illegal' gloves in the first match. How would we get away with this? The answer was secrecy. The fewer people who knew about it, the better chance we had of bypassing the FIFA regulations. My greatest fear was that if more FAI people knew about it, it would quickly be leaked to the media.

Niigata and Cameroon

By Friday, 31 May, the day before the match against Cameroon, it was time to leave Izumo and travel to Niigata. The preparations were over and the World Cup was about to start. JAWOC were providing a charter flight from Matsue Airport (near Izumo) to Niigata, a flight of just one hour, up the western coast of Japan. The trip was uneventful. The only issue we had to manage was that a significant number of our skips had to be sent by road directly to Chiba. They would not all fit on the plane and, in any event, there was no point in bringing all the equipment with us to Niigata, when it would not be needed until Chiba. One of our FAI security people travelled to Chiba with the skips and thus missed the match in Niigata.

We arrived into Niigata at lunchtime and went straight to the hotel. It was modest by previous standards, with small bedrooms. However, we were only going to spend one night here. I had to go to the FIFA hotel to meet the Cameroon Football Association President, in order to swap the complimentary tickets we had for the Cameroon v. Germany and Saudi games, for their complimentary tickets for our games against the same two teams. Having access to an additional 100 complimentary tickets for both games gave us a lot more flexibility.

On the day before each match, there is a formal meeting between the two Associations and the FIFA match delegates, to discuss a wide variety of issues, ranging from the expected number of fans to the security arrangements, media management, refereeing arrangements, doping control and team equipment. The meeting was held at the Swan Stadium and thus provided us with the opportunity to see yet another magnificent stadium. It was only twenty minutes from the team hotel. The FAI were represented at this meeting by Eddie Cox (FAI commercial manager), Martin Walsh (team doctor), Eddie Corcoran (team liaison officer), Joe McGlue (security), Chris Ryan and me. We were also accompanied by two of our JAWOC liaison officers.

There must about been at least forty people at the meeting, as the local police chief, fire officer and health official and any number of

FIFA administrators attended. The meeting was chaired by the FIFA-appointed match delegate. The referees and the FIFA referee delegate, a former referee who assesses the performance of the officials, were also there. Similar meetings, but on a smaller scale, happen before each competitive international match and, indeed, before each European Champions League and UEFA Cup match. It is a good practice and ensures that everyone knows what will happen and that all arrangements have been made. It is a case of making absolutely sure that there will be no hiccups, as most people in attendance are experts in their area and are very experienced in match arrangements.

One of the key elements of such meetings is the inspection of the gear, mainly to ensure that there is no clash of colours. Cameroon was the 'home' team for this match and thus had first choice of strip and access to the home dressing-room. However, there was no clash of colour, and Mick decided to use the green strip. Cameroon's attempt to use sleeveless shirts had been ruled out by FIFA. Our only issue was Shay Given's gloves, with their oversized logo. We decided not to bring goalkeeper's gloves with us to the inspection, relying on the previous week's inspection in Izumo. We 'confirmed' that all our gear had been inspected the previous week and had been found to be in order. We got away with it, and Shay used gloves in the match the next day that were not compliant with the FIFA regulations on gear advertising.

Good luck telegrams flooded into the team hotel the night before the match, including messages from the Archbishop of Dublin, Desmond Connell; the Irish rugby team, who were playing in New Zealand; and GAA PRO Danny Lynch.

*****

Each team are entitled to train at the stadium on the evening before a game. Mick brought the team to the stadium that evening for a light training session.

The day of the Cameroon game, 1 June, dawned bright, sunny and hot. However, the humidity was less that we had been told to expect.

I don't know what it was like for the players, but the hope was that the two weeks' acclimatisation had worked. One of the problems of this game was the afternoon kick-off. It would be very hot in the stadium. This would suit the Cameroon team. However, we were also aware that the Cameroon's arrival in Japan had been delayed by disputes over contractual payments with the players. Mick had seen them play England in Osaka the previous Sunday, and had been impressed by their mobility and physical strength.

Before the game, Milo Corcoran and I walked around the Irish section of the stadium. We were again amazed by the number of supporters. We had expected between 6,000 and 7,000 Irish fans, based mainly on our own direct ticket sales, which were not far short of 4,000. However, it looked as if double that number had turned up, swelled to no small extent by Japanese supporters who had adopted the green. A significant number of supporters had travelled up from Izumo for the match, including Mayor Nishio, who was wrapped in a tricolour. Everyone was in great spirits, with the Roy Keane departure largely, but not quite, forgotten.

The FAI security people mounted an operation at the entrances to the stadium. They confiscated five anti–Mick McCarthy banners – five out of a possible 2,000 banners and flags. Most people wanted to move on. The flags were returned to those supporters after the game. However, with the good result against Cameroon, it was the last dealing we had with the very small number of fans in Japan on the anti-Mick side.

Watching a game like Ireland v. Cameroon in the World Cup finals is not enjoyable. Tension dominates. It was vital that we got a result. Defeat would make qualification very difficult for us. Cameroon started well, but there were very few clear-cut chances for either side until they scored in the thirty-eighth minute. Steve Staunton got turned on the left-hand side of our box and we were undone. One–nil to Cameroon at half-time left us feeling very tense and insecure. Could we get back into the game?

Early in the second half, the shadow of the stadium began to extend across the pitch. The temperature dropped somewhat, but it was still very warm. This helped the Irish team. We did not have long to wait for Matt Holland to equalise from the edge of the box in the fifty-second minute. The shot didn't appear to be that hard and it was a long way out, but it beat the Cameroon goalkeeper low at the near post. Delight, relief and many other emotions were quickly at the surface. Could we go on and win, which would almost certainly guarantee us qualification for the second phase? We finished the stronger team, but in the end had to settle for a draw. Robbie Keane almost did it for us in the eighty-first minute with a shot that came off the post. From my angle in the stand, it looked like it had gone in. We also had a good claim for a penalty for hand ball turned down.

We learned that Germany had thumped Saudi 7–0. This put the Germans in pole position. Qualification would now depend on Cameroon's and Ireland's relative results against Germany and Saudi Arabia. It was a satisfactory start. We had proved that we were a good team and would be competing strongly for qualification out of the group.

*****

The media constitute a very significant part of the World Cup, and FIFA devote a huge amount of resources to keeping it this way. The World Cup is 80 per cent a television and newspaper event, with the fans who actually go to the matches taking a back seat. Sometimes, I feel that the fans, who incur huge costs, are short-changed by FIFA. The media emphasis is driven by financial considerations. FIFA make nearly all their money from the television rights of the World Cup and sponsorship by leading multinational companies. This income has to last for four years, until the next World Cup.

There are a number of media zones at each stadium; one of these is called the mixed zone. The players have to exit the stadium through the mixed zone. There is no other way out. The mixed zone consists of a room with a roped-off passageway, which the players must use to pass by the different media: first the written press, then radio and finally television. The players must leave the stadium through this passageway, but it is up to them whether they stop and talk to the press or simply move on. The Irish players were very open with the media in the mixed zone throughout the tournament, and most stopped when requested to. Of course, some of these interviews were pre-arranged and may have been commercially motivated. In addition, both Mick McCarthy and an Irish player, in this case Steve Staunton as captain, were obliged to give a television interview, which was available to all the media in the stadium via a video link. The mixed zone system works well. It cannot be operated in Lansdowne Road due to the lack of space and facilities. In Lansdowne, there is usually a scramble between the media and the players to get the after-match quotes.

*****

After the match, we travelled by charter to Tokyo (Hameda airport), wanting to get settled into the New Otani Hotel in Chiba as quickly as possible. We had fought hard with JAWOC to procure this charter. It was only four days to the next match against Germany in Ibaraki. The purpose of travelling straight after the match was to make the following day, Sunday, a day of preparation rather that a day of travel. When the media interviews were over, the team went straight to the airport. The team bus and the officials' bus were brought straight onto the tarmac at the airport. It looked like things were moving very efficiently. Wrong! We had to wait quite a while on the tarmac. The Japanese organisers probably assumed that we wanted to keep the team segregated from the fans, who would also be using the airport. We would have been much better off if we had used the normal check-in desks and had access to the facilities, including toilets, in the terminal. We had to wait on the tarmac until the media who were travelling with us reached the airport. They had to file their reports and stories from the stadium.

If we thought that being driven straight onto the runway was going to reduce the check-in formalities, we were again wrong. The Japanese set up a check-in desk and a security (metal detection) gate at the plane and everyone had to go through the procedures, as if we were in a terminal building. Then, as the players, technical staff and officials were queuing, it started to rain. Umbrellas appeared from nowhere and were held over us by the Japanese airport staff. It was all quite funny in a surreal way. Everyone took it in good spirits, as we were all happy with the result.

Reports had already reached us about Eamon Dunphy's behaviour on RTÉ during their World Cup programme. The general reaction was that it was par for the course for Dunphy. One person was certainly not going to let old rows subside and provide committed support to the team during the World Cup.

There were no hitches on the trip to Chiba, apart from it taking slightly longer that we had hoped. When our escort was taken over by the police from Chiba, at the city boundary, the speed of travel increased. For one of the few times in Japan, the speed limit was exceeded. We arrived into the New Otani in Chiba at about 11 pm. We were greeted by all the hotel staff, who lined up to applaud the team and wave the tricolour. Eddie Corcoran had, as usual, travelled directly from Izumo to Chiba to ensure that all the players' rooms were correctly allocated and that normal check-in procedures could be avoided. I can only assume that the players' comment in the Genesis Report that 'our eyes were out on sticks' refers at least in part to the New Otani Hotel. I doubt if any other team in the World Cup stayed in a better hotel. It was our fixed base for the next twelve days.

Ibaraki and Germany

The following morning, the team trained at the Inage Seaside Park. Again, I am sure that the players' eyes were out on sticks at the quality of the facilities and the attention they received from our Japanese hosts. Every pitch used in the World Cup had the same type of grass; the training pitches also used this grass. They were all developed especially to meet this standard. It was a thicker and heavier grass that we are used to in Ireland. The pitch was fully fenced off, and there was the possibility of erecting a 6-foot canvas screen to make the area private. The media had their own secure benched area separate from the fans at the training pitch, where they could observe training. Perhaps 2,000 Japanese and Irish fans watched every Irish training session. The local authority had set up a ticketing system to control the crowds. Demand for these tickets far exceeded the supply. Many of the Japanese fans dressed in green for the training sessions. They reacted with enthusiasm to everything that went on.

After the training sessions, there was a daily press conference, using the media facilities we had agreed with Chiba. There was a large interview room, more than adequate to accommodate all the media comfortably, with a platform for television cameras at the back. There were separate rooms for one-on-one interviews, if required. There were about thirty work stations for journalists with the required telephone lines, ISDN lines and e-mail connections. These facilities were especially installed by Chiba City for our use during the World Cup and would be removed immediately afterwards. There were free hot and cold drinks. Not one journalist complimented the FAI on the standard of these facilities or thanked us for arranging them.

*****

One of the first issues we had to deal with after arriving in Chiba was to do with the players' families. It had been agreed well in advance that the players would make their own arrangements for their families and that the FAI would look after them on match days by providing transport and tickets. As usual, the family members would join the players for the after-match meal in the team hotel. Mick usually gave the players the night after the match off. I was aware that the arrangements for the families had been poor in 1994, and was anxious to avoid a repeat. If the FAI were not making the arrangements, we could not be blamed if things went wrong. Therefore, the FAI had no direct input into the arrangements, but gave commitments on transport and tickets, which were more than met. The players made the arrangement through a travel agent. However, reports had reached us in Chiba that the arrangements made for the players' families were very poor. Many of the families included very young children. The trip out had been a disaster, with lengthy delays and a bad flight service. This has been well reported in the media. The hotel they were using in Tokyo was reported to be below standard. Maybe some of the players now respect the lengths to which the FAI go to get things right. The players took responsibility for the travel and accommodation arrangements of their families and these were a disaster.

Unhappy families meant distracted players. Between Ray Treacy and Chris Ryan, alternative accommodation was found in Chiba and the necessary transport arranged. The problems were solved. Thus, for the duration of the stay in Chiba, it was not uncommon to see the players strolling around Chiba with their wives and children during their time off. The fans based in Chiba totally respected this. The FAI should have no responsibility for the travel and accommodation of the players' families. However, in this case, we very quickly came to the rescue and no further difficulties arose. I find it extraordinary that Genesis recommended that the FAI should make travel arrangements for players' families. This is a recipe for further criticism. How the mess between the players' families and their travel agent was sorted out, I have no idea.

*****

It was at the first officers' meeting in Chiba that the rows over the World Cup review and the accreditation arose. Some of the officers had obviously discussed and decided on a World Cup review amongst themselves, prior to the officers' meeting in Chiba. The review would examine the problems encountered during the World Cup. Milo Corcoran and I opposed the review on the basis that, whether it was needed or not, this was not the time to decide on it or announce it. It would only keep the rows going. We wanted to wait until the World Cup was over, when we could have a better overall view. However, the decision about the World Cup review was mainly about political power, and precipitated a part-temporary and part-permanent shift in allegiances among the officers. It quickly brought it home to me that my position within the Association was going to be undermined and that a public autopsy on Saipan was the lever that was going to be used. We had only been in Japan for three days. All arrangements were first class, but power politics dictated that fingers of blame had to be pointed. The members of the Association do not unite at times of crisis; rather individuals seek to position themselves to their own advantage.

What was extraordinary was that some of the officers wanted the World Cup review announced immediately prior to the Germany game. Whether this would undermine Mick and unsettle the team and the players was irrelevant. John Delaney was leading this charge and I was the target. I believe that Delaney's support for Mick was lukewarm, despite many professions of friendship. He made many attempts to publicly undermine my relationship with Mick. His father, Joe, had been one of the two people on the five-man manager selection committee in 1996 that had opposed Mick's appointment.

Throughout the World Cup, John Delaney was very close to the group of Sunday newspaper journalists who were critical of Mick McCarthy.

Milo Corcoran argued strongly against the World Cup review. He had been the only officer in Saipan and was totally supportive of Mick. Despite being a fan of Manchester United, Milo put the blame for Saipan firmly at Roy Keane's door. Milo and I succeeded in having the announcement postponed until after the Germany game. At least, if only for the short term, the needs of football took priority over internal political considerations.

*****

The Germany game came fast. The four days between the first two matches was the minimum allowed between World Cup games. Mick decided not to train in the Ibaraki stadium on the Tuesday evening, preferring not to subject the players to a two-hour bus journey the evening before the game. The usual pre-match meeting took place at the stadium in Ibaraki. The key issue was travel time to the stadium for both teams. The Germans were staying somewhat nearer to the stadium than we were. The Japanese police claimed that it could take between two and a half and three hours for the trip from Chiba. This was absolute nonsense. We had timed the trip in February at approximately one hour and had verified it that day, travelling at the permitted speed limit of 55 mph.

There was a protracted discussion. We asked that there be no police escort, so that we could exceed the speed limit if required; this was a non-starter with the organisers. In Japan, police escorts are for security and to ensure that you obey the speed limits; they obey all traffic signals. In Ireland, the object of a police escort is to get from A to B as quickly as possible, moving other traffic aside if needs be. Mick agreed to leave a half hour earlier than planned, and as a result arrived at the stadium a half hour earlier then he wanted to. This was two hours before kick-off, rather than the normal ninety minutes. The Germans arrived exactly ninety minutes before kick-off.

The stadium area is very secure. You cannot get into any area without having the correct pass. We had a pass for the team bus, two cars and a minivan for the VIP parking area. We parked as directed. As the officials were leaving the cars and buses and examining their tickets to see what part of the stadium they were seated in, the German team coach arrived. We stood and watched. Security people were panicking, moving people out of the way. This led to an allegation by FIFA's head of security, at a post-match press conference, that the Irish had transported fans on the team bus and these fans had therefore got into a restricted area. Unfortunately, no one checked with the FAI before making these comments in a public arena. I found out about them through the media and it led to a series of telephone conversations and faxes between FIFA and me until a correction was issued.

The team bus is sacrosanct. Not even the President or General Secretary of the Association will travel on it without the express permission of Mick McCarthy. In six years as Honorary Treasurer and

General Secretary, I was on it twice, once in Estonia when I inadvertently got left behind at the stadium, and again on the journey to the homecoming in the Phoenix Park after the World Cup. Apart from the team and technical staff, there were only two other people on the bus, Monsignor Liam Boyle from Limerick and Fr Paddy O'Donovan from New Jersey, who are unofficially part of the technical staff and have been so for years.

Unbelievably, our security people were asked to remove Irish flags and banners that mentioned a product, a pub or anything that smacked of a commercial enterprise. It was in the World Cup regulations that stadium advertising was reserved for the World Cup sponsors and these flags and banners conflicted with the sponsors' exclusive rights. What a load of rubbish! Our security people refused to assist in removing the 'offending' banners. Any attempt would have created chaos.

With the evening kick-off, the temperature for the Germany game was somewhat lower than in Niigata and the pitch was in shadow for the most part. Even more Irish fans had turned up than for the Cameroon game.

The Germans started very strongly and we were quickly under severe pressure. We only held out until the nineteenth minute, when Klose headed in a cross from Ballack on a quick German counterattack. Our defence were nowhere. It was very much a damage-limitation exercise in the first half. We had some chances, but so had the Germans. We got to half-time just 1–0 down and it could have been worse. We were aware that Cameroon were struggling somewhat against Saudi Arabia, which was some good news.

We were transformed in the second half. We attacked the Germans, and for the most part they defended their lead. They had a few opportunities on the break, but we were dominating, creating chances but failing to equalise. With twenty minutes to go, Mick made a brave tactical decision. He took off Ian Harte and Gary Kelly and brought on Niall Quinn and Stephen Reid. We were committed to attack in a 3–4–3 formation. However, Oliver Khan was not rated the world's No. 1 goalkeeper without just cause. He brought off a string of outstanding saves.

Time was running out for us, as the game entered additional time of three minutes. There was time for one last attack. Steven Finnan played in a long ball towards Niall Quinn, who nodded it into the path of Robbie Keane. Robbie squeezed the shot between Khan and his near-hand post. Khan got his hand to it but could not keep it out. The stadium erupted. Apart from the photographs of Robbie scoring, the undying image from this moment is the photograph of Mick McCarthy as he realised that Robbie had scored. His jaw has dropped in disbelief.

John Treacy, Chairman of the Irish Sports Council, had joined us in Chiba and stayed with us for the duration of the tournament. After the match, he described it as one of the best ever Irish sporting occasions, ranking it with Sonia O'Sullivan's World Championship victory.

Two points from two draws with the top two teams in the group kept us very much in contention. We heard that Cameroon had beaten the Saudis 1–0. Qualification was now in our own hands. If we beat Saudi by at least two goals, we would qualify for phase two, no matter what happened in the match between Germany and Cameroon. We were a very happy camp as we made our way back to Chiba. The Germany game was one we could have lost, which would have made qualification difficult. In the end, the Germans were trying to hold out, which they failed to do.

One of the after-match events was the mandatory doping test. Two players from each team were selected by lots at half-time to give an after-match urine sample, which was then tested for FIFA's extensive list of banned substances. Robbie Keane and Richard Dunne were the unlucky two after the Germany match. Robbie had played the full ninety minutes in blazing heat and had exhausted most of his body fluids. Despite a significant intake of fluids after the match, it took Robbie well over an hour to supply the sample. During this period, he was secluded from the rest of the squad in the stadium medical room. Dr Conal Hooper was with the players throughout this period.

It was after Ireland's very strong finish in the German game that we realised that the Irish team were very well acclimatised. Saipan had achieved what it was supposed to have done in terms of fitness for Japan's climate. At subsequent press conferences, the Irish players continually stated that Saipan had been great for acclimatisation and they were comfortable playing in Japanese conditions. This was also the conclusion of the Genesis Report.

*****

Back at the New Otani in Chiba, the normal after-match meal took place in a private room upstairs. The players were joined by their extended families. Steve Staunton had just won his 100th cap for Ireland and Milo Corcoran presented him with a Waterford Glass trophy to mark his achievement. This trophy had been especially brought out to Japan by the FAI in anticipation of this event.

Not all the officers of the FAI attended this function. The FAI had decided to open the bar downstairs to all comers at the expense of the FAI. This had been done this without consulting the President, Milo Corcoran, the Honorary Secretary, Des Casey, or me, as General Secretary. We were not aware that it had happened until we received reports of it the following morning. My initial information came by e-mail from a friend in Ireland, commenting on press reports that the FAI had opened the bar in Chiba for the night. Why we were celebrating two draws is still beyond my understanding. Surely, the appropriate time for such a celebration was when we had qualified for phase two.

However, none of the fans, players or media who attended the boozing session objected to a night-long supply of free drink, especially when a bottle of beer cost €9. No controls were put on who could benefit from this 'generosity' and I believe no limit was put on what could be spent. This was the FAI at their most outlandish, and publicly confirming all the impressions of an organisation out of control. The rule appeared to be that if you were in the sports bar of the hotel on that night, then you were lucky. I know this, as my daughter and my sister were two of the beneficiaries for a while. They told me the next morning that their information was that Chiba had opened the bar. I was at the meeting with Chiba when the bar bill was discussed. While Chiba City may have ended up paying for the bar tab, it was an FAI decision to open the bar. At that time, the FAI could not have known that we would later pressurise Chiba to meet this part of the bill.

My firm recollection is that the bar bill came to €20,000. This was the figure used by Chiba City officials. It was also the figure used in the exposé by Paul Hyland in the *Evening Herald*. I suspect that most Irish journalists who were at the World Cup attended that boozing session. It was months later, in early 2003, that Paul Hyland decided to write about it.

The FAI PR spin was that I had leaked the story. This is nonsense, as the story was in the public domain for months before. On the morning of publication of Hyland's article, I received a phone call from Paul asking me to confirm that the bar bill in Chiba was between €35,000 and €40,000. He already had the story. I told him that this was way too high and that a figure of half that would be more accurate. My approach was that, if a story was breaking, then provide an accurate estimate to reduce incorrect speculation. The FAI PR spin machine went into overdrive, denying key elements of the story. I received another phone call from Hyland the following day. He had obviously come under a good deal of pressure. I confirmed to him that the story as he had written it was largely correct. There is little point in trying to re-invent facts when dealing with the media. That will eventually lead to more problems.

On the morning we were leaving Chiba, John Delaney, Peter Buckley and I sat down with Tsatumi Ono to reconcile the hotel bill, and to clarify what Chiba City would pay for under our agreement and what was for the FAI account. Ono stated that Chiba would not pay the bar bill, as it was not part of our agreement, which covered accommodation, food, soft drinks, transport, laundry and access to the fitness club. Alcoholic drink was excluded. However, we were below budget on these other areas and Ono was eventually persuaded that the bar bill should be included as part of Chiba's budget. Chiba City Council had treated us brilliantly and been very generous; it was highly embarrassing trying to extract this money from them. However, it allowed John Delaney to claim that the boozing sessions had not cost the FAI, even though he could not have been aware of this at the time it was decided to throw open a night-long free bar to all comers.

*****

During our time in Chiba, the issue of Mick McCarthy's additional bonus arose and this had significant ramifications later. It is dealt with in detail in Chapter 7. The officers of the Association were told by John Delaney, who had spoken to Mick and his agent, Liam Gaskin, that Mick would not sign off on his new contract without the payment of an additional bonus for exceptional performance – even though the contract had been operational since February. Both Milo Corcoran and I had spoken separately to Liam Gaskin the previous day and had been informed that there were no issues with the contract and that Mick would sign it at an opportune time. In any event, it had been agreed and was operational.

What had caused this *volte face*? What we were not told at the time was that, during his conversations with Mick and Liam Gaskin, John Delaney had suggested that Mick should seek an additional performance bonus of Stg£100,000 from the FAI before signing the contract. It was reported in *The Sunday Times* that John Delaney's initial conversation with Mick took place late at night in a bar. This appears to have been during the famous boozing session after the Germany game. However, Delaney did not disclose his conversation and bonus offer to his fellow officers or to me as General Secretary. He misled us by stating that the bonus was required to achieve Mick's signature on the contract, and that this issue had arisen due to my delay in getting Mick to sign the contract.

*****

The morning after the Germany game, John Treacy informed me that the new Irish government had been announced. The FAI had developed an excellent working relationship with the previous Minister for Sport, Jim McDaid. We were surprised by the appointment of John O'Donoghue. Apart from being aware that he had been the previous Minister for Justice, was from Killarney and most likely had a GAA background, we knew nothing about the new minister. We sent him a message of congratulations. John Treacy also informed me that if Ireland progressed to the second phase, Minister O'Donoghue would travel to Korea to support the Irish team.

John Treacy had an additional piece of good news: the Programme for Government was committed to building a new national stadium.

*****

There was a five-day gap between the German game and the Saudi game. We did not need to move base. The squad quickly settled into a routine. We just had to defeat Saudi Arabia by two goals and we were moving on to Korea.

I used this time to make contingency arrangements for travelling to Korea. The likelihood was that we would finish second in the group and would be playing in Suwon, close to Seoul. If, by a freak set of results, we won the group we would be playing in Jejou, a holiday island off the south coast of Korea, which we knew had excellent hotels and facilities. For phase two, we were going to locations that had previously been used by other teams. Hence, there should be few difficulties.

Eddie Corcoran and Ray Treacy travelled to Seoul to assess hotels and facilities. It was an overnight trip. This time, Mick decided on a centre city location to again change the environment for the players. When Eddie and Ray returned, they had selected the Westin Chosun Hotel for the team, one of the best and most expensive hotels in Seoul. It was not feasible to negotiate preferential terms with our host city for phase two. Hence, we were relying on FIFA's daily allowance and the additional $1.7 million we would earn for qualifying for phase two. Neither Ray nor Eddie had managed to inspect the allocated training facilities. This would have to be sorted as soon as we arrived. As at least four teams had been based in the Seoul area for phase one, it was unlikely to be a problem.

*****

We made the final decision that the team would travel to Yokohama on the morning of the Saudi game and have the pre-match meal and a rest in the Yokohama Sheraton. This was the best decision and was well within the normal travel patterns for professional footballers. However, it was an expensive decision for the FAI, as the hotel required full room rates, although the rooms would only be used for a few hours. It worked well for the team and that was what was important.

We had our usual pre-match meeting at the stadium in Yokohama on the Monday evening. We ran into an unforeseen problem. The Saudi goalkeeper had opted for a black jersey. This was a change from what had been specified prior to the World Cup and was a direct clash with Shay Given's normal black jersey. Saudi were the nominated home team and they, therefore, had choice of colour. Under World Cup rules, a clash of colour had to be avoided for goalkeepers in case, for example, one of them decided to come into the opposing penalty box for a corner kick. None of us at the meeting knew the colour of Shay's reserve jersey. I nominated yellow. After the meeting, I spoke to the match delegate, who was a very understanding gentleman, and agreed with him that I would telephone him with the actual colour when I got back to the team hotel. I assured him that we would avoid a clash of colour.

On our return to the team hotel, we discovered that Shay's reserve jersey was a combination of blue and grey. However, it had been packed into the skips and sent to the airport for onward transportation by DHL, either to Seoul or Dublin. I could not believe this. There could be any number of reasons why a second supply of kit could be needed at a match, but ours was in transit. Eddie Cox got in touch with DHL and went to the depot at Narita airport. With their help, he found the correct skip and rescued the jersey. Contact was made by phone with the match delegate and approval was received to use the blue/grey jersey.

A number of people had travelled out from Ireland specifically for the match. Among them were my son, Ronan, two of his friends, Damien and Chris, my cousin, Yvonne, and two of her family, Paul and Lisa. They had discovered a €250 fare out of London. They spent less than twenty-fours hours in Japan before returning to Ireland. They spent more time in the air than on the ground, but they all thoroughly enjoyed the occasion.

Despite the 72,000 capacity of the stadium and the small number of Saudi fans, the game was sold out. There was a significant number of Irish fans without tickets for the match. I was getting reports to this effect from the FAI security people out among the fans. I approached FIFA's ticketing people and they made whatever tickets were left available to Irish fans. They went out and sold the tickets directly to the fans, rather than dealing through the FAI, which was a relief. The good reputation of the Irish fans helped in this regard, as I am sure that FIFA would not have been so obliging for fans from some other countries.

The match against Saudi was again an evening kick-off. For the first time, the forecast Japanese humidity had arrived. It was very hot and clammy and, I suspect, the players found it more difficult. There was a sticky, light drizzle.

We needed two goals and got off to the best possible start, when Robbie Keane volleyed home Gary Kelly's cross in the seventh minute. The Saudi goalkeeper probably should have saved it, but no one was complaining. The task was now to score the second goal. During the first half, the Saudi's created quite a few chances, as we lost our usual pattern of play. At half-time, we heard that Germany were beating Cameroon. This was good news for us, as in these circumstances any Irish win would do. We relaxed a little bit in the stand. Gary Breen put us totally at our ease with a goal in the sixty-first minute and Damien Duff completed the scoring two minutes from time. We were definitely through and the celebrations started well before the final whistle.

Robbie Keane's name again came out of the hat for the doping control test. He was far from impressed.

We travelled back to Chiba in a great mood. We were celebrating, but were also aware that we were very much in a new phase. Our opponents in the second round would not finally be known until the next day, but Spain were odds-on to win their group. We definitely would be playing in Suwon on the following Sunday. The after-match meal again took place with the players, their families and officials. The following day was a day off, as we had made the firm decision that, whether we qualified or had to go home, we would not travel until the Thursday.

Seoul, Suwon and Spain

The transfer between Japan and Korea was always going to be potentially difficult. We were aware of this and tried to cover all angles in advance. However, while problems did occur that delayed our departure from Hameda airport, they were not too significant.

The problem arose because the organising committee provided us with a smaller plane that they had promised. I am not sure whether this was the Japanese committee (JAWOC) or the Korean World Cup Organising Committee (KOWOC). We did not become aware of this until check-in at the airport. Despite the skips being sent on in advance by DHL, the plane could not carry the rest of the luggage. There was committee meeting after committee meeting between the Japanese, but nobody seemed to have the authority to resolve the problem. The Japanese were blaming the Koreans, who were not there to defend themselves. With Ray Treacy's advice, we decided that the media luggage could not be accommodated on the plane and would travel separately. This allowed us to depart Hameda after a delay of close to one hour.

The FAI provided two of their security personnel to accompany the media luggage. It would travel from Narita airport on the other side of Tokyo, which meant a two-hour road journey. JAWOC tried to charge us for the cost of transporting this luggage, but we refused to pay for it. The luggage arrived into Seoul later that day and was delivered to the media personnel at their hotel. A problem that should not have arisen was well resolved.

Despite not having all the luggage with us, there was a shortage of transport for the luggage at Seoul airport. Apparently, the vans had initially gone to the wrong airport. My memory of this is a lot of luggage on the pavement outside the terminal and Mick Byrne dancing a jig of annoyance and giving out about the FAI. (I thought he was part of the FAI.) The team went on their way to the hotel, about an hour's drive into the centre of Seoul. The luggage vans came along shortly afterwards and everyone's luggage was with them not long after they got to their rooms. We would all have been better off, if people whose responsibility it was to sort out the problems, had been left to do their job. It is unrealistic to expect that there would be no minor glitches, and this proved to be the case. From the day of arrival in Japan to the day of departure from Korea, the organisation on the FAI's part was excellent.

The Westin Chosun Hotel was five star and well above the standard required. Eddie Corcoran had again travelled a day in advance and all was ready for the team when they arrived. The key issue was to ensure that the training facilities were satisfactory. Mick and I arranged to inspect the allocated facilities that evening. We were accompanied by our Korean liaison officer, who was called Woody. We were brought to the facilities that had previously been used by the Chinese team. They were located in a small stadium about forty minutes from the hotel. Our first impressions were reasonably favourable. However, the pitch was terrible. I never saw the pitch in Saipan, but it had to be better than this. I do not understand how the Chinese accepted it, nor how these facilities were approved as an official training camp by KOWOC. Roy Keane would have been very unhappy and justifiably so.

We immediately entered into discussions with KOWOC to identify alternative facilities. The Korean Army's Academy of Sports was recommended. Mick and I arranged to inspect this facility first thing in the morning, before the team went training. Korea has compulsory military service, and all the country's top sports people were posted to this camp on conscription. In a country like Korea, the army facilities were likely to be superb. This proved to be the case. The facilities were on a par with Japan, and, needless to say, we would have no difficulty with security. We could even have kept the media away if we wanted to. The Korean army were delighted to welcome the Irish team. Their facilities had been turned down as an official training camp. How this had happened, I do not understand.

The camp commander watched the Irish training sessions and had his son's photograph taken with Mick McCarthy. He ordered a large ice-box of cool drinks for the media, which was much appreciated by them. He gave permission for the regular pre-match kick about between the FAI and the media to take place at his facilities. I watched one of these events in Chiba and to call it football would be contrary to the Trades Description Act. If the commander had turned up at that, he would have fallen off his chair with laughter.

The commander was extremely hospitable not only to the team but also to the media entourage. I believe that if you treat people with courtesy and respect their traditions and customs, then they will push the boat out for you. This was certainly the case at the army training facilities in Seoul. They could not do enough for us. For example, as soon as the Irish training session had finished, the pitch was cut and re-marked in preparation for the following day. In addition, a detail, obviously either of raw recruits or those with demerits, cleaned the place of all litter, including the media's empty drink cans.

*****

The FAI, through our officers, decided that we should be the ticket providers for the Irish fans for the Spanish game – a throwback to the bad old days of 1990 and 1994. I still do not understand this decision. The tickets were freely available at FIFA offices in Seoul.

The match was not a sell out. Ticket prices were the same in Japan and Korea, despite Japan being a far wealthier country. The stadia in Japan were full, but many Koreans could not afford the tickets. We had managed our ticket situation very well up to this point. But now we were going to lose money on this unneeded venture, and create other serious problems for ourselves. Why did the officers feel we needed to do this? Did they not remember the Bastow Charlton Report? The evidence of the three matches in Japan proved that we did not need to get involved.

The first issue was to persuade FIFA to provide us with the tickets. We were the only Association looking to do this. They must have thought that we were mad. Eventually, they provided us with 500 tickets on a sale and non-return basis. We sold, perhaps, 300 of them. The average price of a World Cup ticket for a round-of-sixteen match is probably close to $100. Thus, the FAI lost some $20,000 on this venture. These figures are approximate. I have no doubt that the less than 300 people who queued up outside the Westin Chosin Hotel on the Saturday morning would just as easily have acquired the tickets directly from FIFA. There may have been 12,000 Irish fans in Suwon. The FAI's operation, as was the case in the US, had little impact and it again cost the Association money.

The tickets were priced in dollars and the FAI ticketing decision was that only dollars and euro would be accepted in payment. Many of the fans who queued only had the local currency – the Korean won – with them and were initially refused tickets. I heard that fans had been refused tickets because they had the wrong currency. It was only with my intervention that the won was accepted in payment. We had considerable expenses to meet in Korea, so there should have been no problem with accepting won. It was Saturday morning and the banks were shut. Why go to all the trouble of setting up a ticketing system and then impose silly little rules that make it difficult for the fans?

We also had to deal with the people who had pre-ordered tickets from FIFA before travelling to the World Cup. These would have been team-specific tickets. The purchasers were guaranteed a ticket for each Irish game. The tickets were given to the FAI for distribution, which was not the original plan. If time had permitted, the tickets would have been posted directly to the purchaser by the FIFA ticketing agency. There were about 200 fans who had to collect these tickets at the hotel. Thus, there were two queues at the rear of the hotel early on that Saturday morning, and, of course, they got mixed up at times. This led to one serious incident, which has subsequently resulted in legal action being taken against the Association.

One fan collecting pre-purchased tickets from the FAI got anxious about the different queues and entered the ticket distribution area for the second time at about 9.30 am. Ticket distribution was due to commence at 10 am. When the fan was asked to leave without having his queries answered, there was an altercation between him and an FAI security official. I do not know the rights and wrongs of the situation, but the motto that the customer is always right did not seem to apply in this case. The fan sustained some minor injuries and required medical attention, which was provided by the hotel. The hotel manager and his security and medical staff were involved in resolving the problem.

I became aware of this issue later that morning. The fan knew of me, and early the following morning, the morning of the match, he requested to see me. He made a formal complaint about his treatment. At this stage, he was still very upset and felt unable to travel to the game. I asked Dr Conal Hooper, who was our second team doctor, to examine him. As it was 10 o'clock on Sunday morning, the team mass was starting in the hotel and Dr Hooper brought him and his friend to the mass. I spoke to the fan again later in the morning and persuaded him to travel to the game, providing him with transport on an official bus. He was satisfied with this and we agreed to be in touch on his return to Dublin. He wanted the FAI security official involved to be dismissed immediately, but this was impractical and unrealistic as the evidence was disputed.

I thought that that would be the end of the matter. However, John Delaney gave the story to John Lee of *The Sunday Times*, who published it. I had taken a few days off on our return to Dublin and had agreed to contact the fan on the following Tuesday. However, publication of the story in *The Sunday Times* precluded this. It resulted in immediate legal action being taken against the Association for damages and defamation. What benefit it was to the Association to leak this story, I do not know. The rest of Lee's article had a series of negative comments about me, most of which were incorrect.

It was decided that this claim against the Association would be treated as an insurance matter rather than a legal matter. Thus, it was taken from our legal advisers and given to our insurers to deal with. The claim for damages would be covered under our employers' liability insurance. Any settlement for defamation would have to be met out of the FAI's own pocket. The fan also took action against *The Sunday Times*. *The Sunday Times* quickly wrote to the FAI stating that, as an official of the FAI (John Delaney) had been the on-the-record source of the information, the paper would countersue the FAI if it had to pay damages for defamation.

Being an insurance matter, it was passed to Michael Cody, a director of the Association who had recently retired from a senior position in the insurance industry, to deal with. The FAI's insurers agreed to pay a substantial settlement to the fan. However, in addition the FAI had to pay €10,500 out of our own pocket to settle the defamation – the cost of a big mouth.

An interesting aside to this story is that John Lee of *The Sunday Times* telephoned me in early 2003, asking me what the situation was with the FAI as regards the claim. I was not acting as General Secretary of the Association at that time, so I suggested that he direct his enquiries to Kevin Fahy. Ironically, at the time of the phone call, I was in the company of my solicitor, deciding to take legal action against *The Sunday Times* for the many inaccurate pieces of information about me that had been published in that paper by John O'Brien.

*****

The new Minister for Sport, John O'Donoghue, his wife and some officials from the Department of Sport joined us in Seoul for the match. It was an ideal opportunity to meet and get to know the Minister and inform him about the FAI and our plans for the future, including our support for the National Stadium. At that stage, it looked as if both parties in the coalition government were committed to the stadium. The Minister and his department insisted on meeting all their own costs, including the flights home on the team charter. We also spent a very enjoyable evening at a barbecue at the Ambassador's residence. There are a lot more Irish people in Korea than in Japan. This is mainly due to the fact that a significant number (49 per cent) of the Korean people are Christians. An Irishman is the football correspondent for the local English-language newspaper.

On our second night in Seoul, Korea were playing Portugal. It was live on a big screen in a large square right beside the team hotel. About 250,000 Koreans had assembled there to watch the match. It was an extraordinary sight. Everyone was wearing red. Some had been there for hours to get the best view. The chants for Korea were phenomenal. Korea won the match with a late goal and the celebrations were out of this world. This win confirmed Korea as a qualifier for phase two. As soon as the match was over, the crowd dispersed in a very orderly fashion, taking all their litter with them. Thirty minutes after the final whistle, the square was empty and clean.

Before the Spanish game, Eddie Corcoran did a scouting mission to Gwangu, which would be the venue for the quarter-final match if we beat Spain. It was a four-hour road journey south of Seoul. It would be quicker to travel by road than by air, despite the length of the journey. It was only at this stage that our potential itinerary for the rest of the tournament became clear. Eddie's report was that conditions were going to be difficult. He had been shown around by an Irish priest based in Gwangu. He had identified one suitable hotel from those on FIFA's list, but it was well below the standard we had used to date. Training facilities would be limited. Roy would not have been happy, but at least this time he could only blame the Koreans! The stadium, as always, was superb. In these circumstances, we would delay our departure from Seoul to Gwangu for as long as possible, most likely two days, before the quarter-final match.

The Association were getting demands for tickets from many sources. One of the most unusual was from Michael Flatley, who intended travelling from his home in Monte Carlo with his girlfriend, Lisa Murphy, and secretary to support the team. I provided him with three category 1 tickets. I later had to argue within the Association that these should be complimentary, even though after the match, Michael paid for the drinks for the team for the night, which I assume cost a sizeable sum. Michael attended the after-match meal with the players as a guest of Mick. It was interesting to see star football players queuing up to speak to Michael Flatley and in some cases to get his autograph – a complete reversal of roles.

*****

It was now a matter of waiting for Sunday evening and the game against Spain. At this stage, we feared no one, even though the Spanish team was full of world-class players. In Korea, the police escorts actually move other traffic aside, unlike in Japan. On our way to the match in the officials' minibus, one of our escorts got knocked off his motorbike in a collision with a learner driver. In trying to move her to one side, he obviously confused the driver and collided with her when her car veered in an unexpected direction. We later found out that the policeman had suffered a minor fracture of his leg, but no serious injuries.

The official party had been joined by Ben Dunne and a companion, who were also travelling in the official bus. Ben had been provided with complimentary VIP tickets by the Association. He was fully togged out in 'unofficial' Irish gear. During the trip to the stadium, Ben was on the telephone to his bookie, placing a large bet on Ireland beating Spain by a good margin within ninety minutes. He was certainly optimistic of Ireland's chances. Prior to the Saudi game, we had never scored more than one goal in a World Cup finals match, so I hope he got very long odds on us scoring three.

The game against Spain followed a similar pattern to those against Cameroon and Germany. We were under pressure from the outset. Morientes scored with a flicked header from a right-wing cross in the seventh minute. Morientes has always been one of my favourite players, but he went down in my admiration on this occasion. Could we get back into the game? Damien Duff was brilliant. Mick switched him to the right wing when he brought on Niall Quinn in the fifty-fifth minute, with Gary Kelly losing out in the substitution. We had chances and they had chances. If they scored a second, I could not see any way back for us. Then in the sixth-third minute, we were awarded a penalty for a trip on Damien Duff. He had been continually fouled as he went past Spanish players, but this time it was in the penalty box. The Spanish couldn't cope with his close control. Ian Harte hit a poor penalty and it was saved by Casillas in the Spanish goal. Football is full of 'what ifs'. What if Robbie had taken the penalty? He would surely have scored and it would have been 1–1 with twenty-seven minutes left. Would we have gone on and won, as we certainly dominated the rest of the game?

The Irish formation remained 4–4–2 until a further substitution in the eightieth minute, when David Connolly replaced Ian Harte. It was now all-out attack in a 3–4–3 formation. For the last ten minutes, the pressure was really on the Spanish, but we couldn't score. The game went into injury time. As a cross from Steve Finnan came into the Spanish box, Hierro, the Spanish central defender, was hanging out of Niall Quinn, so much that his jersey nearly came off. I suspect that Niall's experience had a lot to do with the penalty award. The Spanish defender probably expected Niall to jump for the ball but he didn't. Thus, the jersey pull became very obvious. The Swedish referee, Anders Frisk, awarded a second penalty – a brave decision in the last minute of a World Cup match against one of the bigger teams! Robbie Keane duly scored and we were into extra time.

Extra time seems to change the psychology of games. I think that this is a consequence of the golden goal rule. There is great excitement when the golden goal is scored, but I believe it results in negative play rather than positive play, as there is no way back. We became more cautious, and despite continuing to press more than the Spanish, our clear-cut chances were few. No goals at half-time.

I realised that the Spanish had only ten men on the field. I checked the Spanish formation as they lined up for the kick off, to determine whether it was defensive or offensive, and could only count ten players. I felt that we should really have a go at them. I now know that Mick and the Irish bench did not realise for some time that Albeda had come off injured and the Spaniards had used all the substitutes allowed. The Spanish played it quietly. We had a few half chances, but no real scoring opportunity. About halfway through the second period of extra time, a draw and a penalty shoot-out began to appear inevitable. I do not know what it is, but players seem to prefer the lottery of a penalty shoot-out to taking risks during extra time.

The penalty shoot-out took place at the end in front of the Irish supporters. I spoke to Anders Frisk after the game and he told me that he had spotted Paddy Daly, who looks after visiting referees for the FAI, in the crowd behind that goal, and that was the basis on which he made the decision on which goal to use. We scored just two (Robbie Keane and Steve Finnan) out of our five allotted penalties with Matt Holland, David Connolly and Kevin Kilbane all missing. Having missed our second and third, we were always chasing the Spaniards. However, in the end it came down to 2–2, with Spain's final penalty to be taken by Mendieta, another of my favourite players. Damien Duff had destroyed him when he came on as a second-half substitute, but his was to be the last act of the match. He put a badly struck shot low into the centre of the net. Shay Given, having dived to his right, had gone past the ball and missed it with his trailing leg by just a foot. Spain had won; Ireland were out.

This had been the best and most exciting match of the World Cup to date. The Irish were glorious in defeat, but was this a cause for celebration or disappointment? In the World Cup there can be only one winner, in this case Brazil. All other thirty-one teams lost at various stages of the competition. As a small country with limited resources, we had performed well. We were ranked twelfth in the World Cup tournament and our FIFA world ranking had improved to thirteen. Let us take pride in what we had achieved, but avoid complacency for the future. The match against Spain in Suwon was glorious despite the penalty shoot-out defeat.

One of the strangest myths to come out of the World Cup was the story that Ireland had not practised penalties. I have a video, taken by our video analyst Ian Rogers, of penalty practice at the army training grounds in Seoul, showing the Irish players taking penalties against Shay Given, Dean Kiely and Alan Kelly. They had a very high success rate. Mick also refers to penalty practice after the training session in the Suwon stadium, on the night before the game. Three Irish players – Steve Staunton, Ian Harte and Gary Kelly – who would be in consideration as penalty takers, had all been substituted during the match.

*****

On the day after the match, I was called down to the lobby of the hotel by our liaison officer to meet a representative of the Korean government. He had a present for the Irish team. It was a beautiful presentation box of ginseng products for each member of the official party. He extolled the beneficial health and energy properties of ginseng. I replied that it was a pity we had not been given the ginseng some days earlier, as we had lost the game last night. I am not sure that Irish humour translated well into Korean.

The next day involved planning to go home, rather than travelling on to Gwangu. We had tickets from Seoul to Dublin via Amsterdam on KLM, but it was going to be impossible to get the full party on one flight. There were at least fifty-five people, including players, technical staff, FAI officers and FAI staff. The alternative was to charter a flight. The cost would be very high, but at least everyone would travel together. Through Ray Treacy, KLM agreed to charter a

747 to come out to Seoul and bring us directly to Dublin on the Tuesday, at a cost of $200,000. This was a lot of money and would eat into our World Cup profits. Nonetheless, the decision was quickly made to charter the plane. We used KLM rather than Aer Lingus because Aer Lingus do not fly to the Far East. It was the same reason that we had been using KLM from the outset. I have no doubt that KLM were very pleased with the positive publicity they received. They certainly deserved it, as they had been very helpful to the Association since we had qualified for the World Cup.

During that day, I strolled around the streets of Seoul with Linda and my eldest daughter, Aisling, for an hour and a half, my only real time off duty while in Korea. In Seoul, there is an underground city, as well as an overground one. In the underground pedestrian street crossings, there are hundreds of shops and I am sure that this network continues for miles. Space is in short supply in Seoul, so they have created additional space by going underground. Did no one in Dublin ever think of this? My overall impression was that Korea remains fairly poor, despite its massive industrialisation over the last thirty years.

*****

As I re-entered the hotel, I was descended upon, or more likely ambushed, by a group of journalists asking me for some final views on Ireland's participation in the World Cup. Mick had not scheduled a press conference, so stories were in short supply. However, Mick did hold one later than day. What I did not realise at the time was that the group was largely made up of British journalists with a tabloid bias. If I had known this, I might have been slightly more cautious with my comments. Despite our many differences, there is some degree of trust between the FAI officials and most Irish journalists.

Towards the end of a wide-ranging interview, I was asked the inevitable question about Roy Keane and whether he would play for Ireland again. I replied that Roy was now in his thirties and had only a limited time left with the Irish team in any event, given his age and injuries. Sooner or later, the Irish team would have to learn to do without him, as it had in the World Cup. Of course, one of the

English tabloids had a field day with this, twisting what I had said to mean that Roy Keane would not play for Ireland again. Given subsequent events, what I said in Seoul has proven to be completely accurate. Roy decided for himself that, because of club commitments and injuries, he would retire from playing international football for Ireland. Nonetheless, my comments caused another controversy. As soon as I disembarked the plane in Dublin the next day, I did an interview with Colm Murray of RTÉ to try to clarify what I had said. I had been forewarned by colleagues in Dublin to expect this.

As an interesting aside, it is worth considering how John O'Brien dealt with this story in *The Sunday Times*. In his article of 23 June, he quotes me as saying:

> *'That's the end of it now. The Roy Keane issue has gone away. It's an irrelevance.'*

These words were within quotation marks and thus purported to be the actual words spoken by me. They are a fabrication. I can't recall John O'Brien being present when I spoke to the journalists in the hotel lobby. He never contacted me to verify what I had said.

*****

At this stage, we were becoming aware that a welcome home jamboree was being planned. Initially, there was little enthusiasm for it among the players or from Mick McCarthy. The view among the senior players was that the 1994 homecoming in the Phoenix Park had been disastrous. If there was to be a welcome home, then an open-deck bus through the streets of Dublin was by far the preferred option. However, these decisions were being taken in Dublin. Paul Brady was representing the FAI in the organisation of the event. For safety reasons, it was going to be the Phoenix Park.

The flight home was part bedlam. There was a continuous sing-song, including some very out-of-tune journalists and players. As the alcohol consumption increased, the singing got worse. The singers had assembled at the bottom of the stairs to the business-class cabin, thus ensuring that they disturbed everyone on the plane: upstairs, downstairs, front and back. At least three journalists, one of them very drunk indeed, approached me about getting a PR job in the FAI. God help us – weren't things bad enough? One journalist had to restrain another from throwing cushions at Linda and Aisling, who were trying to sleep at the rear of the plane.

During the flight, the last of the arrangements for the homecoming were put in place. The attitude of the players in general was not very favourable, but as it was a *fait acompli*, Mick agreed that everyone would attend but that their appearance should be short. We would make a quick pit stop at the Holiday Inn Hotel at the airport, where the players would be staying that night and where they would meet their extended families. Then we would travel to Áras an Uachtaráin to be greeted by President Mary McAleese and other dignitaries. Finally, we would be bussed to the 15 acres, where Mick McCarthy and the team would be presented on stage. It would be a long evening for the players, after twelve hours of travel. We were already hearing that thousands of fans were turning up at the Phoenix Park.

As we landed at Dublin airport, the pilot of the KLM plane requested for a tricolour to fly out of the roof of the plane. There seems to be some kind of hatch that can be opened in the cockpit. I believe that it was the flight engineer who flew the flag. We were escorted down the runway by the airport fire tenders, with lights flashing and horns blazing, to a reserved area to the left of the main terminal, where a reception area had been cordoned off. Mick McCarthy and Milo Corcoran were first off the plane, with Steve Staunton and Mick Byrne not far behind.

I did my interview with Colm Murray on the tarmac at the bottom of the steps. I have little recollection of the ceremony on the tarmac, other than that it was thankfully very brief. I believe that it was little more than a photo opportunity.

We were quickly put on buses and brought to the Holiday Inn Hotel. There were a large number of people at the hotel to greet the players. We had tried to limit the numbers to four per player, but this was impossible. One of the technical team threatened to sue the FAI because his wife was initially refused entry by security and got caught up in a crowd. Everyone was going on to the Phoenix Park and was being accredited to the VIP area by a system of infrared coded wristbands.

The players needed to shower and change into their Louis Copeland suits, which had been provided to them by Louis prior to their departure. It was taking an extraordinarily long time for the luggage to arrive from the airport and we were falling seriously behind schedule. There were 100,000 people waiting for the team in the park, and we still had a courtesy call to make to Áras an Uachtaráin. One suggestion for the luggage delay was than the Aer Rianta van had run out of diesel on its way to the hotel. I cannot confirm whether this story is true. Tensions were mounting in the hotel. In the end, we could not wait for all the luggage and one member of the team, David Connolly, had to travel without his official suit.

The trip from the Holiday Inn to Áras on Uachtaráin was only the second occasion that I travelled on the team bus. We had a police escort all the way. On the M50, all the cars were stopping, with people leaning out of the windows and waving flags. As we entered the Phoenix Park, there were streams of people making their way to the 15-acre site.

We were warmly welcomed at the Áras. President McAleese had met the team at the Holiday Inn on the Wednesday prior to their departure. The President had also attended some of the home international matches. While probably not the keenest sports fan in Ireland, the President always takes an interest in the performance of the team and recognises their role as ambassadors for the country. There was a large invited group in the Áras. I cannot recall who exactly was present, but I know that some members of the government were there, as was Mark Durkan of the SDLP. There were short speeches of congratulations. Everyone was aware of the very large crowd waiting for the team, so the visit to the Áras was short. As we were leaving, the President's daughters were setting out from the Áras to walk to the homecoming. I offered them a lift on the team bus, which they were only too delighted to accept.

David Connolly's wardrobe was an issue. He would stand out a mile from the rest of the nattily dressed lads. Simon Doyle, the team chef, offered him his suit, as he would be in the background. Simon is a good deal taller than David, but it was the only solution. A quick exchange of clothes occurred at the back of the bus.

The homecoming was a fantastic event. I know that the players' reservations about the event were instantly dispelled when they saw the size and enthusiasm of the crowd. As we drove through the Phoenix Park, we could see more and more people making their way to the site. Any latecomers would be miles away from the stage. We heard that some fans had been there since early afternoon to ensure a good view. Despite the controversy at the start of the World Cup, the fans had united behind the team.

Being up on stage, facing a crowd of perhaps 100,000 people, was an incredible experience. No matter what direction you looked you saw a sea of faces, flags and colour. Reading some of the banners near the front of the crowd, which seemed to be predominately female, it was not surprising to see that Damien and Robbie were the superheroes.

Peter Collins and Joe Duffy introduced Mick and the players individually to the crowd to a tumultuous reception. Then some of the players were interviewed. I thought that some of the questions asked by the interviewers were inane, and I could see that Damien Duff was totally non-plussed by a reference to his mother and Padre Pio. The time on stage was quite short. The players were delighted to be there but wanted to finally finish with the World Cup and commence their summer holidays, which were going to be unusually short that year. Once off the stage, they would be free after a total of thirty-seven days with the squad. I believe the fans were delighted with the event. Nonetheless, I felt that it was too short and quick, especially for the fans who had been there for hours. You eventually learn that the fans are the givers in these situations and will go to extreme lengths to support their team. I wonder if the players fully appreciate this. It is the fans who cough up money in so many different ways to pay the large salaries of our elite players.

After the on-stage show, it was back into the VIP area where there was drink and food. The media were present in large numbers, but their focus was on the homecoming event. The players spent about twenty minutes there before departing back to the Holiday Inn and the break up of the squad.

I went back to the Holiday Inn, but at that stage exhaustion had set in, due to jetlag and the twenty-four hours that had elapsed since we had left the hotel in Seoul. A lot had been fit into one day, as we had gained eight hours on the trip from east to west. It was straight into a car and home. It had been twenty-seven days since I had left. It was great to be back, but thoughts still lingered about the possibilities if we had just beaten Spain in that penalty shoot-out.

*****

On the following Sunday week, there was one final World Cup job to perform. RTÉ were doing a World Cup review in the evening after the final and I was to represent the Association in a panel discussion with Ray Houghton and Eamon Dunphy. It would be chaired as usual by Bill O'Herlihy. This was going to be fraught with difficulties, given Dunphy's affiliation to Roy Keane and RTÉ's general anti-FAI stance, even though the imminent Sky TV deal had not even been announced yet. My decision was that it was important that the FAI be represented and put their position across.

I watched most of the show within RTÉ, as I was only going to join the panel for the last twenty minutes of discussion about Ireland's performance. Obviously in RTÉ's view, football administrators are not qualified to talk about or give their view on football matches. The fans' views are also largely ignored. The views of the 'experts' are the only legitimate ones. Yet, I was the only one who had actually seen the matches live.

I was in the studio, off screen, when the *Après Match* skit came on. Eamon Dunphy featured significantly in it. I had the privilege of watching Dunphy watching himself being taken off by the *Après Match* team. He was smiling and laughing, but his body language suggested that he was not enjoying it in the least.

I am reasonably experienced at TV interviews but less so in panel discussions. However, I went through a few training courses in a previous career and know some of the tricks. A key one is to know when to shut up. Dunphy only wanted to concentrate on the negatives. In my view, he either likes you or dislikes you, and if it is the latter, then he will give you a hard time. If he likes you, you can expect an easy ride. I had moved from someone that Dunphy 'liked' during the Eircom Park saga to someone who was now in his bad books. Bill O'Herlihy was also interested in the rows and was anti the FAI. I remember that, at one point, Ray Houghton was saying how far things had come in the FAI in recent years in terms of hotels, travel arrangements and facilities. A two-way debate ensued between Houghton and Dunphy. I told myself quietly to stay out of it, as Ray Houghton defending the FAI would have a much better impact than if I was doing it. I believe that Bill O'Herlihy realised what was happening, maybe he even saw me smiling to myself, and interrupted their debate with another negative question directed at me. I do not believe that this discussion added anything. People had entrenched opinions on the Saipan/Roy Keane saga and debate would not change anyone's mind. RTÉ people, including Bill O'Herlihy, came up to me after the show and said that I had performed well in a difficult environment. Did this mean their expectation was that I would be a lamb to their slaughter? I was certainly one who had failed to go meekly.

I adjourned to the RTÉ bar for a drink after the show. The whole of RTÉ's Sports Department were there celebrating a month's work. There was a brief mention of the need to finalise the new TV contract. The penny still had not dropped with them. The announcement of the deal with Sky was just five days away. Being human, I took some pleasure in knowing this. While I did not see or hear RTÉ's coverage of the World Cup, my impression in general was that they had been negative towards the FAI. They had facilitated Dunphy, who was totally prejudiced against Mick McCarthy.

*****

So my World Cup came to an end. It is a very positive memory that will always be with me. I am an upbeat person, a realist, who wants to make the best of situations. Roy Keane can have no memory of the World Cup. I suspect that in time this will be a matter of regret for him.

Brazil won the World Cup, beating Germany in the final, a Germany we had matched in our second game. If we had beaten Spain, how would we have fared against Korea? It would have been a fifty-fifty game in my estimation. If we had won that, it would have been on to play Germany again in a potential semifinal. They certainly would have respected us this time round. This is the realm of 'what if', a largely pointless exercise. However, let me state that I believe that it is unrealistic to expect Ireland to get to a World Cup final. We are a small football nation, with limited resources, but we have made the best of them. My unwritten target, prior to the World Cup, was that success would be getting to the quarter-final, equalling what we had achieved in Italia '90. We didn't quite achieve this, but so what? We performed well and can be rightfully proud.

Would Roy Keane's presence have made any difference? There is no realistic answer to this question. Roy was not psychologically or physically ready for the World Cup, and I think this was the key factor in his decision to go home. I believe that, after initially being persuaded to stay, Roy managed the situation so that he would be sent home. He had changed his mind once and did not want to do so again. Why did a media-shy Roy Keane, in effect, seek out Tom Humphries to do that interview, which he must have known would lead to problems. Roy is not stupid and must have anticipated the consequences of his actions.

Roy was, at that time, our best player and our captain. I believe he would have been eclipsed by Damien Duff's performances during the World Cup. He was the leader of the team, yet not part of it. He left the hotel on the morning after the Iranian game in Dublin, without talking to any of his team-mates. He roomed alone. He led by example on the field. It was a haranguing type of leadership. I know that it intimidated some of the younger players. I know that there was a general sigh of relief in the camp when the news arrived that Roy was not returning.

In Izumo, I coined the phrase that 'new leaders and new heroes' will emerge. They did in Steve Staunton, Damien Duff, Matt Holland, Robbie Keane and Shay Given. In fact, there was something heroic about the performance of the whole team in the circumstances. France lost their de facto leader in Zidane and failed. We lost our leader and succeeded. A team can be greater than the sum of its individual parts. Did Ireland's greater cohesiveness and team spirit overcome the absence of Roy Keane's individual contribution? Nobody knows.

The best team won the World Cup, but they were far from a great Brazilian team. Germany were a poor team by their own standards; they were missing some of their top players, but still managed to reach the final. The other key features of the 2002 World Cup were the emergence of Japan and Korea, the good performance by the US, the failure of France and Portugal, two of Europe's top teams, and the lack of progress by the African nations.

In my view, it will be the next World Cup in Germany in 2006 before we get a proper assessment of how much progress Japan and Korea have really made. Remember that the other Asian teams, China and Saudi, were the two worst performers in the tournament. Japan and Korea had the advantage of playing at home. Home teams have always performed well in the World Cup. In addition, their preparations were more akin to a club team, with the squads being together for months before the World Cup, compared to just two weeks for most other squads. The Americans were the other team that exceeded expectations. Korea and Japan had two excellent European managers. How will they fare with the departure of Troussier and Hiddink? I will have a personal and professional interest in this in my new role as a consultant to the Asian Football Confederation on their Vision Asia development project.

Only Senegal of Africa's five teams made it through to the second phase. All of Africa's top players are now playing in the top leagues in Europe, so their relative failure in 2002 is somewhat surprising. The African Championships took place in February. Was participating in two major tournaments within four months too much for the African teams? International football is levelling off, but still only about six countries (Brazil, Argentina, Germany, Italy, France and Spain) are capable of winning the World Cup. These are the countries with the depth of talent and resources to underwrite potential success. Africa is not yet ready to mount a serious challenge. That could change when South Africa host the World Cup in 2010.

France was missing Zidane, but this alone does not explain their quick demise. Their team was still loaded with world-class stars. Perhaps it was the absence of competitive matches for two years because, as world champions, they qualified automatically. In general, the European teams performed poorly at the end of a long season. This is possibly a reflection of too much football for the top players. The big clubs would love to see a cut back in international football, but this would impoverish the Associations, particularly the smaller ones, and jeopardise the development of future stars.

This commercial clash between the big clubs and the Associations in Europe is probably the most critical issue in world football today and will eventually explode into a major row. Will the selfish commercial interests of the big clubs prevail over the solidarity principles of UEFA and the Associations? The clubs would prefer it if World Cups and European Championships did not exist. Thank God they do.

6

The Sky TV Deal

Let me upset a lot of people at the outset. I believe that the Sky TV deal was the right one for Irish football and, if I had the chance, I would do the same deal again. The only thing I would change is how we announced it and I would be better prepared to respond to the public reaction. I believe that those who are involved with and support the game at all levels in Ireland broadly concur with this view. Those who believe that football in Ireland does not go beyond the senior international team and the English Premiership, don't want to understand the full implications of the deal. As long as they have access to football on the box, they don't really care.

The relationship between the FAI and RTÉ was always fraught. RTÉ wanted the rights to the Association's international games and had little interest in the League of Ireland, friendly internationals or U21 internationals. The competitive international matches were commercially attractive to RTÉ and were always ranked in the top-ten sporting events televised in Ireland, frequently leading the charts.

RTÉ had a monopoly in the Irish television market prior to the arrival of TV3 and Sky satellite television. In effect, they still have a virtual monopoly, as TV3 have a lot less resources than RTÉ, and Sky have only really penetrated the sports viewing public. At its simplest, all the television licence revenue in this country goes to RTÉ, while TV3 have to rely solely on advertising revenue. This gives RTÉ significant commercial dominance in the market-place and this dominance has always coloured RTÉ's stance in negotiations with the FAI.

Prior to 2002, the FAI never had a television partner other than RTÉ. In the more recent agreements, the relationship had become realistic. For example, it was only in the 1996 agreement that the FAI had retained the rights to the footage of their international matches. Prior to this, RTÉ retained these rights and exploited them commercially for their own benefit, for example through videos and sales of highlights packages to other stations.

The FAI were commercially naive; we owned these rights but gave them to RTÉ for nothing. In late 1995, the FAI retained Laurence St John as their television consultant. Laurence has significant expertise and widespread contacts in the international television market. Nothing would be the same again. The Association began to generate realistic commercial income from television rights and sale of highlights packages, both at home and abroad. The nature of the agreements with RTÉ changed fundamentally.

Traditionally, the deal between the FAI and RTÉ covered both international matches and domestic football, including, from 1998, *The Soccer Show*. Let me put it simply: RTÉ wanted the competitive international games and the attractive friendly international matches. They did not want to cover the League of Ireland or U21 games. They only televised league matches because it was an integral part of the overall contract.

The FAI largely funded *The Soccer Show* from sponsorship they acquired and from their own resources, with RTÉ only making a partial contribution. *The Soccer Show* was an imposition on RTÉ and was duly resented. It was an external production by a company called FAI Productions, with the FAI having editorial control. This was not what RTÉ was used to. *The Soccer Show* was usually broadcast at off-peak hours, such as after the *Late Late Show* at 11.30 pm on a Friday night, with a repeat at lunchtime on Saturday. No wonder audience figures, usually around the 100,000 level, were unsatisfactory. I often wonder what financial and broadcast arrangements RTÉ had with other major sporting organisations, with regard to their magazine programmes. I doubt that we were all treated equally.

RTÉ had a limited number of hours on their two channels reserved for sport and had a limited budget to pay for it. One commentator has estimated RTÉ's overall budget at €150 million, of which, perhaps, 20 per cent, or €30 million, goes to sport. If this figure is in anyway accurate, then RTÉ's offer to purchase the rights to Ireland's international games was appallingly low. The FAI's international games were important to them, but domestic soccer ranked low in RTÉ's priorities, both for air time and resources. Despite being a state company, with a public service broadcast brief funded by licence fees, RTÉ put domestic football well down their list of priorities. Many minority sports have also suffered at the hands of RTÉ, with little or no coverage of these sports on the national television station. As we entered negotiations with RTÉ in mid-2001, *Saturday Sports* was due to be axed.

From my point of view, negotiating with RTÉ was always difficult. The problem was trying to persuade RTÉ to provide adequate coverage of the domestic game. Both sides were usually fully aware of the other's position, and, while it might take a long time and a lot of posturing, both sides knew that they would eventually end up in bed together. Neither side would be fully happy. The year 2002 was going to be different.

The approach of RTÉ is best illustrated by a quote attributed to Niall Cogley on his appointment as RTÉ Head of Sport in January 2002 and published in *Ireland in Sunday* on 14 July. Mr Cogley is reported to have boasted openly about RTÉ's tough negotiating team and their success in brokering deals:

> *Any federation or sports association who has done business with us, leaves thinking 'we got away with it'. They go away thinking 'Jesus, I can't go back thinking this is the best deal that I could cut'. They tell us what they want, we offer a sum and always, always, they say no. So we wind up doing concessions – extra previews, stuff like that. That is why it appears as if we devote our schedule to the big sports. It is not that we necessarily want to, but it is what gets us the contract.*

That is one negotiating model that is unlikely to be used again. It basically says that RTÉ offer the minimum they can get away with. Even the EU Television Without Frontiers Directive insists that sports bodies should receive a market-related fee for their TV rights.

The FAI's existing contract with RTÉ was due to expire at the start of September 2002. Laurence St John and I decided to get negotiations on a new contract started early, with the first meeting with RTÉ taking place in July 2001, thirteen months in advance[1]. Even at this early stage, Laurence and I discussed possible alternative deals, now that TV3 had become established and Sky television were becoming more widely available via cable and satellite TV. We also had a meeting with TG4.

Our objectives were simple – to get more coverage and more money. There were other perceived advantages of a Sky/TV3 deal. Soccer would become the number one sport for TV3, and we were confident that we would get increased news coverage for the domestic game. This happened, not only with a dedicated Monday night show, but increased news coverage on the TV3 sports news bulletins. RTÉ television frequently ignores League of Ireland soccer and on occasions does not even provide the results in news bulletins.

Having said this, I would like to distinguish between RTÉ television and RTÉ radio, where the attitude is completely different. With the advent of commercial and local radio, RTÉ radio have competed in an open market for a number of years. RTÉ radio, which have a separate deal with the FAI, recognise the need to offer a competitive package.

The television coverage from Sky/TV3 would have a more tabloid approach, which we saw as a positive development. The editorial approach would be upbeat and constructive. A focus on personalities, an aspect that had been sorely missing to date, could be a key issue in promoting the League of Ireland. This had the potential to be a true

---

1. The role of the General Secretary on an issue like this was to carry out the negotiations, involving the officers and committees as required.

partnership and would contrast sharply to the situation with RTÉ. As the national broadcasting station, RTÉ somehow believed it had the right and the duty to be the final arbiter of the national conscience. It decided that the Irish public should be shown the English Premiership rather than Irish football.

Sky TV were the experts in televising football, and hence the production quality of football coverage would improve, for example, by having more cameras at Lansdowne Road. This also happened. No matter which way we looked at it, a Sky/TV3 deal was much better than an RTÉ one – and this was before we took the financial package into consideration.

At this time, RTÉ were going through the financial horrors. When it came to discussing money with RTÉ, their initial offer on a new contract was 37 per cent below the previous one. Not a good opening gambit when the negotiations got serious, particularly when the FAI were sitting on a very much higher offer from Sky.

Laurence St John made an initial off-the-record contact with Sky Television to see if they were interested. The response was positive, but secrecy was paramount. At this stage, I decided to keep knowledge of the talks with Sky confined to Laurence and myself. I was well aware that some of the officers would be extremely annoyed when they found out, as proved to be the case. However, the FAI leaks like a sieve and, as soon as the circle of knowledge was widened, the story would be given to the press. Yet again, this proved to be the case.

Thus we had a twin-track approach: open negotiations with RTÉ and secret talks with Sky and TV3 to develop an alternative strategy. Right to the very end, RTÉ seemed to be oblivious to the possibility that the FAI could be speaking to anyone else.

The early negotiations with RTÉ went nowhere. The national broadcaster wanted to agree the financial fees for the international matches before discussing coverage of the domestic game. They knew we would never accede to this. When we discussed coverage of the domestic game, the RTÉ offering, in terms of content, was unacceptable. The FAI position was the usual one of securing satisfactory coverage of the domestic game first, before selling the crown jewels – the polar opposite of the RTÉ approach. We went around the houses in this regard at a number of meetings, without making any real progress.

At the same time, we *were* making progress with both Sky and TV3. Sky TV were prepared to offer a very significant fee for exclusive coverage of our home international matches and, in effect, to become our host broadcaster at Lansdowne Road. The fee has been reported at €7.5 million over four years. This was at a time of a weak market for TV sports rights. The fee was in addition to the pre-existing arrangement (and fee) with Sky for the UK rights, which had been agreed in 2000. Sky were already broadcasting our matches under the UK agreement and the games were, therefore, already available on Sky in Ireland. The new element which Sky were paying for was the exclusivity.

In late autumn 2001, I informed FAI President, Milo Corcoran, of the state of the negotiations and the possible involvement with Sky. He agreed that, at this stage, it should go no further in case of leaks. By early spring 2002, the Sky/TV3 deal looked a runner. I then informed Honorary Treasurer, John Delaney, of the discussions with Sky. I believed that we could be close to a deal and would need to put it through the normal FAI approval procedures. Four people in the organisation were now aware of the discussions with Sky. Four people in the FAI having access to information means that it is no longer a secret. Shortly afterwards, *The Star* newspaper had an exclusive on the possible deal with Sky.

On 7 May 2002, Paul Lennon announced in two-inch banner headlines across the back page of *The Star*:

Sky TV Deal. FAI's €8m TV Boost. New Deal to Include TV3.

Incredibly, there was no reaction from RTÉ. They mustn't read *The Star* in Donnybrook. If they did read it, then they dismissed it. Right up to the end of negotiations with RTÉ, I believe that they assumed that they were the only player. They saw themselves as having a monopoly and acted like monopolists.

We were making progress with RTÉ on some issues. At one stage, there was the possibility of a dedicated highlights programme for the League of Ireland on Sunday evening, for at least part of the season. However, this quickly became subsumed into a general sports programme. The idea of having a programme called *Sunday Soccer* appeared to be an anathema to RTÉ. RTÉ's ability to service the matches during the main summer months also became an issue. Football's switch to summer soccer would overload RTÉ's broadcasting resources. However, if RTÉ's financial offer had been at all realistic; these issues would probably have been resolved.

Sky wanted to bring negotiations to a quick conclusion. Our problem was that we had no concrete offer from RTÉ. In early spring, RTÉ requested more time to firm up their proposals. The key meeting with RTÉ took place in April 2002. Verbally, RTÉ offered the FAI a fee of €400,000 per annum to include all international matches, the FAI cup semifinals and final and live televising of a minimum of five domestic league games. This compared to a fee of €637,000 per annum for the same package under the previous contract, a reduction of 37 per cent. I have no difficulty in quoting these figures, as they were made public by both FAI and RTÉ sources during the bitter public debate that ensued after the FAI announced the Sky deal in early July.

RTÉ were represented at the April meeting by Niall Cogley (Head of Sport); Stephen Alken (a producer in the Sports Department), who is a good supporter of Irish football; Frank Whelan (RTÉ Finance Department) and Cathal Goan (Head of Programming). The FAI people present were Michael Hyland (Chairman of the Eircom League), Laurence St John and I. After a brief discussion we got down to the meat of the negotiations. Despite ten months of preliminary discussions, this was the first meeting in which money was discussed.

RTÉ offered €400,000 per annum; the FAI wanted €1.5 million. Did we live in the same world? RTÉ were at 27 per cent of our level! The FAI proposal of €1.5 million was based on our assessment of the commercial value of an average of six competitive and friendly matches a year. We included not only the commercial revenue from sponsorship and advertising, but also an allocation of RTÉ's licence fee. Our premise was that the licence fee was for making programmes and, hence, the televising of matches was entitled to a pro-rata allocation. Our proposal was based on our estimate of RTÉ's net revenues.

Although the proposal was below what we believed we had from a deal with Sky Television, the FAI were prepared to accept the lower figure if RTÉ agreed. The RTÉ delegates were aghast, got up and left the meeting, ending negotiations there and then. On parting, Cathal Goan diffused the situation slightly and said that they might be back in touch.

The RTÉ offer and reaction cleared the way for the Association to conclude the deal with Sky and TV3. The RTÉ offer was an absurd one. I know that RTÉ were in severe financial difficulties and the government were holding off on the licence fee increase. Nonetheless, there can be little doubt that RTÉ were endangering control over one of the jewels of the Irish television market. I do not know how RTÉ came up with a figure of €400,000 per annum as an appropriate commercial value for the international games. For example, I believe Sky Television pay Stg£600,000 (€900,000) for each live Premiership game. It is reputed that RTÉ pay €1.3 million for the Premiership programme of highlights, with other costs, including remuneration of the pundits, pushing the total figure up to €2 million. Their offer certainly pushed those of us in the FAI who wanted the Sky/TV3 deal further that way.

There were no further real negotiations with RTÉ prior to our announcement of the deal with Sky on 5 July. The World Cup intervened, but by early June we had, in effect, agreed to the Sky deal. RTÉ wrote to the Association on 4 July, putting their offer of April in writing.

By this stage, it was irrelevant. We were geared up to announce the Sky deal on 5 July. In their letter, RTÉ recognised that the FAI had rejected their offer of April. There was no way we were going back into negotiations with RTÉ. The financial gap was too large to bridge and, in any event, the coverage being offered under the Sky/TV3 deal was way ahead of what RTÉ were proposing.

We had achieved our aim of more money and more coverage. All our international matches would be covered live, with improved production values. There would be delayed full coverage on TV3. Our U21 competitive internationals would also be televised live. This had never happened before. We had a dedicated Monday night soccer show on TV3, plus good coverage on their sports and news bulletins. We had at least five live League of Ireland games being broadcast a season. We had substantially more money to develop the game.

All in all, we had a very good deal. One of the possible issues was the quality of TV3's live production of matches, an area where they had little experience. However, their first match, a vital league game between Bohemians and Shelbourne, was very successful. So much so that someone from RTÉ Sport complimented the standard of production they had achieved. Praise from the enemy camp is praise indeed.

From April onwards, we worked to put the final dimensions to both the Sky and TV3 sides of the deal. The Sky element was easy as we had worked with them before and knew the format of their contract. TV3 were more difficult, as they were entering a new area. What we had to negotiate with them was coverage – their financial contribution was small. Eventually all the pieces were in place. We had had no further contact from RTÉ until their letter in early July.

During the World Cup, when the FAI were in Japan, Laurence St John put the final details together. Sky were informed that the FAI agreed to their proposals.

After the World Cup, nearly everyone in the FAI took some time off. However, the matter needed to be brought before the Board of Management at the July meeting, on the first Friday of the month – 5 July. We were aware of the need to tie up the loose ends with RTÉ, but if we alluded to the fact that we had an alternative deal in place, then we would lose control of the situation. We knew RTÉ would be far from happy.

Laurence St John made contact with RTÉ on our behalf. The result was the putting in writing of their ridiculous offer of April. This we received on 4 July and we rejected it immediately. RTÉ had failed to move one inch in the ten weeks since the meeting in April. There were just two months to the expiry of the existing contract and the start of the Euro 2004 campaign. RTÉ were aware of the urgency of the deal. They were assuming we had nowhere to go and had to come back and agree a deal with them.

We were at all times aware of the Broadcasting (Major Events Television Coverage) Act 1999, based on the EU Television Without Frontiers Directive of 1992, covering the designation of major sporting events for terrestrial television. The EU directive was not binding, but it was open to individual governments to introduce legislation if they wished to. The Irish government passed the relevant act in 1999, but did not designate any events in the act or afterwards by ministerial order. The government did give the power to the minister to do so in the future. However, when we agreed the deal with Sky, no events had been so designated by the Minister for Communications.

Let me quote you the words of the then Minister for Communications, Síle de Valera, in the Dáil on 13 October 1999:

There is no reason not to expect that such an order will be made. That is the object of this bill. It gives me the power to make such an order.

No order was made. When questioned by Deputy O'Shea on the issue that the legislation did not address the situation where broadcasters have acquired the rights of certain events into the future, the minister replied 'there can be no retrospection'. In the end, the government did introduce retrospective legislation to overturn the Sky deal.

Reading the Dáil debate of October 1999 is instructive. All the politicians from all parties who spoke were concerned about the rights of viewers. No one mentioned the rights of sporting organisations that depend on funds from the sale of television rights to fund their activities.

There seemed to be no legal constraint on the FAI doing a deal with Sky. Once the deal was done, we believed that there was nothing that anyone could do about it legally. We thought retrospective legislation to be unlikely, as there was no history of this in Ireland and the constitutionality of such legislation is doubtful. The Irish constitution and legal system gives strong protection to property rights. The TV rights of Ireland matches were the property of the FAI. We had strong and expensive legal advice supporting this view.

We were set to seek approval within the FAI on Friday 5 July. The procedure was to get the proposal passed by the Television Committee, followed by the Board of Management and finally the FAI National Council. This was basically a rubber-stamping exercise. Getting the deal through the Television Committee was a good start, as it was extremely unlikely that the larger Board and Council would change a recommendation of their peers. There was little opposition, with a decisive factor being the very large gap of nearly €6 million between what was on offer from Sky and RTÉ. In fairness, two Council members, Bill Attley and former President, Pat Quigley, pointed out that the deal could encounter public opposition.

The role of the FAI is to administer all aspects of the game. The international team is the commercial jewel and we needed to exploit this to provide the funding to develop the next generation of players. The FAI underage international programme is very expensive and is on a par with that of Europe's leading football nations. The FAI has twenty-five people working in the Technical Department, with only partial funding from the Irish Sports Council. The lure of Sky's additional money for development was enticing.

I still fully support the Sky deal. A poverty-stricken FAI would gradually weaken the senior international team and weaken its commercial attractiveness. Just as there was a constructive cycle after qualification for Euro '88 – when a successful international team led to more players in the game, more commercial revenue, more money for development and thus self-sustaining success – the danger is that if the FAI cannot continue to invest in the game, then it could quickly revert to the pre-1988 days of near bankruptcy and a cycle of decline. At one stage back then, the FAI had to borrow money from one of its affiliates to meet its financial commitments. Given its overall responsibilities and obligations, the FAI made the correct decision in accepting Sky.

There is a related debate going on at present between the big European clubs (known as the Group of 14) and the national associations. The clubs resent their star players playing in international matches. The clubs pay the players' salaries. By comparison, the players get a pittance for playing in international matches. However, what the clubs conveniently forget is the investment by the associations in developing young players. The associations need the international matches to raise the finance to invest in the development of the next generation of players. The clubs are not going to do this unless it is to their commercial advantage. Where would Roy Keane have ended up, were it not for Rockmount FC, Cobh Ramblers and the FAI FÁS Academy? The responsibility for developing young players is falling on the national associations.

We informed key people in the late afternoon that we had done a television deal with Sky. This included the government. RTÉ were telephoned by Laurence St John to inform them that we were announcing the deal with Sky that day. Unsurprisingly, it caused consternation in RTÉ. They had lost the crown jewel of Irish sport. The Irish international team had consistently drawn the highest audience for live sport. RTÉ claimed that they heard the news on the bulletins of competitor stations. This is untrue. We had pre-recorded a news item for TV3, but this was not broadcast until after RTÉ were informed. I can understand that not everyone in RTÉ had heard the news before it was on the airwaves.

What the FAI had underestimated was the public reaction to the deal. We had focused on its positive impact for development. I had not factored in the upset caused to armchair supporters. A lot of the reaction was orchestrated by RTÉ, who felt aggrieved. However, the deal split the football public into those who accepted the arguments of the FAI and took an overall view and those who had a narrow focus on the international team and wanted armchair access in the comfort of their own home. These people contribute little or nothing to football in Ireland and want free access to the FAI's only valuable product. The argument quickly became emotional. RTÉ led the way. They were furious. They had been caught out badly – and it was largely their own fault.

I was travelling to Sligo that evening to attend the annual prizegiving and dinner of the Sligo and Leitrim District League. En route, I received a request from RTÉ to do an interview on the nine o'clock news. Getting to Sligo in time was difficult on a Friday evening. Linda drove most of the way, as I was in constant demand for interviews.

I arrived at RTÉ's Sligo studio at about ten past nine. It is a very small studio. I was put sitting in front of a backdrop of Ben Bulben, advised not to look at the TV monitor and I was on air. The interview was live with Anne Doyle, who was in the Dublin studio. To say that there was steam coming out of her ears would be putting it mildly. Such were the glares I was receiving from Ms Doyle across 150 miles, I was finding it difficult to keep my eyes from straying to the monitor. The questions were very aggressive. Obviously, the Sky deal had hit RTÉ where it hurt – in their pride and in their pocket. All guns were blazing, with the FAI as the target.

I believe that I gave Anne Doyle as good as I got. Having survived the training ground of the Keane saga during the World Cup, a few aggressive questions from someone who knew little about football wasn't going to upset me. In addition, I had got good training for the interview earlier in the evening with George Hook on Newstalk Radio. George, of course, is a rugby journalist and has strong RTÉ connections. At that stage, I was unfamiliar with the format of Newstalk and went on air to do the usual ninety-second sound bite. Twenty minutes later, I was still being harangued by Mr Hook. The

FAI had betrayed the Irish people. Thirty pieces of silver were mentioned. We were joined on air by Tom McGurk, another rugby journalist who does a lot of work for RTÉ. Do these people really know anything about Irish football? I doubt it. They took the populist stance and, naturally, the RTÉ stance and were not interested in discussing the real issues and reasons why we had dealt with Sky. We were being set up. No counter views were allowed. We had upset the status quo, and those who benefited from the previous comfortable arrangements were seeking their revenge.

Indeed, most phone-in shows I did over the next week featured Mr McGurk as the voice of the aggrieved public. At no stage did McGurk declare his interest in the situation and the fact that he did work for RTÉ. All I can say to this self-appointed conscience of the people is 'get a life'. In fact, you should give yourself the Sick Parrot of the Week Award.[2]

The gloves were off. While some commentators understood the rationale behind the deal and gave us fair coverage, others, led by RTÉ, who had a vested interest in the situation, lambasted the FAI. The debate became purely emotive. We were corrupting the youth of Ireland by forcing them to go to pubs to watch Ireland play. We were depriving the old and sick of enjoyment. The spending of the money on encouraging kids to play football and providing improved facilities was irrelevant; viewing the game was more important than playing it. Even TV3 news took a critical stance. Here we had a situation in which the TV3 Sports Department were overjoyed, while their News Department took an opposite tack. TV3 were nothing if not populist! In our decision to transfer to TV3, we had at least got that right.

The newspaper coverage was not all opposed to the deal. Writing in *Ireland on Sunday* on 14 July, Donal Keenan attacked RTÉ and defended the deal. In an article entitled 'Sports Bodies Must Unite

---

2. When Tom McGurk hosted the RTÉ *Sunday Sports* programme, he gave a weekly award, called the Sick Parrot of the Week Award, to the person whom he thought had made the silliest performance or comment of the week. I was awarded it on one occasion for some clichéd comment I had made.

and Ensure Right to Sell their Wares', his comments included the advice that the sports bodies – especially the big three of the GAA, FAI and IRFU – should come together as a community and resist any efforts to deny them the right to sell their product to the highest bidder. 'The FAI has conducted their business. Now they must prove themselves capable of investing the money wisely.' Keenan was also highly critical of RTÉ, writing:

> Not only did the masters (RTÉ) lose the rights to the Republic of Ireland's home internationals through crass stupidity and incompetence, but their attempts to defend their actions and pour scorn on the FAI were embarrassingly pathetic in recent days. Their coverage of the story on both radio and television was completely unbalanced and unprofessional.

Later, he wrote that the RTÉ team believed that they could do what they want and get away with it.

The RTÉ coverage became personal. I remember a comment being aired on RTÉ about the way I walk, as I made my way from Merrion Square to government buildings, through a media scrum. I have an artificial hip and, particularly in situation of crowds, I walk with my head down to be sure of my footing. At least the RTÉ journalist concerned had the good grace to apologise to me later. Advised by our newly appointed PR consultants, we adopted a policy of going by car, even the 100 yards from Merrion Square to government buildings. We were advised that being chased across busy streets by TV cameras and radio microphones was not the image we were seeking to portray.

RTÉ quickly described satellite television as pay-per-view, which it is not and which was specifically excluded in our deal with Sky. It is subscription television. Not too dissimilar to RTÉ, where people subscribe through the licence fee. At this stage, RTÉ were arguing strongly for a massive hike in the licence fee to rectify their financial problems.

The government quickly entered the fray, criticising the FAI. The populist view was that the Irish international games should be shown live on free-to-air TV. The government threatened to introduce legislation to this effect, if the FAI did not somehow renegotiate a legally binding agreement. There was an initial meeting with the Minister for Sport John O'Donoghue, followed by a summit meeting with the Taoiseach, the Minister for Sport and the Minister for Communications, Dermot Ahern, which was amicable and in which we stated our rationale for the deal. I know that the government were very unhappy with RTÉ and felt that they were at least partly responsible for losing the FAI deal. The meeting also covered other items such as the National Stadium and Euro 2008. The matter was quickly transferred to the Minister for Communications to sort out. Television and broadcasting were his responsibility.

The public stance of the government remained populist; they wanted the deal reversed. Quickly, the Minister for Communications produced his draft proposals for legislation to guarantee that certain games are shown on so-called free-to-air TV. All competitive international soccer games were to be included, including the World Cup and European Championships. In rugby, all six-nation matches and the Rugby World Cup were to be guaranteed on free-to-air television. The GAA were getting off relatively lightly, with only the All-Ireland Finals included. Cultural significance was the key criterion determining what events should be included in the legislation.[3] Soccer had arrived in Ireland. A competitive match against Albania was of more cultural significance than the Munster Hurling Final.

The Association explained that it had no control or influence over away games. These rights belong to the host association. Including them in the legislation would be meaningless. Let me bring you back to 1998 and the away play-off against Turkey. RTÉ were the only player in the market at that time and refused to meet the financial demands of the Turkish TV station that had acquired the rights. As a

---

3. My understanding is that a ministerial order designating the events was insufficient, as the contract with Sky was signed. Hence, the threat of retrospective legislation.

result, the match was not shown live in Ireland. Are we in for more of the same, if the legislation restores a virtual monopoly situation?

The Sky TV deal took place against a background of the development of television broadcasting in Ireland. Sky were providing a digital broadcasting platform in Ireland, through their satellite system, and the RTÉ channels were already available on it. Sky needed the government and the government needed Sky. The danger was that the FAI would be the small fry in this bigger picture and could easily be squeezed out.

The FAI double-checked its legal position and got expert advice on the EU's Television Without Frontiers Directive. The best advice in both Dublin and London was that our position was rock solid. We had a legally valid contract with Sky Television and it was consistent with the EU directive, as the Irish government had not issued a ministerial order under their own legislation.

Sky Television were not too happy with the adverse publicity, as they were being painted as the greedy bad boys. Their ownership by Rupert Murdoch and his News International empire was another problematic aspect. This fact alone was enough to ensure that many newspapers took a negative stance. We had a number of meetings with Sky and the agreement was to hold firm. The first match was due in October and if this were successful, then much of the opposition could dissipate. However, the government remained involved and their statement that they would ensure that all competitive matches would be available on terrestrial television left very little room for manoeuvre.

There were a series of meetings with the Department of Communications, but these did nothing to solve the impasse. The FAI had a legally binding agreement with Sky, which would leave the Association very exposed if we tried to unwind it. The department could not persuade us to renegotiate with Sky, despite the threat of legislation. We thought that it was unlikely that any legislation would be applicable retrospectively.

The October home match against Switzerland passed off successfully, except for the result. The combined viewing figures for Sky and TV3 compared favourably with those achieved previously on RTÉ. However, the government commitment and the proposed legislation meant that the matter could not be left. In the absence of any movement towards a renegotiation, the government accelerated the legislation through the Dáil.

The government were betting that, when they enacted their additional legislation, the FAI/Sky deal would not be challenged in court – retrospective legislation can and probably should be challenged. There were three possible outcomes to the whole issue:

- The Sky TV deal would hold, despite the legislation, as the courts would confirm the validity of the deal.

- The new legislation would become operable. Sky would still hold the rights to Ireland's games but would have to negotiate a sub-licence agreement with a terrestrial television station to show the matches simultaneously.

- The FAI and Sky would wilt under government pressure and the threat of the new legislation. This is what seems to have happened, based on the media reports. Both the FAI and Sky agreed to walk away. A new deal was negotiated giving RTÉ the rights to broadcast the matches live. The financial remuneration from this deal to the FAI was significantly reduced, amounting to €2.5 million over the remaining three years, compared to Sky's €7.5 million over four. RTÉ would pay just over €800,000 per annum, double their initial offer. It was an increase of just over 30 per cent on the deal agreed four years earlier.

Who got the better part of this deal? I have no doubt that in the end, RTÉ got the rights for a sum way below their true commercial value. Politics rather than football won. Who will make up the financial shortfall for the FAI? Who will provide the resources for investment in the next generation of players that will ensure our continued success? No one will.

7

Mick McCarthy's Reign and Resignation

Mick McCarthy's appointment as Irish team manager in February 1996 was surrounded by controversy. Similarly, his departure in November 2002 was also controversial. I became acting General Secretary of the Association just two weeks after Mick was appointed. I stood down as General Secretary in November 2002, one week after Mick resigned. His tenure as Irish international team manager largely coincided with my time at the top echelons of the FAI. Mick lasted one week more than me.

After six months as acting General Secretary, I served three and a half years as Honorary Treasurer of the Association (between November 1996 and May 2001), before becoming General Secretary in May 2001. During those six years, I never got close to Mick. That wasn't my job. I sometimes wonder if the controversy surrounding his appointment caused Mick to keep the FAI in general at a distance. Mick kept his inner circle very tight and very close. I did, however, learn to respect Mick very much. He is a very honest and principled person. I do not know of any other manager in football who resigned because he felt his team would perform better without him. What a brave decision!

In the latter days of Jack Charlton's reign as Irish manager, I had a peripheral involvement in the FAI. I represented Home Farm at the four meetings a year of the FAI Council and served on the

Association's Finance Committee. The National Council, although supposedly the supreme body of the Association, was, and still is, irrelevant. My one claim to fame is that at a Council vote on whether the infamous abandoned match against England of February 1995 should be replayed, I was against it – the lone dissenter in a vote of 44 to 1 in favour.

I had travelled as a fan to Germany, Italy and the US. I was disappointed with the performance of the team in the US. In my view, that was our best-ever side, but it failed to realise its potential. We should have pushed on in the third match against Norway in the Giants Stadium. If we had beaten Norway and topped the group, we would have stayed in New York through to the semifinal. What might we have achieved in the cooler, less humid climate, and with much greater support, against teams such as Bulgaria and Nigeria? Instead, through a lack of ambition, we had to return to the heat and humidity of Orlando to face the Netherlands. The heat and lack of access to water for the players became too much of an issue in Orlando. As a fan, I felt that Jack should have stood down after the 1994 World Cup.

Euro 1996 was going to be in England. Jack probably felt that his team had one last tournament in them. However, it was not to be, as Ireland lost 2–0 to the Netherlands in a play-off in Anfield in November 1995. Again I felt that Jack should have used that defeat as his opportunity to retire. I remember being at Anfield and the huge cheer that went up for Jack as he made a circuit of the pitch after the match. I believe many people were cheering because they believed that it was probably Jack's last match.

Jack didn't resign but was pushed out by the FAI officers just one month later. The crunch meeting between Jack and the officers is reported to have taken place in the car park of the AUL Complex in Clonshaugh, near the airport. Jack didn't want to go, but the decision had been made by the political powers of the Association.

*****

The FAI appointed a five-man committee to select a replacement. This committee would recommend a candidate, or candidates, but the final decision would be made by the FAI Executive Committee (later replaced by the FAI Board of Management). The members of this selection committee were Louis Kilcoyne (FAI President), Pat Quigley (FAI Vice President), Joe Delaney (Honorary Treasurer), Michael Hyland (Chairman of the National League) and Finbarr Flood (FAI Executive Committee).

The proceedings descended into farce. The process and meetings were supposed to be secret but at least two of the officers were continually speaking to journalists. Speculation was rife. Reviewing the newspaper coverage of the time shows just what a farce it was. Kenny Dalglish's name was mentioned. He was then manager of Blackburn Rovers. Blackburn refused the FAI permission to speak to Dalglish. Howard Wilkinson's name was also mentioned. Joe Kinnear, one of the favourites, withdrew after a second interview. There were conflicting reports about Joe's withdrawal. The FAI stated that Joe had said that the time was not right for him. Joe appears to have been annoyed that the interviews had become public knowledge. As he arrived at the secret venue in London, he was met by television cameras. Perhaps it was the case that Joe recognised which way the wind was blowing and wisely got out of the contest.

In the end, the vote came down to a choice between Mick McCarthy and Kevin Moran, Ireland's two centre halves for many an important match. Kevin Moran had been a late entry into the race. In the end, Mick got the vote, but only just. It was a 3–2 split decision. What made the matter worse was that immediately after Mick's appointment, FAI President Louis Kilcoyne volunteered that Mick had not been his first choice. Whatever about the decision-making process, it was important, once the decision was made, that the Association was unified behind the new manager. This was not to happen.

Joe Delaney is reported to also have supported Kevin Moran, not too surprising given Delaney's Manchester United connections. The

FAI then refused to appoint Mick's chosen assistant, Ian Evans, on a full-time basis. Merriongate exploded two weeks later. What a start for the new manager! Mick must have been extremely annoyed with the FAI before he even started the job.

It is interesting to note that the five-man selection panel excluded Sean Connolly. Sean was the General Secretary of the Association at the time. Sean would set up and attend the meetings but would not be part of the decision-making process. This illustrates the balance of power within the FAI prior to Merriongate. Nothing had changed six years later, when Brian Kerr was appointed to replace Mick. The officers run the Association and the General Secretary/Chief Executive carries out their decisions. The decision on the appointment of the manager is made solely by the politicians in the Association. That is the way the FAI have always been run. It is unlikely to change, as the non-implementation of key recommendations of the Genesis Report confirms that the power will remain with the politicians.

There was one other issue about Mick's appointment that needed to be sorted out. As stated in Chapter 1, one of the first pieces of correspondence I received when I became Acting General Secretary was a letter from solicitors acting on behalf of Mick's former club, Millwall FC, seeking compensation for the loss of their manager. Millwall believed that Mick's contract had been broken. Mick believed that he had an opt-out clause. No one in the Association knew for sure. The FAI had appointed a manager, without being aware of the financial consequences of their actions.

Donie Butler, then commercial manager of the Association, and I visited Millwall at the New Den in London to discuss the issue. Little progress was made. Mick was adamant that he had an opt-out clause; Millwall was adamant that he didn't. We had no idea where we stood, as we could not get sight of the contract from either party. We denied that the Association was in any way liable. We then got lucky. Millwall FC went into financial administration shortly afterwards, which involved a change of administration and the resignation of the directors. That was the last we heard of the matter. Millwall's difficulties proved to be timely for the Association.

Mick's managerial career got off to a rocky start, with defeat against Russia at Lansdowne Road. His newly appointed captain, Roy Keane, was sent off for kicking out at a Russian opponent. Mick's decision to appoint Roy Keane as his captain was obviously an attempt to mend their difficult relationship. However, as there was little ongoing communication between them, this decision may have backfired on Mick in the long run.

Mick's career as manager is well documented elsewhere. I will skip forward to the decision to reappoint him for a further two years in February 2002. Let me state that the Association are always faced with a dilemma in appointing a manager. Top Premiership managers earn millions of pounds in salary. The Association cannot afford to compete in this market. Thus, the position of Irish manager, while well paid, does not compare financially to that of Premiership managers. It does have a number of compensatory perks, however. It is a full-time position, but the team plays only about eight matches a year. Moreover, since Jack Charlton's days, the manager has augmented his salary through commercial income from sponsorships and promotions.

The FAI had extended Mick's contract early in September 1999 on the expectation that we would qualify for Euro 2000. We failed to do so in Macedonia. Thus, in late 2001, the Association was reluctant to move on a new contract before the final outcome of the World Cup qualification was determined. This also suited Mick. My opinion is that he believed that his value as a manager would increase greatly if Ireland qualified for the World Cup.

He achieved a substantial increase in salary when agreement was reached in January 2002. While the figures on Mick's salary have been in the public domain through leaks from within the Association, I am not going to repeat them here. Mick's remuneration was always denominated in sterling, reflecting his residence in the UK. Once Ireland had qualified for the World Cup, there was never any doubt that Mick would be offered a new contract. However, I was also convinced that Mick wanted to stay as Irish manager. He loved the job and took great pride in it.

John Delaney and I were appointed to carry out the negotiations with Liam Gaskin, Mick's agent, and Andrew O'Rorke, Mick's solicitor. Mick never got involved in these negotiations. The objective was to have a new agreement reached by early February 2002, when Mick's existing contract expired. There were some initial discussions in November and December 2001, but the real negotiations took place in January 2002, with agreement being reached on 29 January.

The negotiating positions were very different. Liam Gaskin wanted to achieve a high salary for Mick; the FAI, while willing to concede a substantial salary increase, wanted a significant bonus element included in the overall remuneration package. The principle for the FAI was that if Mick qualified the team for Euro 2004, then the FAI's income would increase and they could afford generous bonus payments.

The key meeting took place in the Alexander Hotel in Dublin. There had been a meeting with the FAI officers earlier in the afternoon in Merrion Square, where Mick's contract was discussed and the parameters of the negotiations laid out. At the officers' meeting, it was agreed that there would be a three-tier element to the contract: salary, a qualification for Euro 2004 bonus and a progress during the World Cup bonus. Surprisingly, Mick's previous contract had not included any bonus for progression through the World Cup or European Championships, although there was a qualification bonus.

Agreement was reached quickly once the salary level was set. The qualification bonus was agreed, as was a bonus of Stg£50,000 per round for progression in the World Cup. It was agreed that, as previously, Andrew O'Rorke would draw up the draft contract and that it would be signed as soon as possible. For a number of reasons this did not happen.

*****

Let me state categorically that the Stg£50,000 per round bonus for World Cup progress was discussed at the officers' meeting of 29 January and agreed at the meeting with Liam Gaskin and Andrew O'Rorke at the Alexander Hotel later that afternoon. Liam Gaskin has confirmed these discussions in the Alexander Hotel with me. This became a contentious issue later, when *Ireland on Sunday* published incorrect information in its 26 January 2003 edition. This has since become the cause of solicitor's letters being sent on my behalf to *Ireland on Sunday*.

Let me quote the extract from *Ireland on Sunday*:

> The contract was subsequently renegotiated a second time to include a Stg£50,000 per round bonus to the manager for progression in the World Cup. It has transpired that this was negotiated without the knowledge of the Treasurer.

Solicitors acting on behalf of *Ireland on Sunday* wrote to my solicitor stating that, prior to the publication of the article, Mr Delaney confirmed to their clients (*Ireland on Sunday*) that the proposed bonus payments were negotiated and agreed without his knowledge. He has done so again since.

In subsequent correspondence, *Ireland on Sunday*'s solicitors were able to reproduce verbatim an extract from a private and confidential document entitled 'Officers' meetings in Japan and Korea' which dealt with the Mick McCarthy bonus issue. My question is, if they were given a copy of this document by the FAI, why did they not publish it in full? I am constrained from doing so.

The negotiations regarding the Stg £50,000 per round bonus took place and were agreed at the meeting on 29 January 2002 in the Alexander Hotel. The Honorary Treasurer of the Association was present at this meeting. *Ireland on Sunday* has disclosed that the source of its information was the Honorary Treasurer of the Association, John Delaney. At the time, Delaney was under pressure within the FAI over his role in offering the exceptional performance bonus of Stg£100,000 to Mick McCarthy. Presumably, providing *Ireland on*

Sunday with this incorrect information was an attempt to create a diversion. It is interesting that the story that Brian Kerr was to be appointed as Irish manager was also leaked on that weekend.

*****

A draft contract was received from Andrew O'Rorke in early March. This was passed to the FAI solicitors to vet. This procedure was somewhat unusual for the FAI, as our solicitors normally drew up contracts. However, previous practice had been that Mick's solicitor drafted the contract and there was no reason to change this, on this occasion. The new terms of Mick's contract were implemented immediately by the FAI, in advance of the contract being formally signed off by Mick or the FAI.

Two issues subsequently arose. The first was a change in the wording governing Mick's entitlements to exploit his commercial value; the second was that the World Cup progression bonus was omitted from the contract. The latter issue was not identified until during the World Cup when it was quickly rectified. However, the former element caused a delay in both parties signing the contract, a fact that was exploited in a very strange way during the World Cup.

The FAI could not sign the contract as provided because, when compared to the previous contract, the revised wording could open serious commercial conflicts between the FAI and one of their main sponsors, Umbro. The rule of thumb was that the manager was free to do commercial promotions, as long as they did not conflict with the Association's existing portfolio of sponsors. Umbro had been fully protected in the previous contract, but this protection had now been diluted. The change in wording had not been discussed and the FAI could not concede to it. Umbro are one of the Association's most valuable sponsors.

The basic problem was that Mick had an offer to promote Adidas football boots. Having the Association promote Umbro and the manager promote Adidas would not work. It would dilute the impact of Umbro's sponsorship. A major part of the promotion of Umbro is that the manager and players wear the gear. When the players and technical staff are with the Irish squad, it is an unwritten rule that they wear Umbro clothing in all public appearances and not the gear of their club sponsors. Indeed, in a few cases, players have individual sponsorship deals with clothing companies. This public promotion of Umbro clothing by the manager and players is one of the critical ways in which this sponsorship deal delivers value to Umbro and, thereby, revenue to the Association.

I did not identify the proposed change in the wording until I received the contract back from the solicitor in April. New discussions were required to resolve the issue. FAI commercial manager Eddie Cox got involved and brokered a deal between John Courtenay of Umbro and Liam Gaskin. Mick could represent Adidas Predator boots, but not their clothing. This was a satisfactory solution, but it took some time to work out. As a result, Liam Gaskin was not given a contract for Mick's signature until just prior to Mick's departure for the World Cup. For whatever reason, Mick travelled to Saipan and Japan without having signed his new contract. This was not a problem, as everything had been agreed and both sides were operating under the new terms.

I was asked at an FAI officers' meeting in Japan whether Mick had signed his contract. I stated that I would speak to Liam Gaskin and ascertain the position. This I did. Liam stated that there were no issues with Mick's contract and that he would get Mick to sign it at an opportune moment. Independently, Milo Corcoran had a similar conversation with Liam Gaskin on the same day. This was reported to the officers at a meeting on 7 June in Chiba City, Japan. Imagine our surprise at the subsequent officers' meeting on 10 June, when John Delaney stated that it was his information that Mick McCarthy would not sign the contract without the payment of an additional bonus for exceptional performance.

*****

Before describing the events of Mick's resignation, I would like to review some of the key issues surrounding the opening games of the Euro 2004 qualification campaign.

The draw for Euro 2004 was made in Oporto, Portugal, in January 2002. Ireland were a top seed. We had risen from a third seed to a top seed on the basis of our unbeaten performance in the qualification group for the World Cup. This was a huge advantage, as it meant we would avoid other top seeds such as Spain, France, Italy and Germany in the qualification matches. We would be playing four teams who were ranked below us. There were many good teams among the second seeds, such as the Netherlands, Russia and England.

We were ranked sixth in Europe, excluding the hosts, Portugal, who qualified automatically. With any sort of a decent performance, we would maintain the top ranking for the World Cup 2006 draw. Being a first seed meant we would again miss the commercially attractive countries such as Germany, Spain and Italy. From a commercial perspective, our group – Russia, Switzerland, Georgia and Albania – was very poor. We would only get peanuts in television revenue from the Russian, Georgian and Albanian markets. Luckily, we had pre-sold some of our television rights to a pan-European television rights company and this provided for a minimum fee, which we would now earn. Switzerland, while wealthy, is small and thus is also of limited value from a television earnings point of view.

The financial returns from this group would be low. In addition, there were ten five-team groups. Thus, we would only have four home fixtures, compared to five in previous qualification campaigns. Our total match revenue would also be adversely affected by this. UEFA put the ease of the mathematics, (ten group winners, five play-off winners plus Portugal to create the sixteen qualifiers) ahead of the need to create revenue for their members. The additional new members from Eastern Europe and the decision not to grant automatic qualification to the reigning champions had reduced the size of the qualification groups.

The draw was a mixed bag: the Russians are always dangerous, the Swiss were improving, the Georgians were unknown and I could not believe that the Albanians were only ranked as a fifth seed. In recent years, we had not been drawn against countries from the old Soviet bloc, with the exception of the three Baltic republics, which are highly developed. The Baltic states also have beautiful capital cities with good hotel facilities. Trips to Moscow and Tbilisi, with Tirana thrown in, made it an unattractive group for the fans. The distances were also an issue, with Tbilisi being a six-hour flight from Dublin.

The first event after every draw is to agree the fixtures. The countries in each group get together for a fixture meeting. This is a convoluted process. If the countries cannot agree among themselves, then UEFA will determine the fixtures by means of a draw. This is how England ended up playing Turkey away in their last fixture of Euro 2004 qualification campaign. I suspect it was their least attractive option.

As the first seed in the group, we invited the countries to come to Dublin for the fixtures meeting. It was held in the Burlington Hotel on 13 February 2002. The fixtures have to be played on the designated competitive international dates specified in the official FIFA international calendar. These are basically early September (fixtures on a Saturday and the following Wednesday), mid-October, late March and early April (two fixtures) and early June (two fixtures).

We had a number of constraints. The first was that Lansdowne Road would not be available for the first match in September, as a new pitch was being laid and would not be ready. We managed – surprise, surprise for the FAI – to keep this quiet. In addition, the rugby internationals would still be on in late March and thus the state of the pitch and the need to convert the stadium to its all-seated format meant that the March and April dates were also not available for home matches. We did not want to play away in Moscow or Georgia in the summer or in the winter, given those countries' extremes of climate.

In addition, the Irish team tend to perform strongly in September and October, when the players are fresh, and poorly in the summer, when the players are out of season. All in all, our options were limited.

I had discussions about our options with Mick prior to the meeting and had established the parameters of what we would accept. Mick did not attend the fixtures meeting, as had been the case for the World Cup qualification group. We would need to be clever and to bargain hard to achieve a satisfactory fixture list[1].

We persuaded the other countries that Des Casey, FAI Honorary Secretary at the time, but more importantly, a UEFA Vice President, should chair the meeting. Our fear was that the Russians, Georgians and Albanians might have pre-agreed fixtures and out-vote the Swiss and ourselves at the meeting. The Russians did come with a suggested fixture list, but we managed to have it shelved very quickly. The other consideration in the group was that there were five teams, which meant that there would be only two matches on each date, with one team idle.

Des proposed that Albania, as the fifth team in the group, would sit out both the opening and the closing sets of fixtures. Thus, it was Russia, Switzerland, Georgia and Ireland for the first set of games. I proposed that we would travel to Moscow for the first fixture in September 2002, if Russia came to Dublin the following September (2003). The Russians were very surprised but quickly agreed. None of the other countries knew that we could not play in Dublin in

---

1. The following are the results since 1996, under Mick McCarthy: in September, we beat Lichtenstein (away 5–0) in 1996, Iceland (away 4–2) and Lithuania (away 2–1) in 1997, Croatia (home 2–0) in 1998, Yugoslavia (home 2–1) in 1999 and Holland (home 1–0) in 2001. We drew with Holland (away 2–2) in 2001, and our only defeat was 1–0 away to Croatia in 1999. This is an impressive record against mostly top-class teams. In June, we beat Lichtenstein (home 5–0) in 1997, Macedonia (home 1–0) in 1999 and Estonia (away 2–0) in 2001. In 2001 we also drew at home with Portugal, 1–1. We scraped two victories against Georgia and Albania in Lansdowne Road in June 2003. Our most infamous June result was the 0–0 draw with Lichtenstein in 1993. While the results were in general good, they were, with the exception of Portugal, against weaker opposition. I believe that these results justify the conclusion that the Irish team perform better in the autumn and that is when we should play the stronger teams.

September 2002. Thus the other opening fixture became Switzerland v. Georgia. This was a good start.

Mick wanted to play Switzerland away early in the campaign, but given our limited options, this was not feasible. My key objectives were to avoid Albania and Georgia away in June and to play the strong countries in the autumn. In particular, we wanted Russia at home in September 2003. We agreed to play Switzerland at home in October 2002. The focus was then on the fixtures against Albania and Georgia. The preferred dates for these were away in the spring and home in the summer. Playing the two countries away on one trip would cut down on the total amount of travel. Climatic conditions in these countries were optimum for us in the spring. Playing the two weakest teams at home in June, when we were most vulnerable, also seemed like a good solution.

The fixtures meeting pushed on in this fashion, with us achieving most of what we wanted. We knew we had to travel to Switzerland, and October 2003 was as good a date as any. Within one hour we had agreed almost all of the fixture list. The only problem was the fixtures between Georgia and Albania. The weakest teams had been forgotten in the manoeuverings of the stronger teams. The only dates left were the two September 2003 dates, home on the Saturday and away on the Wednesday. They agreed to these dates, but then there was disagreement on where the first match would be played. Des Casey suggested the toss of a coin and both sides reluctantly agreed.

The fixtures were finalised in a little over one hour, which I would claim is a record for such meetings. At least three of the ten groups failed to reach any agreement and UEFA subsequently drew their fixtures. Imagine the problems this might have caused us, given the restricted availability of Lansdowne Road. We had got most of what we wanted. The Russians and Swiss also seemed to be satisfied. The weaker countries lost out. But, in the nature of such meetings, it is everyone for themselves and a matter of getting the best deal for your country.

*****

Once the World Cup was over, it was a matter of focusing on the Euro 2004 qualifiers. Mick was very confident that we would top the group. We played a friendly against Finland in August 2002 and won easily. A friendly in August is important, as it is the first get-together of the team for the new season. It avoids going straight into a competitive match in early September. It was an excellent, confident performance as befitted a team ranked thirteenth in the world. Everything was positive with the team and it certainly seemed we could go on and build on our World Cup achievements.

The Finnish game was a lovely trip. Helsinki is beautiful and in mid-August the weather is generally warm and pleasant. A friendly international has no tension attached to it. There is very little work to be done, although I took the opportunity, with Brian Kerr and Packie Bonner, to brief the other officers present on progress on Brian's Technical Development Plan for Irish football. This was an off-shoot of the Association's strategic plan, *One Game One Association,* launched in 2001. We have a very good relationship with the Finns and spent a very pleasant evening in their company. At the dinner, I got the distinct impression that they believed our joint bid with Scotland for Euro 2008 was doing a lot better than the Nordic bid.

After Helsinki, it was on to Moscow in early September for the first qualification match for Euro 2004. A huge number of fans travelled. I suspect that for many it would be their only excuse ever to go to Moscow. There were serious difficulties for the fans throughout the trip, starting with a neighbour of mine who had made it to one Moscow Airport, only to discover his passport had landed at another. What I believe happened was that the friend who was travelling with him was somehow 'minding' the passport, but they didn't realise that the flights were landing at different airports. The Irish Embassy personnel were brilliant in looking after the fans. There were many difficult incidents, including gang attacks on fans, leading to injuries and in one case hospitalisation.

The UEFA match delegate, who was from Austria, was made fully aware of these incidents and he included them in his official report to

UEFA. I have no idea whether UEFA took any further action. They probably did not as the incidents took place in the centre of the city rather than at the stadium.

The Russian game was probably the most badly organised match I have ever come across. It was not for want of manpower. Everything was 'over the top' and hence was slow and delayed. The first incident was with the U21 team, prior to the senior match. The team and accompanying officials, of which I was one, were coming directly from the U21 match, which we had agreed to play on the same day to facilitate the Russians. The team bus was parked a long distance from the stadium and the players were obliged to walk at least one kilometre to the stadium. This is unheard of at international matches. The Russian liaison officials who had been allocated to assist us had, of course, disappeared by this time.

I was aware that a large number of Irish fans were still queuing outside the stadium as kick-off time for the senior international approached. I complained to the UEFA match delegate and requested a delayed kick-off time. This is virtually unheard of for a competitive international match, as it upsets television schedules. The Russians were furious. However, I persuaded the match delegate to view the situation for himself, which he did. At eight o'clock, there were still lengthy queues at the turnstiles leading to the Irish section of the stadium. The queues were caused by over-the-top security checks by the Russian authorities. The match delegate requested the Russians to speed up their entry procedures. They ignored him.

However, the match could not start without his permission and he had instructed the referee to keep the teams in the dressing-rooms. By the time we got back to the dressing-room area, most of the spectators had got in. The match started about ten minutes late.

There was similar chaos after the match. The Russian system for emptying the stadium was very slow, on a section-by-section basis. Each section had to be fully emptied and time given for the spectators to disperse, before the next section was allowed to leave. They started with the Russian supporters, leaving the Irish fans until last. One hour after the game, all the Irish supporters were still locked into the stadium. I again complained to the match delegate and persuaded him to speak to the Russians about it. We went to the Irish section of the stadium and spoke to the Russian in charge. He was a large man in a very impressive uniform, bedecked with plenty of medals. He listened to us, without saying a word. Afterwards, I wondered if he spoke English at all. He totally ignored what the UEFA official had said to him and adhered to his own system.

It really was disgracefully inept. It was the imposition of power, simply for the sake of it. It was also a very poor reflection on the Russians. They had no trust in their own supporters or in their own ability to deal with large crowds. When the Irish fans were leaving the stadium, they were escorted by Russian security to their buses parked about one kilometre away. It was the worst stadium management I have ever come across. It was at least two hours after the final whistle, before the last Irish fans were on their bus.

My other abiding memory of Moscow was the smog. Forest fires were raging on the outskirts of Moscow and a heavy pall of smoke pervaded the city. Even with tightly closed double-glazed hotel windows, there was a smell of burnt wood. The media were speculating on a postponement of the match, but this was never a possibility. Luckily, on the night of the match the air was much cleaner than previously. This is a good example of how the media create stories to fill space. When I arrived in the team hotel in Moscow, I telephoned Linda. She was listening to the 4 pm news headlines, which declared that the Irish team were still on the plane, circling Moscow Airport and unable to land because of the smog. This purported to be a live report from Moscow. I do not know how editors let some of these guys get away with such nonsense.

On the morning of our departure from Moscow, I received a phone call at about 5 am from three female Irish fans, one of whom I knew quite well. They had supported the team everywhere. When they arrived at the airport to get their flight home in the early hours of the Sunday morning, they discovered that their exit visas had expired at midnight on Saturday. They were not allowed to board their plane and were now stranded. I can understand the importance some countries attach to entry visas, but to me, exit visas are an absurdity. Why not let the people travel and get rid of the problem? In Russia, rules are rules and hence the three fans were stranded. There is also another reason why they were not allowed to travel. It provided the Russian airport and immigration officials with an opportunity to rip them off.

I contacted FAI travel agent, Ray Treacy, as I knew that we had some spare seats on the team's return flight and that he would accommodate them. Ray was able to get tickets issued for them. That was the easy part. The difficult part was getting them new exit visas. I met them when we arrived at the airport. They were still stuck at immigration. They had been instructed to go to a bank and purchase new exit visas. This they did. They paid $75 dollars each and were given official-looking documents in exchange, stamped by the bank. When they presented these at immigration, along with the new flight tickets, they were not accepted. The bank, or more likely the teller, had taken their dollars and given them a receipt for a foreign exchange transaction. Of course, he had not given them any roubles.

The girls were now collectively over $200 worse off and no nearer to getting out of Russia. Trying to correct the 'error' was impossible, as everyone involved had forgotten how to speak English. The easiest solution was to pay up again. However, this time, with the FAI looking on and the use of one of our liaison officers, the girls succeeded in getting the exit visas and travelled home with the team. I got a present of a couple of bottles of wine for my involvement. I have no doubt that very few of the Irish fans who attended that match would voluntarily go back to Russia.

*****

The performance on the field by the Irish team was poor. Nobody can fully explain the transition from Japan, or indeed Helsinki, to Russia. Perhaps there was one factor, the impact of which had not been fully assessed. With the retirement of Steve Staunton and, to a lesser extent, Niall Quinn, the team had lost their leadership, both on and off the field. When problems arose, these were the players who would have stood firm and rallied the team. This was missing in Moscow.

With the loss in Moscow, the media pressure on Mick McCarthy intensified. At the end of the game, it was obvious that a small section of the fans were dissatisfied, as shouts of 'Keano' rang out. I do not understand why some fans put one individual above the team. This was Ireland playing. It was Keane who had chosen to absent himself. Whatever the circumstances, the players on the field deserved full support.

For many in the media, the issue was not whether Mick was the best manager for Ireland, but simply how to keep the Saipan row going, create stories and sell newspapers. For a small minority of journalists, they had a simple agenda – hastening Mick's departure as manager. A few real football journalists fully assessed the story and gave an honest view. Media coverage of significant stories can be strange. Some newspapers will allocate one journalist to each side of the argument for the sake of balance and fairness. Hence, in the same paper, there will be one journalist allocated to support Mick and one to oppose him.

The defeat away to Russia was not too significant in the overall group, as a point would have been a bonus. Only France, as world champions, had won in Moscow in the past twenty years. However, it intensified the importance of the home match against Switzerland on 16 October. Mick needed a win to restore confidence in him as manager. The team needed a win to stay in contention to win the group.

It was not to be. Whatever malaise had infected the team, it had not gone away between September and October. Ireland played poorly against the Swiss. We were a goal down and struggling when we got a lucky break. We equalised through an own goal, with fifteen minutes left. Mick then gambled and lost. At the time, I felt we were playing so badly that to escape with a draw would be a good result. Mick made the same change that had worked against Germany and Spain. He took Ian Harte off and brought Gary Doherty on, changing to the 3–4–3 formation. This time it backfired. We were exposed in the left back position and Celestini scored the winner for Switzerland.

As the final whistle went, a section of Lansdowne Road booed. My gut instinct at the final whistle was that it had gone sour on Mick and it was difficult to see him remaining as manager. His facial expression and body language gave the same message. Non-football issues were intruding too far and the team were suffering. The players were very committed to Mick and knew the importance of a result against Switzerland. Maybe this added pressure contributed to their poor performance.

*****

There was another dramatic occurrence at the Swiss game. As the crowd were entering the bucket seats on the Havelock Square (North) Terrace at the start of the game, a small section of the seating, containing twelve seats, collapsed and six people fell, some quite a considerable distance, to the terrace below. Luckily, no one was badly injured. The people involved received immediate medical attention with two people being taken to hospital. This immediately raised significant safety issues. I was told of the incident about fifteen minutes into the game, when I was called to a meeting with my safety and security people under the stand.

As General Secretary of the Association, I was the event controller at international matches. Thus, I was responsible for key decisions. The one I was faced with here was a major one. Was the seating safe? Should the Havelock Square Terrace be evacuated? This would mean halting the match and possibly abandoning it. Was this another potential Bastia in Corsica incident? In 1992, sixteen people died and over 600 were injured at a French Cup semifinal against Marseilles at the Furiani Stadium. That incident had been a key factor in FIFA banning temporary seats, as a rule. The temporary seats at Lansdowne Road are allowed on sufferance.

The FAI run a very good safety and security operation at Lansdowne Road, with extensive medical back up. The incident with the seats occurred with very few of the 35,000 people in Lansdowne Road being aware of it. I wasn't aware of the incident until I was told about it at the emergency meeting below the stand. The temporary seats are fully checked by competent people each time they are installed. They are issued with a safety certificate by Dublin Corporation.

This time there was a glitch. Our investigations suggested a most likely cause, but I will not disclose it as the incident may be subject to litigation. Our safety personnel sealed off the area and reallocated people as required. Our deputy safety officer is a civil engineer by profession. There were also experienced personnel from the seating contractors present. The information I received was that the problem was an isolated one, confined to the one section of twelve seats, an area that was now sealed off. It was not a general safety problem. On the basis of that expert advice, no further action was taken and the match proceeded unaffected. During the rest of the match, I spent as much time watching the North Terrace as I did the action on the field of play.

This incident could have had serious consequences for the Association. It could have lead to the banning of the temporary seats by FIFA, thereby reducing Lansdowne Road's ground capacity to 23,000. This would not have been financially that serious for the Association, as the cost of installing and managing the seats, added to the percentage of ticket sales to be paid to IRFU, is close to the revenue generated from using them. However, the ticket allocation problems would become insurmountable.

I told the FAI officers of the incident at half-time. This was a mistake. During the second half of the game, I overheard one of the officers describing the incident to a government minister sitting beside him. He was directly behind and within earshot of the UEFA match delegate, who was the last person in the world I wanted to learn of the incident.

A negative official report would almost certainly cause us difficulties in using the seats in the future. The officer was far from impressed when I suggested that he keep the information to himself. In the end, the UEFA match delegate did not find out and we escaped. The story made the following day's evening papers, but it had lost most of its momentum at that stage. This is one of the few occasions where we managed to control information to the benefit of the Association – despite the behaviour of at least one of our senior officials. Information is power. Within the FAI, disclosing information and appearing important takes precedence over the interests of the Association.

*****

After the Russian game, the official position of the Association was that we were fully supporting the manager. However, cracks began to appear in the support after the Switzerland game, even though there had been no discussion of the issue within the Association. In the *Sunday Tribune* (20 October 2002), just four days after the Swiss game, 'sources' within Merrion Square were quoted as saying that they:

> expected (Mick) McCarthy to do the decent thing and resign. It's understood that there is strong resistance to offering him any kind of severance package, with some officials believing he has done very well financially out of the Association.

This was one senior official acting on his own and without consulting his fellow officers.

This was typical of the FAI. It is important to lead the charge in whatever direction it is going. Position yourself from an internal political position, so that you look good. The merits of the issues are often irrelevant. What a change, from granting Mick an *ex gratia* bonus of Stg£100,000 in June to forcing his resignation without a penny compensation in October. This must be a record for long-term strategic planning, even for the FAI!

Mick went to Portugal on holiday after the Switzerland game. This took him out of public view for two weeks and quietened immediate speculation about his future. However, behind the scenes, things were moving. I received a phone call from Liam Gaskin, asking for a meeting to discuss Mick's position as manager. I was not surprised. Mick was away, so there was no immediate rush, but there would be only one result: Mick would be resigning as Irish manager. This decision by Mick suited the FAI, as I certainly wanted no hand, act or part in forcing him out. I was prepared to soldier on with Mick if that was his desire. His record of success and achievement demanded that.

At this stage, I had informed Milo Corcoran, as FAI President, of this contact and we agreed to keep it confidential. If we widened the circle, it would leak and we would not be able to manage the situation. When we did widen the circle the following week, it did leak and we lost control immediately. Once again, a media frenzy ensued and key issues were discussed through the media rather than across a table. Mick McCarthy kept himself removed from this and acted with great dignity throughout what must have been an extraordinarily difficult time for him.

I met with Liam Gaskin on 30 October, two weeks after the Switzerland game. Mick was due home on the Sunday. Liam informed me that Mick was no longer enjoying the job and that he could no longer perform as manager the way he wanted to. It was affecting the players, who were no longer enjoying playing for Ireland. The legacy of Saipan was intruding. Rather than going away with the excellent performance in the World Cup, the row over Roy Keane had intensified with the poor start to the Euro 2004 campaign. Mick was being advised to stay until he had an alternative job lined up, but he did not want to do this.

There was an initial statement of the terms of departure from Liam, but these were far from the key issue at this stage. It was agreed that nothing would happen until Mick's return. Liam was in contact with Mick throughout this period, but the distinct impression I got was that Mick had decided to resign, even though he loved the job. As

I have said previously, a manager deciding to resign in the interests of the team and their performance is a very rare occurrence.

After the meeting on the Wednesday, I spoke again with Milo Corcoran and updated him on my conversation with Liam. At this stage, it was necessary to bring the other officers into the information loop. One or two were annoyed that they had not been involved from the beginning, even though no decisions had been made. At this point, the situation spiralled out of control, justifying the decision to initially keep the information tightly under wraps. The story was in the media the following day and was the lead story for most of the weekend papers. Rather than controlling the situation and creating a dignified space for Mick, the FAI was led by the demands of the media. Everything had to be dealt with in a few days, rather than managed over a longer period as originally planned. The decision that Mick would announce his resignation on Tuesday, 5 November, was forced on both Mick and the FAI by the media. The FAI had brought this on both themselves and Mick, through the lack of confidentiality.

It was planned that the FAI would meet with Mick on the Tuesday, sort out all the remaining issues, plan for the announcement and make the separation dignified. Unfortunately, every plan we made was thwarted by leaks to the press. We fed the story to the media that Mick would not be in Dublin until the Thursday or Friday of that week, as he was due in to promote his *World Cup Diary* on those days. We had in fact arranged to meet him on the Tuesday in an out-of-Dublin location: Kilkea Castle near Castledermot, owned by Shane Cassidy, a good friend of Mick's and a great supporter of Irish football. The date and venue were leaked. I received a phone call at home from a journalist late on the Monday night, informing me that the media would be present in numbers at Kilkea Castle. I was left wondering how anyone could do this job properly. There was no chance that the media would back off and give the FAI and Mick some breathing space. The hounds were loose and baying for blood.

We had to change plans. The decision we reached was that we would hold the resignation press conference that evening. We had not yet met with Mick face to face, but both sides knew that the sooner it was ended the better. This decision was solely made on the basis of halting the media circus as soon as possible. Mick was en route to Kilkea Castle, when the plans were changed. Instead of Kilkea he would meet us in Merrion Square, walking in by the front door, facing the media. From Merrion Square, it would be on to the Burlington Hotel for the media conference.

At this stage, nothing had been agreed between Mick and the FAI over the terms of his departure. There was a contract with fifteen months to run. Relationships between Liam Gaskin and some FAI officers were deteriorating, as the terms of Mick's departure were being debated in the media, even before we had met him. The payment of the exceptional performance bonus of Stg£100,000 became a focal point of dispute.

Mick's financial demands were small. However, as bad relations had developed between Liam Gaskin and John Delaney, even these caused difficulty. As Mick was speaking with the FAI officers in the Board Room in Merrion Square, Liam Gaskin and John Delaney were having an angry exchange upstairs. It was close to becoming petty. In the end, it was Mick's dignity that resolved the problem. Mick puts certain things, especially his integrity, above money.

Mick was more concerned for Ian Evans, his assistant manager, who was also represented by Liam Gaskin in these negotiations. Ian had not been well remunerated by the Association during his six years, nor would he have accumulated much wealth during his playing days. As he said to me afterwards: 'Just as I was on a decent salary for the first time, I am forced to resign.' I spoke with Ian on the day following Mick's resignation. I wonder if anyone else from the FAI has been in touch with him to thank him for his efforts on our behalf.

From Merrion Square, it was straight on to the Burlington Hotel for the press conference, via a media scrum on the steps of Merrion Square. We were able to use a back entrance into the press conference room, but again the media were waiting with television cameras. What it adds to the coverage of an event to see people getting out of a car and having to push their way past photographers, I do not understand. Perhaps it is the media creating a sense of occasion for their own purposes and artificially increasing the pressure and stress on the individuals involved. The media are full of such tricks. I remember on one occasion being waylaid by a reporter and a cameraman late one evening at the back gate of Merrion Square. I agreed to speak to him. However, the cameraman kept setting off his flash in my face. I doubt if there was even film in his camera. It was a deliberate attempt to distract and disorientate me. I told the journalist that I would not answer another question unless his cameraman desisted.

The news conference was brief. Milo made a short introduction saying how sorry we were about Mick's resignation and what an excellent job he had done for us. Those sentiments were true for some of us, at least. Thankfully, the media had some sense of occasion and having claimed his scalp, the anti-Mick brigade kept largely quiet. No one was interested in what the FAI had to say and neither Milo nor I, who sat beside Mick at the top table, were asked any questions.

After the press conference, Mick adjourned to the Berkeley Court Hotel to have a drink with his technical staff. No one from the FAI was invited or attended. I telephoned Mick to congratulate him on his appointment as Sunderland manager, but only got his answering machine, where I left a message. I have had no other contact with Mick since his resignation and I suspect that few other people in the FAI have either.

*****

Mick's departure in November 2002 was not the end of controversy in the FAI involving Mick. Let me bring you back to the issue of Mick's contract as we departed for the World Cup the previous May. All elements had been agreed and Mick had been given copies for his signature.

Two days after Mick's resignation, on Thursday, 7 November, Liam Gaskin telephoned me and told me that John Delaney had initially raised the issue of the additional bonus in Japan, first with

Mick, and subsequently with him: Delaney had suggested the payment of this bonus. At the time, I wrote down the exact words used by Liam Gaskin during the telephone conversation. These were:

> 'John Delaney incited the renegotiations in advance.'

> 'The figure was agreed in advance before Milo and you met with me.'

Again, unfortunately for reasons of confidentiality, I cannot reproduce the letter I subsequently wrote to Milo Corcoran or the notes I wrote up on the officers' meetings in Japan. This is despite the fact that these notes were given to the *Ireland on Sunday* newspaper. This is one of the ironies of the situation. I will observe my legal obligations to the FAI as a former employee. Someone should tell the FAI that contracts normally have two parties and each has obligations to the other. I believe that the FAI, as my employer, was frequently in breach of its duty to me and also breached my contract of employment. In my opinion, some of the information put out by the FAI defamed me. Let me quote Philip Quinn in the *Irish Independent* of 23 January 2003, in which he wrote about an FAI Board meeting to hear the allegations by Liam Gaskin that John Delaney advised him to seek the addition bonus:

> At each step, the two FAI officers have consulted legal advice in their efforts to find the root of the Gaskin allegations, which not only cost the FAI £100,000 but may have slighted Menton's reputation.

In the *Sunday Tribune* of the following Sunday, Paul Howard wrote about the spin being put out by the FAI:

> The clear implication of these stories was that the delay had allowed the FAI to be held to ransom and that Menton was to blame.

I believe that I have the right to set out the facts to protect my reputation. I wrote to the FAI on a number of occasions in 2002, expressing concern at the leaks from within the FAI and the negative spin about me that was put on much of this information. However, yet again the FAI chose to do nothing about the situation.

This made their threats of legal action against this book appear hypocritical.

I had reported to the officers in Japan on 7 June 2002 that I had spoken with Liam Gaskin the previous day and that he had told me that there were no problems with Mick's contract and that he would sign it at the opportune time. I recall that Milo Corcoran stated that he had received the same information from Liam. Three days later, John Delaney told the officers at their subsequent meeting that Liam Gaskin had informed him that Mick McCarthy would not sign the contract without payment of an additional bonus.

What had changed between the two meetings? It was only much later that we discovered that John Delaney had approached Mick, who had referred him to Liam Gaskin, and offered him an additional bonus for exceptional performance. With the possible exception of some of the Eircom Park happenings and the ticket scam perpetrated by George the Greek on Joe Delaney during the 1994 World Cup, this is probably the most outlandish and bizarre incident that I came across during my time with the FAI.

The truth of this matter is set down in an affidavit by Liam Gaskin, drawn up when he threatened legal action against the Association in defence of his and Mick's reputations. The legal action was threatened in response to information put into the media by the FAI, to the effect that Liam Gaskin and Mick McCarthy had held the Association to ransom over payment of this additional exceptional performance bonus. It was also reported that Gaskin was annoyed at the unnecessarily triumphant way Delaney described the severance deal he had negotiated with McCarthy. An unnamed source is attributed with saying that the manager would receive no payment, as he had already taken the Association for enough money during the summer. It was reported in the *Sunday Tribune* (26 January 2003) that when Delaney mentioned the bonus, Corcoran is reported to have replied 'Jaysus, this is ransom'. It is interesting to note that this was not a direct quote from Milo, rather it was alleged that these were his words. The only possible place these words could have been uttered, if indeed Milo said them, was in the 'privacy' of an FAI officers' meeting. Therefore, the President's alleged words at a private meeting were given to the media by one of the six most senior FAI officials present at that meeting. Let me also say that I cannot recall whether these words were actually said at such a meeting.

At no stage did Delaney disclose to me, nor I presume to his fellow officers, that it was he who had suggested the additional bonus to Mick and Liam. It has been reported that Delaney's initial approach to Mick occurred in the bar in Chiba. This appears to have been during the infamous FAI booze up on the night of the match against Germany (see Chapter 5).

Milo Corcoran and I sat down with Delaney and Gaskin to discuss this additional bonus, not having been informed by Delaney of the full circumstances. This cost the Association Stg£100,000, equivalent to €160,000 at the time. I believe it has cost significantly more since, in terms of legal costs in settling the matter between Gaskin, Delaney and the Association. I believe the Association met all legal costs and the total bill is now well over €200,000. I was excluded from this 'facilitation' process and this remains an issue of significant disagreement between the Association and me.

The story is really outlandish. I missed the Finance Committee meeting of September 2002. However, I have heard from members who were present that, in response to a question that was probably planted, Delaney told the Finance Committee that a major bonus had to be paid due to a contract with an employee not being signed. The Committee was also told that the officers had been informed that the contract was signed. I was, in effect, being accused of being responsible for the cost of this bonus to the FAI, when in truth the Honorary Treasurer had offered this bonus to Mick McCarthy.

The officers had never been assured that the contract was signed and they accept this. The President, Milo Corcoran, reported his conversation with Liam Gaskin in Japan to the officers. What had been stated was that there was no difficulty with the signing of the contract. I can only guess as to who announced publicly that the contract had been signed. It certainly was not me, as I believed that the contractual situation was a private commercial matter and should be treated as such. However, the information on the details of the contract, which was known to very few people in the Association, did of course get into the media.

No sooner had we agreed to pay Mick the exceptional performance bonus than it also appeared in the papers. Some senior source within the Association had given this information out, in the context of the non-signature of the previously agreed contract.

I cannot speak for Milo Corcoran, but I certainly entered into the renewed negotiations, which took place in Seoul, based on the information provided by the Honorary Treasurer. Liam Gaskin's position probably was that this had fortuitously landed in his lap, and he was not going to ignore the opportunity to benefit his client. Of course, John Delaney supported the payment of the additional bonus as he saw this as an opportunity to create a stick to beat me with in the mindless game of internal FAI politics. Unfortunately, it has cost the Association more than €200,000, money which could have been used very productively in other areas of football in Ireland. But as was typical of the Association, when they were provided with the facts and asked to investigate it, they ducked it.

This was the issue on which I legally challenged the coverage in *The Sunday Times*. They ran for cover, issued a clarification, which accepted that the delay in the contract was not due to administrative errors as they had reported, and agreed to pay my legal costs. *The Sunday Times* could not defend the story by John O'Brien as they had published it. Similar errors were made by other publications, including the *Sunday Independent* and the *Irish Independent*. They were fed incorrect information, and they published it without checking. Indeed, the *Irish Independent* attributed the bonus to administrative hold-ups, even after one of their senior reporters had been briefed by Liam Gaskin on the full facts of the issue.

I am aware that the picture painted here is one of absolute chaos. This is typical of the FAI. Short-term internal political gain is put ahead of the interests of the Association. It is impossible to manage issues appropriately, when the people who are supposed to be your colleagues and advisers are undermining your position and actually misleading you, to the detriment of the organisation you both represent.

After the suggestion that Mick McCarthy had held the FAI to ransom over the payment of the exceptional performance bonus appeared in the media, Liam Gaskin wrote a solicitor's letter threatening to take legal action against the Association, unless an apology was forthcoming. He included an affidavit, in which he gave a detailed account of the circumstances of the exceptional bonus. I did not see this affidavit, as the Association refused to show me a copy of it, despite many requests and my close involvement in this matter. I believe that it fully confirms my version of events and states clearly that John Delaney approached Mick McCarthy and Liam Gaskin in Japan and suggested that they seek the additional bonus before signing the previously agreed contract. Some of the officers of the Association met with Mick McCarthy, and I believe he also confirmed verbally what Liam had stated in his affidavit.

Philip Quinn reported in the *Irish Independent* of 23 January 2003 that:

> *McCarthy met with Corcoran and Fahy before Christmas in Dublin and, I understand, corroborated Gaskin's recollection of events in Chiba.*

The Treasurer of the FAI suggested this bonus, without any referral to or discussion within the Association. Then he suggests a totally different scenario to the Association and in the media. Despite my calling for a full investigation to establish the truth and providing written statements of what had transpired from my perspective, backed up by Gaskin's affidavit, the FAI tried to brush the issue under the carpet. To date they have succeeded. I have informed them that if they do not resolve this matter internally, I will take legal action. It was the key unresolved issue at my severance from the Association in July 2003. As the FAI refused to deal with the issue and as I would not give an undertaking not to take further action or make a claim against the Association, my final separation from the Association was acrimonious. Believe me, I have no difficulty with this, given the nature of the organisation.

When the matter was brought to the attention of the FAI Board of Management in January 2003, they ran for cover. Within the FAI Board of Management, three people being vocal on any issue is normally sufficient to prevent a decision being made. The other twenty will sit on the fence, as if it were of no concern to them. Delaney looked for a vote of confidence at this meeting, but this was denied him.

In appraising the stance the Board took on the matter, the reader should bear in mind two quotations:

> *Somebody has to be held accountable because the Association is going down the tubes.*

This quote was attributed to an unnamed Board member in advance of the Board meeting to investigate the issue on 24 January.

The following quote from John Delaney appeared in *The Sunday Times* of 23 June 2002, when the topic was the proposed report into World Cup preparations. O'Brien wrote that:

> *Delaney has said categorically that he will resign if there is any attempt to cover up what went wrong in Saipan and wants the findings to be made available before the end of August:*
>
> > *'We can't do the old-style thing, circle the wagons, which would have been the previous way of doing things,' he said, 'that's not for me.'*

Once again, what the FAI said and what the FAI did were two very different things. Not only did they circle the wagons on the bonus issue, with Delaney as lead rider, but they built a moat and bailey as well.

The initial Board decision was that John Delaney be given two weeks to respond to the allegations made about the bonus. However, internal political machinations intervened and a facilitator was appointed to try to amicably resolve the issue with 'all' parties. However, all parties seemed to exclude me. The FAI needed to bury this matter. I found this strange, as what I required was for the truth to be established and put on the record. But unpalatable truths are not welcome in FAI politics. I was now 'outside the Association and history'. On the appointment of the facilitator, the special Board meeting at which Delaney was to respond with his version of events was cancelled. What is even more astounding is that I have heard that the directors of the FAI, for the most part, chose not to read either Liam Gaskin's affidavit or my letter of complaint when they were made available to them at the February 2003 Board meeting. Some €160,000 of the Association's money had been wasted on the bonus and the directors did not want to find out why.

With less than twenty-four hours' notice, I was invited to attend with my solicitor a meeting in the Four Courts, which we did. For close to two hours, a trilateral meeting took place between the solicitors representing Delaney, Gaskin and the FAI, under the chairmanship of the facilitator. Delaney also attended this meeting. I was left waiting outside the meeting with my solicitor and was excluded from discussions. At the end of the two hours, my solicitor was shown a statement which had been agreed between the other three parties, but it made no reference to my situation, the issues I had raised or my demands that the truth be established. We left the Four Courts at this point, believing that the process was flawed.

The 'agreed' statement was used to sweep the issue under the carpet in the FAI. Liam Gaskin got his apology for the 'ransom' remarks attributed to the FAI. He also got his legal costs, as did Delaney. The Association have never offered to meet any of my legal costs. The statement leads to only one conclusion. McCarthy and Gaskin were approached in Japan and offered the exceptional bonus. The statement also added that the bonus was given with the agreement of the FAI. Not so! I was part of the negotiations on that bonus and I believe that I had incomplete information before them. In no way could this be portrayed as agreeing to it willingly.

The official FAI statement was as follows:

> At a special Board meeting of the FAI in February, Mr John G. O'Donnell, B.L., was asked to act as independent facilitator to resolve issues arising from matters raised in relation to contract issues pertaining to Mick McCarthy.
>
> Following Mr O'Donnell's facilitation, the FAI wishes to make the following statement:
>
> 'Further to recent reports in the media and on its own behalf, the FAI is happy to clarify that at no time, before, during or after the World Cup in Korea/Japan 2002, did Liam Gaskin or Mick McCarthy bring any undue pressure to bear on the Association regarding the payment of a bonus. Indeed, the contrary is the position and the FAI was prepared to offer and pay the bonus to Mr McCarthy.
>
> 'The Association acknowledges that the awarding of the bonus was a collective decision and that John Delaney acted at all times in the best interests of the Association.
>
> 'The FAI apologises for any distress or upset which may have been caused to either Mr Gaskin or Mr McCarthy by these media reports. The FAI has no hesitation in confirming that Mr Gaskin and Mr McCarthy, at all times, acted in a professional and honourable manner in all their dealings with the Association.
>
> 'The FAI wishes to thank Mr O'Donnell for his work as facilitator to the parties involved and, as part of the agreement reached between the parties, no further comments will be made on the issue.'

I subsequently wrote to Milo Corcoran, disassociating myself totally from the contents of this statement and reasserting my demand that the full truth of the matter be established and published. It had been used in a very Machiavellian way to damage me. The Association was told that unless they dealt with the matter satisfactorily, I would seek legal redress. They were formally written to by my solicitor to this effect in early June. This remains the situation as at October 2003.

Appointing the New Manager

On the Saturday after Mick's resignation, the FAI officers and I met in Kilkea Castle to receive a presentation on the Genesis Report. At the end of the meeting, there was a discussion on the process for appointing a new manager. As usual there was a scramble for position. At my suggestion, it was agreed that we would bring in an outside football person to assist us in the appointment process. There would be three other members of the appointment panel, but as was the case with Mick McCarthy in 1996, the General Secretary would not have a vote. The decision would be taken by the officers.

The General Secretary is seen as an administrator for the Association and not as a decision maker. At that time, the General Secretary was not a voting member of the Board of Management of the Association and was not a director of the Association. I had raised the issue of amending this situation during a rules revision in the Association in 2001/02 and was basically told to get lost. The partial implementation of the Genesis Report at the 2003 AGM has finally made the Chief Executive/General Secretary a director. However, he remains a lone voice among nine politicians. This is not what Genesis recommended.

The officers appointed to the selection panel were Milo Corcoran (President), Kevin Fahy (Honorary Secretary) and John Delaney (Honorary Treasurer). It was suggested that Liam Brady be approached. However, Liam and some other former international players declined to get involved and in the end the Association turned to Brian Hamilton, former international manager of Northern Ireland, who has wide experience and contacts in the game.

Brian Hamilton was a good choice. The FAI had offered Hamilton the position of technical director in 1996, prior to the appointment of Brian Kerr to that position. After initially agreeing to take the position, Hamilton subsequently declined it for personal reasons. Packie Bonner also came close to being appointed in 1996 but had to wait another seven years before becoming technical director. In appointing Brian Kerr in 1996, the Association reversed a policy decision which stipulated that one person should not perform the two roles of technical director and underage international manager.

Brian Kerr approached me in late 2001 to tell me that he felt that it was no longer possible to carry out both the job as technical director and underage international manager. He wanted to focus on the job as underage international manager. I wasn't too surprised at his decision, as both jobs had expanded greatly. I again informed Milo. We agreed to keep it quiet, even within the FAI, for a few months, as Brian had some time remaining under his existing contracts. I wanted to avoid a situation where he would be undermined if it were known that he was not staying on as technical director. I have no doubt that this would have happened as, despite his many successes, Brian had his enemies within football, ranging from officers, to Eircom League clubs, to schoolboy officials.

The FAI are a very public organisation and as soon as any position becomes vacant, the applications flood in, even prior to it being advertised. The applications for the job of Irish senior international manager come from two sources: the jokers and the serious contenders. I do not understand why someone would waste their time and effort writing joke applications, applying for the position of Irish international manager, based on having run an U10 team that lost a cup final. Let me assure these people that they are not original. There are hundreds of you out there. Your sense of humour is pathetic.

Serious contenders indicated their interest very quickly. Among these was Philippe Troussier, the former manager of Japan, a country that had a very successful World Cup. There were other well-known names from the international arena. I was surprised that Aime Jacquet, who managed the French team to success in Euro 2000, took the Moroccan job before the Irish position was determined. Maybe he appraised the situation correctly. Basically, the contenders came from three distinct areas: former Irish international players, out-of-work UK managers and managers with international experience. To these would be added the name of Brian Kerr, an applicant from within the Association.

By the time the formal applications were coming in, I had stood aside as General Secretary of the Association. As such, what I am writing is based on my own opinions and external observations and bits of information that I received from people within football and the media.

None of Ireland's former international players had performed well as managers and, as a category, they looked weak. Kevin Moran was a possibility when he was linked with Brian Kidd as his second in command. Kidd has an excellent reputation as a coach. But once Brian Kidd decided to work with the English team, Kevin's position was undermined. I could not see any of the out-of-work UK managers having the capabilities that were required. Many of them had poor records as managers. In my view, the only one with any credibility was Peter Reid, who had, at times, achieved a lot with Sunderland and Manchester City.

The fact that Brian Robson was the runner-up in the selection process amazed me. If he were that good, he would have had a decent manager's job in England. He had not managed since leaving Middlesbrough in 2001. I had been asked, through a third party, to supply some information on the job to Robson, which I did. I similarly assisted another candidate, who requested some information. The rumour within football is that John Delaney voted for Brian Robson. This is not too surprising, given Robson's Manchester United connections and Delaney's antipathy to Brian Kerr.

My belief was that it would come down to a contest between Kerr and Philippe Troussier. Not only had Troussier worked wonders for Japan in the 2002 World Cup, but his previous record with African countries – Nigeria, South Africa and Burkino Faso – was also good. He brought Burkino Faso to third place in Africa. Philippe was French and had been educated as a coach in France, which would have been a major plus, given the reputation and achievement of

French managers and coaches. I met him briefly in Japan during the lead up to the World Cup. He was a very personable and pleasant man, although his English was not quite fluent.

From what I heard, Troussier did a very credible interview, but there was doubt was about his long-term commitment to Ireland. It was perceived that he wanted to use Ireland as a stepping stone to a better job. We were ranked thirteenth in the world at the time. If he could improve on that ranking, then it would have been regarded as an excellent achievement. The only 'better' job he could have got would have been the French international job. Being manager of Ireland is certainly not a stepping stone to a major club job.

In the end, the decision came down to a clear choice between Brian Kerr and Brian Robson. There could only be one winner in such a contest, although the officers involved were split. As in the Mick McCarthy decision in 1996, it quickly became public knowledge that Brian Kerr had not been the first preference of all the officers involved in the final decision. Milo Corcoran and Kevin Fahy outvoted John Delaney.

Of course, the decision to appoint Brian Kerr to the post was leaked. The Board meeting that confirmed the appointment of Brian Kerr was also the one at which Delaney was under pressure over the Mick McCarthy exceptional bonus payment. Not surprisingly, the Brian Kerr story became the focus of media attention over that weekend, rather than Delaney's internal political difficulties.

I had first met Brian when he was assistant manager to Mick Lawler in Home Farm in the late 1980s. When Mick left Home Farm, he suggested that we appoint Brian to take over. We didn't do this: a decision which now looks very silly, given Brian's subsequent managerial success at every level.

I had developed a good working relationship with Brian during his stint as technical director and my time as General Secretary. We had worked closely together to expand the Technical Department and provide it with the appropriate focus and objectives. I had drawn up a Strategic Development Plan for the Association, entitled *One Game*

One Association, (what a misnomer!) and under Brian's direction a new approach to coaching at all levels was being devised.

Brian was appointed to general acclaim. I knew Brian's capabilities and my hope was that these would translate to the senior international team. I was a spectator at Brian's first international against Scotland at Hampton Park in February 2003, just two weeks after he was appointed. From what I observed from a distance, I was confident that a good group of people was again in charge of the Irish international team.

Brian's selection of Chris Houghton as assistant manager was well received within the Association. The Association had previously considered Chris for the Irish U21 manager's job, prior to the appointment of Don Givens.

I was not the least surprised at Roy Keane's decision not to play for Ireland again. I had predicted it in my comments on the situation after Ireland's exit from the World Cup. The timing of his announcement, on the eve of Brian's first match, left a lot to be desired. It is interesting that in the paperback version of his book, Keane claims that he was close to agreeing his return to the Irish team, but ultimately decided against it, on medical advice. A maximum of five competitive games for Ireland a season was a step too far for Keane. I note, however, that he has no difficulty playing in meaningless friendlies for Manchester United, as they exploit football supporters across the world in search of extra revenue for the club.

Ireland were beaten by Switzerland on 11 October 2003 and will not be going to the European Finals in Portugal next summer. I 'watched' the match on my computer screen through a minute-by-minute report on UEFA.com at 1 o'clock in the morning in Kuala Lumpur. I was disappointed for Brian, the players and the fans. I will always be a fan of the Irish international team. Nothing the FAI do will change this.

8

Departure

I left the FAI in November 2002. Actually, that is not quite accurate. I stood down as General Secretary of the FAI in November 2002. I left the FAI some nine months later in August 2003. As I write (October 2003) significant issues remain unresolved between the Association and me.

There has always been conjecture about the nature and timing of my decision to stand aside as General Secretary, because it coincided with the publication of the Genesis Report. Were the two linked? Not in my mind. Would I have been pushed if I had not stood aside? Certainly, elements within the Association, including one officer, would have continued to undermine me. As John Delaney told Linda in RTÉ the morning after I stood down, it would have been death by a thousand cuts. How many was he planning on inflicting?

I had a two-year contract with the FAI, commencing in June 2001. The two-year period was my choice. At its end, I would know whether or not I wanted to stay. I did not need two years to convince me to get out. The contract also had a six-month work-out clause, designed to allow for a smooth transition if needed. The question of whether my contract would have been renewed in May 2003 is irrelevant. I would not have looked for it to be renewed.

By late 2002, I no longer had the stomach for the job or for the pettiness of the FAI. Those who know me will confirm that it is a decision I have not regretted once since the day I made it. In the months following my decision, I was given the nickname of 'Happy Harry' by some of my former colleagues, who still work beyond the green door. I had my life back and I had a spring in my step again, in spite of my artificial hip!

I had a new sense of freedom. On the morning after I stepped down, I was in the car park of the FAI with my daughter, Ailbhe. She had a garment she wished to exchange in a boutique on Grafton Street. I offered to do it for her. When was the last time I had a chance to walk down Grafton Street? I was going to savour the little bits and pieces of real life again. Oscar Wilde once said 'One's real life is often the life that one does not lead'. I was returning to real life and I could feel it.

In the months after the World Cup, I had begun to hate the job of General Secretary of the FAI and everything associated with it. This feeling was not brought about by Saipan or the Sky deal and all the attendant controversy. That was part and parcel of the job; I accepted that. It was the absence of a spirit of togetherness or unity of purpose within the FAI. It is always a game of finding something wrong, of finding someone to blame and of finding a reason to stop things from happening. It was an environment in which I no longer wanted to operate. There are better things to do with my life.

It does not have to be like this, but there are always people in the Association who will keep it that way for their own gain. I contrast this to the atmosphere and ethos of the Asian Football Confederation – where I now work – in which people work as a team. Football is what drives them on. These people really care about the game.

I nearly quit the FAI about a month earlier. I was playing golf in Portmarnock on the annual golf day with the IRFU, GAA and GUI (Golfing Union of Ireland). I was in the company of Barry Keogh, Vice President of the IRFU and a good friend of mine, and Mícheál Ó Muircheartaigh from the GAA. It was a miserable day, with continuous heavy rain and a strong wind. Good golf was impossible. It was far from being the enjoyable day I had anticipated. As we came up the ninth fairway, we debated whether we should continue. My rain gear had passed its sell-by-date and I was wet and miserable.

Prior to teeing-off, my phone rang before I could switch it off. There was yet another FAI problem looming on the horizon. This was the pattern of the job. You could never escape from the permanent flow of problems. Time to do constructive things was stolen. I began to ask myself was this what it was all about? Is this why I took on this job?

Being on a golf course can give you an opportunity to think about things. That day, I thought seriously about quitting the FAI. I was simply not getting any satisfaction out of the job. I felt that I was being thwarted at every step. No matter what I achieved, it would not be recognised or acknowledged. There were many people in the FAI waiting in the long grass to cause me problems. There were scores to be settled, probably going back to Merriongate, the 'Paul Marney' affair and Eircom Park. In fairness to many of my opponents on Eircom Park, they treated me honestly and fairly. It was some of my supposed 'friends' that were the problem.

In the end, I decided to stay for a bit longer to see if I could change things. This was a mistake on my part. It merely postponed my decision by about a month. It meant that my standing down as General Secretary coincided with the publication of the Genesis Report; the two became linked in the mind of the media and, as a consequence, in the minds of many of the public. At that stage, I simply didn't care. I wanted out of the FAI and I wanted my life back. Moreover, I still don't care. I know that it was totally my decision and that is what is important to me.

I came to dread the Board meetings of the FAI. For me, each month was divided into two elements: the week of the Finance and Board meeting, when FAI politics predominated, and the other three weeks when I could try to do some decent work for Irish football. I knew that at each and every Finance and Board meeting I would be ambushed about some matter or other. This was normally set up well in advance. I am sure that the phones were buzzing before the meetings and the traps were laid. If people think that this was payback for my attacks on Bernard O'Byrne over Eircom Park, I simply do not care. I know my motives on Eircom Park were honest, and I was open and direct in my criticisms. Most of the issues at these Finance and Board meetings were trivial and of little importance for the health of Irish football. We seldom got to talk about serious football issues at the FAI. The atmosphere stank.

I am serious when I say that leaving the FAI gave me my life back. In a comment to me, Dr Tony O'Neill compared being General Secretary to maggots crawling all over you. Let me illustrate the way some of the directors treat the General Secretary: There was one particular director who always wanted his own way and was prepared to bully anyone to get it. I used to receive phone calls on at least three mornings a week from this individual and even more frequently when there was something he badly wanted. He knew that I was on the road at 7.45 am every morning and his calls started before 8 am. They became a standing joke with my daughters, Ailbhe and Niamh, who travelled with me en route to school. His catchphrases are well known to them.

The situation became so bad that I put caller ID on all the phone numbers he used, so that I could ignore his calls. Either that or I would leave my phone switched off until I got to the office, when I could divert it to Vanessa Tucker, my personal assistant. I knew he would catch up with me later. I remember receiving phone calls at 8 am on Saturday mornings, one at home and another when I was teeing off for a game of golf in Galway. On another occasion, a Sunday, I was about to enter an 11 am anniversary mass for my mother when the phone rang. It was the same individual again. I even got a separate personal mobile phone to try and control things.

There are a number of people in the FAI who always want their own way and will intimidate people to achieve this. The easy life would be to concede to them, but then they own you.

I was trying to do a job and stay out of the politics of the FAI as much as possible. I know that malicious rumours circulated that I had involved myself in the contest to elect a new Honorary Secretary in July 2002. It was even rumoured that I had visited Cork to canvas on behalf of one candidate. This was untrue, but then the truth never got in the way of political ambitions. I was delighted that Kevin Fahy was elected, as I know that it was in the best interests of the Association.

I was also aware, as was everyone involved in the FAI, that one officer was running a concerted media campaign to undermine my position. It was invidious. It was not a matter of right or wrong; it was about politics and power. What particularly appalled me was the number of times inaccurate information was provided to certain journalists, who published it without checking its substance. It really does not matter for Irish football. The game will thrive, irrespective of the FAI. The success of football in Ireland is based on the commitment of thousands of volunteers at grassroots level.

During my tenure as Secretary General, I had tried to introduce some reforms into the Association but was continuously thwarted by the Board. I had brought Ray Cass back in for a second consultancy report, but again only a limited number of his recommendations were accepted for implementation. I could not move in any meaningful way without Board approval. If I did, I was setting myself up as a target in the future. A Board member even attempted to impose a certain FAI executive on me as an Assistant General Secretary. Apart from the fact that the director had no responsibility in this area, many other staff members found it extremely difficult to work with the person he was advocating.

After the World Cup, I worked with Ian O'Callaghan, a management consultant who was on secondment to the FAI, to identify what changes we should make in the internal management structures and processes of the FAI. Why did I do this if Genesis were also carrying out a consultancy? The reason is that the Genesis Report was supposed to be confined to the World Cup and the changes required to support the international team and ensure its continued success. I knew that much more than that was needed. I was probably banging my head against a brick wall, but I decided to have another go.

In my view, Genesis exceeded their terms of reference. In principle, I had no problem with this, but the authors of the report never informed me that they were looking at wider structural issues. The structure proposed by Genesis did not differ greatly from the internal structure that was being developed by the internal consultant. The main difference is that the Board immediately endorsed the Genesis proposals in principal; any reforms I might have tried to introduce would have been resisted by the very same people.

My recollection is that during any discussions on reform of Merrion Square, the idea of increasing staff numbers was strongly resisted by Board members. This was the situation in October 2002, just one month before Genesis was presented. You can see the intractable situation I was facing.

Let me further illustrate the difficulties I faced. One of the reforms I did manage to introduce, albeit temporarily, after I became General Secretary, was that FAI senior executives were brought to Board meetings. They were available to contribute to the meeting on their areas of operation. This should be a normal business practice in my view. However, Michael Cody proposed that this practice should desist and that FAI executives had no place at Board meetings. He succeeded in having them excluded. No other director could be bothered to support my position, although it was in their interests.

The Genesis Report is at best a part solution for the FAI. The major structural problem faced by the FAI is that the representation structure simply does not make sense. Most Associations in the world are organised on a regional basis, with the region taking charge of all football in the area, apart from the professional league. The English County FA system is a good example, as is the Japanese Football Association. The parent Association supervises their activities, helps them financially and sets the development policies. The parent Association runs the international teams and a separate body runs the professional league. Let me have one crack at the Eircom League. The league is a separate organisation, but its problem is that the clubs run it. Self-interest rules the day, the night, the week and the season. In an interview on *Prime Time* in early 2003, former league Commissioner Roy Dooney described the league as a disjointed organisation:

> *It was a difficult organisation to work in. I found that there was never any clear definition on who did what, particularly between the volunteer element and the paid full-time staff. This disorganisation suited the political manipulations.*

The FAI have their regional associations: the four provincial football associations. They used to be important in Irish football but are now largely moribund and irrelevant. They supervise junior and intermediate football. They have lost all say or influence on schoolboy, schools' and women's football – the growth areas – because of their inertia. The provincial associations retain their political power, however, and have sixteen seats on the FAI Council. Their main purpose is as a springboard to power in the FAI. If you attend enough meetings and stay around long enough, then you may become President of the FAI. Close to 50 per cent of FAI Presidents come from the provincial associations. Their age profile is much older than the general football population.

In the vacuum left by the inactivity of the provincial associations and their focus on junior and intermediate football, a whole series of other affiliates were created representing schools, schoolboys and women, among others. In all, the FAI Council is comprised of four provincial councils, the League of Ireland and at least eight affiliates. There is duplication of roles in all areas. One organisation represents the universities and another the third-level colleges. There is also a Junior Council for junior football to compete and dispute with the provincial associations, even though the people involved come from the same leagues. Nobody is sure of the Junior Council's role as distinct from that of the provincial associations.

The FAI need to decide what their representative structure should be. It should either be a simple regional structure or, alternatively, be organised around the different areas of football, thereby abolishing the provincial associations. The structure cannot be efficient if it tries to be both. The FAI will, no doubt, choose to remain inefficient. In early 2002, I organised a meeting of the four provincial associations with the officers of the FAI. I was astounded to learn that this had never happened before – even though some of these provincial organisations are over 100 years old.

As part of the reforms, I had proposed that a working group be established, representing amateur football, underage football and professional football, the three strands of the game in Ireland. This caused consternation. It was seen as a threat to long-established privileges. As soon as I had departed the scene, this idea died a quick death. The traditional seats of power and privilege were safe again.

Genesis did not look at the political structures of the FAI. The Cass recommendations were far more radical. The politicians were happy with Genesis because, apart from a reduction in Board numbers, it left their structures, representation and privileges untouched. The main impact would be on the executive staff in Merrion Square. The FAI will not fundamentally change until the political structures are reformed. Most problems arise at the political level, rather than the administrative level.

My biggest criticism of the Genesis Report was that it did not deal with the culture of the FAI. If you are going to change an organisation like the FAI, you have to change their culture. We can all see that this has not happened; hence, nothing will really change. Genesis went further than their terms of reference, but then did not go far enough to solve any of the real issues. The report has stranded the FAI in no man's land. The FAI politicians are happy with this, as it is not threatening to them. They will endorse Genesis with enthusiasm, as it ultimately protects their interests.

*****

Although this is dealt with in Chapter 7, the Mick McCarthy bonus row is important in the context of my decision to stand down. On the Thursday before I decided to get out, I received a phone call from Liam Gaskin, Mick McCarthy's agent, filling me in on the details of what had actually transpired in Japan over Mick's additional bonus. John Delaney, the Honorary Treasurer, had approached Mick in the bar in the hotel in Chiba after the Germany game and offered him the bonus. Delaney then told the officers of the Association and the media that the bonus had been demanded because Mick's contract had not been signed. Who wants to operate within, or have any connection to, an organisation where this type of behaviour is tolerated and protected? The Association refused to face the reality of this in early 2003 and tried to brush the issue under the carpet.

On Saturday, 17 November 2002, the officers and I met in Kilkea Castle to be briefed by the Genesis consultants and to discuss the process for appointing a new manager. I would be allowed to organise the appointment process, but would have no say in the decision. The only people who knew about the location of the meeting were the Genesis consultants, the five officers and myself – and, of course, the media. One of the officers had informed the media of the location and the Sunday papers were there in force.

The following day, *The Sunday Times* reported that I had been put under pressure to resign at the meeting. This is absolutely untrue. There was no such discussion. Obviously, one of the officers had fed this line to John O'Brien and he had swallowed it hook, line and sinker. He had written it without checking the facts. This journalist actually spoke to me after the meeting but never looked for confirmation. He was prepared to accept what was fed to him from his regular source. This was all part of the ongoing campaign from within the FAI to undermine me. I never knew that journalists were so gullible! I can provide a long list of quotes and comments in the papers that are untrue. *The Sunday Times* was particularly bad in this respect.

The morning after the Genesis meeting, I woke up thoroughly fed up. My gut feeling was confirmed. Being General Secretary of the FAI was, as Genesis said, an impossible job. If you tried to change anything, you were prevented from doing so. You were always in the firing line. But worst of all, there was a significant group who simply wanted you out, so that they could control the running of the Association. I have no doubt that if I had agreed with the likes of John Delaney and Ollie Byrne and done what they wanted, simply to have an easy life, I might still be General Secretary of the FAI. But that was not the way I wanted to do it. It was then that I decided to call it a day.

I ran the thoughts through my head again. I came down for breakfast and simply said to Linda: 'I have decided that I do not want to do this anymore.' I listed my reasons: I said that the daily grind of politicking was getting me down. This was not why I had gone into this job. I wanted to do as my father had done and work for football. Apart from a brief spell in the FAI, my father operated where what you did really mattered for football: at club and schoolboy level. I wanted to get out of the FAI and back to working in football, even if it was again on a voluntary basis. I also knew that the Genesis proposals would bring more rows and I had had my fill of these. The role of General Secretary was not for me. Once I had articulated these thoughts, a weight was lifted off my shoulders. It felt good. This was the right thing for me to do.

Buoyed by the relief of my decision, I immediately reached for the phone. Linda asked me to give it an hour. I did not need an hour; this felt right. Linda had independently come to the same view. I told my daughters of my decision. Their reactions varied. They loved the exciting aspects of my job, but at the same time were aware of the downsides. I phoned my son, Ronan, and he told me it was about time!

I then rang Milo Corcoran and told him that I had had enough and intended to stand down as General Secretary of the FAI. I told Milo that the organisation had to change, that I had lost interest, and if my moving aside at this stage helped achieve change, then so much the better. Milo was taken aback; he had not expected this. He and I had worked well together and had developed a friendship, which still endures. However, he said that if this was what I really wanted, he would not stand in my way.

I next phoned Kevin Fahy, the Honorary Secretary. Like Milo, he was surprised, but said he would support me in my decision. Kevin and I had also a very good working relationship – as the General Secretary and Honorary Secretary should. We had been through a lot together in the Eircom Park days. I left it to Milo to inform the other officers.

I offered to stay on and continue as General Secretary until a replacement was found. I thought that this was a sensible suggestion, as it would provide a continuation for the Association and allow the new regime to be brought in when the time was right. I did not expect to be part of this process, but simply to provide a smooth handover. My contract lasted until May 2003, with an additional six months work-out. My staying on would save the Association money. Milo had no difficulty with this.

Obviously the officers spent most of the Sunday discussing this among themselves. At 11 pm on the Sunday, I received a phone call from Milo asking if I could meet with Kevin Fahy and him that night. This was crazy. I was in no mood to go out at midnight and discuss an issue like this. However, some of the other officers were unhappy and wanted things settled immediately – by me stepping down. They needed their petty victory.

Linda and I set out at 11.30 pm to travel to the Great Southern Airport Hotel, arriving about midnight. It must have been at least 12.30 am before Milo and Kevin arrived. We found a quiet corner of the lobby to discuss the issues. It came down to semantics: I would no longer be Secretary General, but I would remain employed by the FAI for the time being. It had yet to be decided what role I would play. As I had little interest in taking the FAI's money for doing nothing, I declined what is commonly called 'garden leave'. We set out and agreed a variety of projects with which I would remain involved. The two interesting ones were the joint bid with Scotland for the Euro 2008 Championship and the UEFA Club Licensing Project.

I felt that I got the better part of this bargain. I would be involved in two worthwhile projects and would be paid my full salary. I would be working, at best, at half pace, but I would have rewarding work to do. It would give me time to sort out my future. I would have time to do other things, like play more golf; indeed, from the spring of 2003, my additional free time allowed me to write this book. Thank you FAI.

In the end, I agreed to what the FAI officers wanted that night. I wasn't simply going to disappear into a black hole. I would stay involved within football (not necessarily the FAI) on my terms.

*****

As a side note, my vacating of the position of General Secretary caused difficulties for some journalists. I recall doing an interview for RTÉ News; before going on air they asked me several times, 'But what will we call you now?' I replied, 'Just call me Brendan Menton'. I hadn't changed; the essential me remained. However, the journalists were not comfortable with the lack of a title, and so I was labelled 'the former General Secretary of the FAI'. The label was more important than the person.

*****

I believe in their rush to get me out as General Secretary, the FAI may not have taken all aspects of my contract into account. It had been agreed with Des Casey and preceded many of the current officers taking up their positions. They all assumed that it was a two-year contract and that I would be out of their hair by next May. I don't think they realised that there was a further six-month work-out clause – the FAI would be paying me for more than a year, until the end of November 2003. In the end, I did even better: at the start of June, I was in dispute with the FAI over their mishandling of the allegations about Mick McCarthy's additional bonus. As a result, the six-months-notice clause was not activated until 1 August. Thank you again FAI!

Thus, the FAI will have paid me at least fourteen months' salary after my standing down as General Secretary. It could end up being more, as I am still in dispute with the FAI over the issue of Mick

McCarthy's bonus and legal action cannot be ruled out. Given their behaviour, I can take their money without a twinge of conscience. I have come to understand that the FAI and Irish football are two very different things, and while I will continue to support Irish football in anyway I can, I owe absolutely no loyalty to the FAI. Their treatment of me over the McCarthy bonus issue was disgraceful and, I believe, broke all the rules of corporate governance. I have heard that many of the directors never even briefed themselves by reading the documentation – shades of Eircom Park. Nothing ever changes beyond that green door.

I am now working in a better and more interesting job in the Asian Football Confederation and am doing very nicely financially. I have read newspaper comments on my remuneration package and smile wryly to myself. It will remain confidential, as the FAI have no access to the information. And I might even make some money from the book. Once more: thank you FAI!

*****

The next day, Monday, 19 November, I informed a few of my close colleagues in the FAI of my intention. They were very surprised, but also very supportive. I know that some friendships will survive all our association with and contamination by the FAI.

That Monday was a long and difficult day in many ways. Linda phoned me several times during the day and asked how I was bearing up. I replied each time, 'You don't know just how good this feels'.

Tuesday was the day of presentation by Genesis of the findings of their report to the Board. The meeting was held in the Burlington Hotel. Again, the whole issue was pressurised by leaks to the media. The FAI had no choice but to call a press conference immediately after the Board meeting. They had no opportunity to discuss the recommendations in detail or to adopt a strategy. The findings would go straight to the media. This nearly did not happen, as the powers-that-be forgot to get legal clearance for publication of Genesis. There was pandemonium in Merrion Square on the Tuesday morning.

Genesis was quite controversial in some areas. In the end, a diluted and truncated version of the report was presented to the media.

The Genesis Report was presented to the Board for about an hour. As I knew what was in it, I did not pay much attention. Instead, I worked on my statement to the Board. I am sure some favoured Board members had been told what was going to happen. There had also been speculation in the press that morning that there would be a resignation.

As soon as Alistair Grey of Genesis had completed his report, there was polite applause. A Board member then proposed that the FAI Board agree to accept and implement the recommendations in full. No discussion and no analysis, just implement them all. The Board members had not even read the report at this stage. We seemingly had turkeys voting for Christmas. But, no, they are more clever than that. In reality, they were protecting their feeding trough. The test will come when the reforms implemented do not match up to the Genesis recommendations. Now remember that the key recommendation of Genesis was that there would be a significant upgrading of the executive staff in Merrion Square and that they would be empowered to carry out their jobs without interference. Also, remember that, just one month earlier, it had been argued that there was no need for additional staff in Merrion Square. Why the Pauline conversion?

The President announced that I wanted to make a personal statement to the Board. I forget the actual words I used, but it was to the effect that I would not be seeking a renewal of my contract as General Secretary of the Association and that I had decided to stand aside with immediate effect, so that the Association could begin the process of change. There was silence. My friends on the Board were stunned, as I had not had an opportunity to tell all of them what I intended to do. I don't know and don't care what the reaction of the rest of them was. I then left the room, so that the directors could discuss my decision.

I retired to an upstairs room in the Burlington Hotel, where I could have some privacy. I worked on the statement I would give to the press conference. I made some telephone calls, telling key people what I was doing. John Treacy of the Irish Sports Council was very surprised by my decision. I spoke to Maurice O'Connell, who had acted as the independent Chairman to the Genesis Report. He, too, was shocked. I had known Maurice since my days as an economist; indeed, he had worked with my father in the Department of Finance. I assured him that my decision was not directly connected to the report and its recommendations.

The media were everywhere: TV cameras, radio people, journalists, snappers, the lot. Many of them know Linda; she knew if they saw her they might take that as a confirmation of my resignation. Linda and my family made their way into the Burlington Hotel, giving the journalists the slip. The girls insisted on buying me a new shirt and tie and brought a change of suit for the press conference. They wanted me to look my best in the glare of the media. I had a cup of tea and a snack. I was very relaxed.

After about forty-five minutes, an emissary from the Board was sent up to me. They were having problems approving what I had agreed with the officers. They did not want me involved in some of the projects that had been identified. In addition, they wanted my longer-term involvement in the FAI to be at the discretion of the new Chief Executive. This was just another example of the pettiness of the FAI Board. They had no time for the bigger picture. They were merely wasting time and delaying the press conference. They were also missing the main point. I had worked for the Association for more than a year and, therefore, had the protection of the employment legislation. I still have. I doubt if any of the FAI directors were even aware of this fact. What I agreed to that day was going to be irrelevant in the end. I wanted out of the FAI, but I wanted to control the situation as best I could. This, I believe, I largely achieved.

Part of the agreement was that I would only talk to the media on a limited basis – one radio interview with Marion Finucane that had been arranged for the following morning and one major press interview (with Emmet Malone, in *The Irish Times*, on 6 December 2002). No one mentioned a book.

In any event, I had no real interest in the detail of the agreement. Unlike my two immediate predecessors, I had sought no legal advice. They both left under a cloud of some sort. I was leaving of my own volition. They had both received pay-offs, one of them a very substantial six-figure sum; I simply wanted my contract to be honoured. I signed their document and returned to the Board meeting. Some people said nice things about me, but there were only a few I cared about: Milo Corcoran and Kevin Fahy of the officers, Ray Gallagher (Sligo Rovers), Paddy McCaul (Athlone Town), Frances Smyth (women's football), Terry McAuley (universities) and, what will surprise many people, former President Pat Quigley.

The next step was the press conference, which my family attended at the rear. The media were agog with expectation, but no one from the FAI was looking crestfallen. They were puzzled. If there had been casualties, then there should be sad faces. Heads turned when Linda and the girls entered the room. Linda described the awkwardness and embarrassment of some of the journalists when they saw her. Some were disinclined to look her straight in the eye. Afterwards some of them approached her and commiserated with her. She was looking at the situation from a completely different perspective. She was, as she says, 'full of the joys' as she knew this was what I wanted.

Pressure was on the media people. Deadlines had passed. The heat from the TV lights in the small packed room was overpowering. Everyone sat in expectation. At last, the FAI Board members appeared from behind the screen. I felt relaxed about my decision, and I must have shown this, as Philip Quinn from the *Irish Independent* remarked on my demeanour and said 'We hacks began to think we had the wrong man'.

I had to sit through a truncated presentation on Genesis for half an hour. Then I was centre stage. I read my statement verbatim, saying that I had decided to stand down as General Secretary of the Association:

> At the start, I would like to thank the Chief Executive of the Irish Sports Council, John Treacy, for his assistance in the development of the review and, particularly, Maurice O'Connell as Chairman and Alistair Grey of Genesis for the depth and quality of the work and for their commitment to the project.[1]
>
> Before anyone saw this report for the very first time last Saturday, the officers and I took the decision to publish the details at the earliest possible time – seventy-two hours later, having briefed our staff and Board, we are now doing so in a frank and open fashion.
>
> All the officers here at the table went to the Board today and recommended acceptance and implementation of the review.
>
> It is clear from this independent assessment that some of the fundamental problems associated with the Association and football in Ireland are not just about Saipan. I took the reigns eighteen months ago and, while I have made many changes across various disciplines within the Association and the game, the review indicates that the issues impacting negatively on the FAI span a long period and much more importantly, looking to the future, require the type of radical and genuine reform which some of you in this room have recently written about.
>
> We are talking about a new organisation, not a service and overhaul, but a much more fundamental change process.
>
> This will take a certain type of leadership and, perhaps, not one closely steeped in football traditions. Having played my own part in the development of football through many different areas, I have indicated to the Board today that I would not consider myself as candidate for the position of Chief Executive.

---

1. My views on Genesis have changed on in-depth analysis.

Indeed, I first indicated the decision to the President on Sunday. In the light of this, I will step aside as General Secretary, as and from this evening. This is not a sudden decision on my part but the timing is opportune.

I will be taking up a different role within the Association initially, bringing to fruition a number of important projects for the Association.

A key point in the Genesis Report cites the need to draw the line, have a clear marker, and create a watershed to provide the Association with a period of stability within which it can implement the most radical change in its history.

As a true lover of football in this country, I hope that the required changes will happen and that the future of Irish football will be a bright one.

Milo then said that he personally regretted my decision and that I had contributed a lot to football. I know that Milo's statement was genuine. Others, for once, had the good grace to keep their mouths shut. I have little recollection of the press conference. I know that there were questions on my decision and on the Genesis Report. I think that I handled it well, but I was glad when it was all over. Being the focus of attention at such a press conference is a strange experience – a glass fish bowl is the appropriate analogy. I declined to speak to the media after the press conference. Enough had been said and I was emotionally drained. Most of the media had the manners to leave me alone. There were others I had to take evasive measures to avoid. I had made my exit from the FAI. I had done it in my own way and under very different circumstances than previous General Secretaries, who had resigned from the FAI. My head was high.

I retired to the bar of the Burlington for a few drinks. It had been a very tense seventy-two hours but now it was over. Many friends and family members came by to support me. Others came and spoke to me. After six years in the FAI, I knew who was genuine and who was not. They also knew that I knew.

I had one duty the following morning – an interview with Marion Finucane. This was a mistake. I had been turning down interviews with Marion since the World Cup. Marion's show was a bad choice, as she knows little about football. She had no interest in the Genesis Report or in my resignation. The interview was to be a rerun of Saipan. There was a copy of the Genesis Report on the studio desk; it looked unopened. During the ad breaks, I tried to suggest that the discussion move on. I wanted the opportunity to explain why I was standing down as General Secretary of the FAI and what Genesis had said. The phone call comments started coming in. The first one was from Cork, with a question about Keane! It was getting ridiculous. I eventually managed to make a few of the points I wanted. I had been badly advised to select the *Marion Finucane Show* for this interview.

*****

Let me deal with the ongoing implementation of the Genesis Report. The FAI have bastardised it. The main recommendation with regard to the management of the Association was that the executive management would be empowered with the appointment of four people to senior executive positions. Together with the Chief Executive, they would form the senior management team. The Board would be reduced from twenty-two to ten in size, which has been agreed. This is one of the few common denominators between the Genesis Report and actual reforms. It is the headline issue, which is being used to disguise the non-implementation of other more important reforms.

Genesis proposed that the composition of the Board would consist of the Chief Executive and two independent non-executive directors, along with seven FAI politicians. It is my understanding that the FAI have dropped the idea of independent directors. More politicians will remain involved instead. The officers and the Chairmen of four key committees will be the new directors. Note the transfer of power from the proposed four senior executives and proposed independent directors to FAI politicians. The new FAI Board will consist of nine FAI politicians and the new Chief Executive (the replacement for the role of Secretary General), Fran Rooney. God help him. Actually, I don't know if even God could help him. All the proposed reforms will achieve is to concentrate power in the hands of a smaller political clique. Four directors acting in concert can now probably control the FAI. I am sure that this is being worked on. And they did it 'for the good of the Irish people'.

I had spoken to the previous Honorary Secretary of the Association, Des Casey, about the General Secretary becoming a director of the Association, and thus having a stronger say and a vote at Board meetings. However, the time was not right for such a reform. In the Scottish Football Association, the Board also acts as the Finance Committee. If the FAI are serious about being professional rather than political, they should do the same. Key expenditure decisions would then be discussed and taken at Board level, rather than by the politically appointed Finance Committee, as is currently the case in the FAI. As it stands, the Board simply rubber stamps the political decisions of the Finance Committee. I can't remember the FAI Board ever overturning a decision of one of the subcommittees. That might upset the cosy club.

I recognise that the FAI had failed in some aspects of the management of high-performance sport, which were highlighted in the Genesis Report. However, our management of the 2002 World Cup was leaps and bounds ahead of 1990 and 1994. We had done everything we had been asked to do by the team management. Ninety-five per cent of the arrangements were excellent. Saipan had its good points but maybe was the wrong location. We had, according to Genesis, missed out on challenging Mick and the technical staff on their decisions. We didn't have the expertise to do this. Genesis said we should have employed someone who had. The role and responsibilities of this position were detailed in the report. Has this appointment been made or is it in the pipeline? I am not holding my breath on this. This appointment would encroach on too many interests.

The Genesis Report was long on expensive recommendations for the senior international team and the staffing of Merrion Square. I hope that all the resources are not diverted away from grassroots development to pamper our international players. They have become rich men on the back of the investment of time and expertise of people involved at the base of Irish football. Rather, the FAI should recognise their responsibility to the next generation of players.

The political row about the Genesis recommendations at the general meeting in September 2003 was over an attempt to curtail the powers of the Honorary Secretary and transfer them to the executive function. These powers are mainly supervisory and I would have thought that good corporate governance would recommend the separation of executive powers from supervisory powers. The Honorary Treasurer is the officer position with the most executive power. Any expenditure recommendation he makes is normally approved. I know because I was there for four years. I know that those who wanted to transfer power from the Honorary Secretary will not apply the same logic to the Honorary Treasurer. It is not about reform or principle, but power.

*****

After the Finucane interview, I took a few days off and relaxed. I played some golf. It was good to get out on the course with a clear mind. The only urgent item on my agenda was the Euro 2008 joint bid with Scotland, with a final decision to be made by UEFA on 12 December. I devoted as much energy as needed to this. I would love to write a chapter on the bid, but time and space do not permit. We were defeated by political machinations within UEFA. We were the only viable alternative to the Swiss–Austrian bid. They scored just one point more than us on the technical evaluation by UEFA.

For those interested in the reality of what happened, I would refer them to the French sports paper, *L'Equipe*, which had a good grasp of UEFA politics and the decision-making process. The coverage in the Irish media was largely superficial. I sincerely hope that a joint bid is made and succeeds for Euro 2012. The Irish and Scottish fans deserve it and the SFA are well organised and has a lot of experience of major events.

I was disappointed with the failure of the Euro 2008 bid, particularly the manner of defeat. After Christmas, I focused on the UEFA club licence system. I was involved in the initial assessment against the licence criteria of twenty of the clubs. This was a consultancy exercise to assist the clubs with the license process. I avoided Dublin City, because of my close association with the club and its relationship with Home Farm, and Shelbourne, where I knew I would not be welcome. The project brought me into contact with genuine football people around the county. I finished my tour of the clubs in March 2003 and had all the reports delivered by early April. Then zilch. I was being moved aside. I was not surprised. I had set up the UEFA club licence system to ensure that it was taken seriously, but seemingly I had nothing more to offer. The official who had done an excellent job in administering the club licence system left. I feared for the success of the project and wrote to the Association expressing my concerns.

As spring turned into summer, I had nothing to do. As I was still being paid and the sun was shining, I was not too upset. My golf improved greatly and I began to play close to my 15 handicap. I played my first competitive round for four years in my home club, Blackbush. Apart from the occasional football-related golf outing, I had not had the time to play over the previous six years.

When Fran Rooney was appointed Chief Executive, I sent him a good luck card offering to brief him on a one-to-one basis if he wanted. No response. I had known Fran Rooney slightly outside of football, but mainly through his brief involvement in Home Farm. The last time I spoke with him was about three or four years ago when I bumped into him in his local pub, Myos in Castleknock.

*****

My final departure from the FAI was as bungled and ham-fisted as everything else to do with the organisation. I knew, when I stepped aside as General Secretary in November 2002, that my involvement with the FAI would come to an end sooner or later. I had no difficulty with this, as I did not want to be associated with an organisation that behaved as the FAI did.

There was really only one outstanding issue between the Association and me. That was the way the Association had handled the Mick McCarthy bonus issue. I was extremely annoyed about my treatment by the FAI over this. I wrote to the Association expressing my complete unhappiness with the events; they had received a solicitor's letter from me in May, threatening legal proceedings if they did not publish the truth and correct the official record of the Association. Their approach was a head-in-the-sand one, hoping I would go away. That was not going to happen. I started to write this book. The two are directly related. My first pages dealt with the McCarthy bonus issue as that was rankling with me. The book went from there; I was determined to expose the truth.

The talks between the FAI and me concerning my departure were supposed to be confidential. They were on a privileged basis until agreement was reached or, as happened in this case, not reached. Before the FAI had received a response from me on their proposals, incorrect information was circulating that I was prepared to accept a cash settlement and drop all other issues. Nothing could have been further from the truth. The only issue that needed to be resolved was establishing the truth on the Mick McCarthy bonus issue. Until that was done, nothing could be settled.

The issue of privilege prevents me from revealing the full details of the negotiations and the only meeting that took place. I am bound by my legal obligations, even if the FAI behaviour was again appalling.

I was dealing directly with one of Rooney's new people. I involved my solicitor from the beginning of these dealings, as I did not trust the FAI, despite the appearance of change and openness. I was correct in my assessment. The approach in the end was an attempt to bully me into submission. Despite my being centrally involved in the FAI for over six years, very few FAI people understand what motivates me.

The people involved in these discussions certainly did not. Despite my years of service to the FAI, my only dealings in these negotiations were with a messenger.

When my solicitor and I met the FAI negotiator in the Berkeley Court Hotel in late June 2003, his opening gambit was *plámás*. What a great contribution the Menton family had made to football in this country. What a lot of respect Fran Rooney had for my father and me. My father, who was a cofounder of Home Farm Football Club and a former President of the FAI, got plenty of praise. I doubt if the person speaking had ever met him. One of his offers was that the FAI would hold a function for me and say complimentary things about me. I could do without such hypocrisy. Rooney had so much respect for us that he had not spoken or met with me since his appointment as Chief Executive of the Association. He had sent his chief executioner instead.

We quickly established that the real purpose of the meeting in the Berkeley Court Hotel was to agree a severance package for me. I think our directness on this issue was a surprise to the FAI negotiator. From facilitator with *plámás* to executioner, however, was a very quick change of character. Let me say just one other thing: during these discussions, the FAI were informed that I was writing this book.

My conclusion from the meeting was that there would be ongoing discussions between the FAI and my solicitor to resolve the Mick McCarthy issue and to agree my termination package from the FAI. I thought that the two would go hand in hand, but I was wrong. The FAI had no interest in resolving the McCarthy bonus issue. As was to become clear later, their objective was to protect an officer of the Association, rather than meet their contractual and employment obligations to an employee. At this stage, I was still an employee of the Association.

Matters accelerated very quickly at the end of July. There was an FAI Board meeting as usual scheduled for the first Friday of August. The key factor remained the Association's obdurate opposition to facing reality over the McCarthy bonus issue. How they thought they could prevent the truth coming out was beyond me. I could publish my side of the story at any time and back it up with supportive documentation, including reference to Liam Gaskin's affidavit, which my solicitor had seen. Indeed, the FAI's own statement after the facilitation between the FAI, John Delaney and Liam Gaskin clearly admits that the bonus had been offered to Mick McCarthy. Simply ask the question: who offered the bonus? It wasn't me and I don't think it was Milo Corcoran. Only one other person was involved. Liam Gaskin has always stated that he would provide his evidence in any dispute I had with the Association.

It suited me to reach an agreement at this stage, as I was preparing to travel to Kuala Lumpur to take up my new job with the Asian Football Confederation in mid-August. No one knew this. My demands were simple. Bring out the truth of the McCarthy bonus issue and meet the terms of my employment contract with the FAI. The FAI had no problem with the latter. It was back again to one issue – the handling and cover-up of McCarthy's bonus by the FAI.

I had played golf with my solicitor in Milltown on the Wednesday evening, 30 July 2003, and at that stage we were confident that an agreement would be reached on my departure from the Association. It was to be a simple one, dealing with my employment contract only and leaving the contentious issue of dispute over the bonus to one side for the present. My hope was that by achieving this, a modicum of goodwill could be established.

Late on the Thursday evening, 31 July, I became aware that the confidentiality accord had been breached by the FAI; any concept of privilege ended there and then. It was put out in FAI circles on the Thursday night that the problem of Brendan Menton had gone away; he was, in effect, being bought off for the measly sum of €20,000 before tax. Nothing could have been further from the truth. At this stage, I had not even discussed the contents of the proposed agreement with my solicitor. I received a phone call from a third party on the Thursday evening, asking in incredulous tones if the issue was resolved. No way! As a family, we felt very strongly about our freedom. Linda, who was undergoing an operation on this Thursday, sent me a text message as soon as she came around from the anaesthetic, which read: 'Don't let them buy you and don't let them gag you.'

When I saw the draft agreement as provided by the FAI late on the Thursday afternoon, 31 July, I knew we had a major problem – the inclusion of the words 'and any other' in front of the word 'claims'. The FAI were trying to get me to agree not to take legal action on any issue, including the public maligning of me over the bonus. No apology, no nothing; Brendan Menton was supposed to walk away. They had some hope.

The other issue in the agreement, which I still do not understand, was the money. At first glance, I thought that the proposed figure represented the complete remuneration package under my contract for six months. I was later informed that it included an *ex gratia* payment of €20,000. Was this to buy my silence? I would love to know whose idea this was. Not anyone who knew me. This only came out during fraught discussions on the Friday morning, 1 August. The figure offered by the FAI did not include my pension entitlements, other fringe benefits or legal fees. My solicitor was promised that they would be met. It was some way of doing business in an acrimonious dispute!

The FAI had a problem and until they addressed it openly and honestly, it would not go away. To many, the bonus issue may seem a minor matter at this stage, but my reputation had been falsely tainted and the FAI had a duty to me as my employer. As was stated clearly to the FAI at the only meeting we had, money was not the issue – the truth was. I had one other major problem with the draft document I received. It was signed off by a consultant to the Association on behalf of the FAI. In my view, under his signature, the agreement was not worth the paper it was written on.

I spoke to my solicitor early on Friday morning and it was quickly agreed that the only real problem was those three words 'and any other'. If they were deleted, then we would have an agreement. The pressure tactics started immediately. The FAI had been told that I would not be available until after 12 noon on the Friday, as it was the first anniversary of my father's death and I would be attending an anniversary mass and a family gathering. I received a phone call from the FAI negotiator at 8.50 am, on the morning of the mass. He had been instructed to deal only with my solicitor, but that was irrelevant to him. I politely told him to contact my solicitor.

The message back to me was that if I did not sign the agreement as presented to me, then everything was cancelled. The FAI were demanding resolution before their Board meeting began at noon that day or there would be no agreement. This was obviously a matter of saving face for the new management. The prospect of no agreement did not perturb me in the slightest, as I had my new job lined up, had most of this book written and still had the option of legal action against the Association.

The more I thought about it, the more I was convinced that my decision was the right one. The quiet contemplation of a period in church reinforced this decision, as did a discussion with Linda, my brothers and sister. I phoned my solicitor to say that I would not agree to the document. The response he received from the FAI was an intensification of the bully-boy tactics. The *ex gratia* payment would be withdrawn, I would have to meet my own legal costs and I would be issued with notice under my employment contract that day. Grand, but I was not for moving. Those who know me well, know that I have a stubborn streak and, when it is aroused, I become immovable. The FAI had badly misread me.

All went quiet on the eastern front for a few hours. I went up to the graveyard on the Hill of Howth, spent some time at the summit and then down to the pier to buy fresh fish for dinner. Contrast this to the long day of meetings and rows experienced by the FAI people as they fought over my termination, among other issues. I had truly escaped from beyond the green door. I was back in the real world.

The best information that I have is that there was a crisis meeting between the officers, with Fran Rooney joining them by phone from abroad. The Board members were kept waiting for at least one hour after the scheduled time. I have heard that Rooney presented the agreement as his, even though he had never spoken to me. It was reported that the breach of confidentiality had caused me to reject the agreement. This was not true. I had no expectation of confidentiality from the FAI and was proven right. I believe that the real reason for the breakdown – my refusal to sign a document agreeing not to take any legal action against the Association in any circumstances – was not conveyed. It was agreed at that meeting that I be given notice of termination under my contract.

I received a letter at home by fax that afternoon, in effect, terminating my employment with the FAI. It arrived just one week before I would have been forced to resign from the Association in order to take up my new position with the Asian Football Confederation. The timing could not have been more opportune. Just to be sure that I was getting the message, I was telephoned by the consultant (despite the fact that he knew that his avenue of communication was with my solicitor) to tell me that the letter had been faxed to my home and would also be couriered to me that day. The document arrived at my home when I was down in the doctor's surgery with one of my daughters. It was left in the letterbox.

The petty vindictiveness of the approach is best illustrated by paragraphs stating that I could no longer use an FAI car, telephone or credit card from that day. No transaction had occurred on my FAI credit card since I had concluded my work for the Association on the UEFA club licensing project months earlier. I was not using an FAI car, but they were paying for a rented one. I switched off their mobile phone.

I am probably one of the few people to be glad to receive a notice of termination of employment. I would be 'unemployed' for two weeks. The future was now sorted, even if there remained outstanding issues. I was fully in control of my own destiny. The FAI were again teetering on the brink of chaos. The split had already occurred.

I celebrated that night and had a few sips from a bottle of Middleton Reserve, a very special fifteen-year-old Irish whiskey I keep for special occasions. Ironically, Paddy Goodwin, John Delaney's solicitor, had given it to me as a fiftieth birthday present. I savoured it well.